THE DIRECTOR IN A CHANGING THEATRE

**ESSAYS ON THEORY AND PRACTICE, WITH
NEW PLAYS FOR PERFORMANCE**

Edited, with an Introduction, by
J. ROBERT WILLS

Mayfield Publishing Company

for Susan, James and Robert

Library of Congress Catalog Card Number: 75–44696
International Standard Book Number: 0–87484–348–0

Manufactured in the United States of America
Mayfield Publishing Company, 285 Hamilton Avenue, Palo Alto, California 94301

This book was set in Vega and Illumna by Applied Typographic Systems and
was printed and bound by the George Banta Company. Sponsoring editor
was C. Lansing Hays, Carole Norton supervised editing, and Gene Tanke
was manuscript editor. Michelle Hogan supervised production, the book was
designed by Nancy Sears, and cover photograph was by Dennis Anderson.

CONTENTS

PREFACE

The Director in a Changing Theatre is a record for our time,
a memorandum of alternatives made possible by the recent (and
continuing) revolution in theatre. Its aims are simple: to provide a guide to
contemporary theory and practice in directing, to provide insights
into the evolution of present-day directing procedures, and to offer a
sampling of plays for directing practice. It focuses on those
ideas, techniques, and plays that are currently helping to transform
the theatre into what it will become.

Many books explore the traditional ways for directing traditional
plays. Because this book presents other avenues of discovery,
and because no similar collection now exists, it should answer a real and
present need and at the same time complement existing works.

Many of the selections included inevitably reflect in some measure
the influences brought into being by what used to be called the
New Theatre. It was a lively period, and it deserves chronicling. But the
inclusion of these works here hinges on a far more encompassing
premise: that aspiring directors will practice their art and craft in the
future rather than in the past. Consequently, even as this book provides
a historical record of the ideas that have motivated specific directors
and particular directing practices in our time, it is also offered as
a starting point for continued innovation and further
individual development.

I am indebted to many people for both direct and indirect help with
this endeavor: to all those at the Mayfield Publishing Company,
especially C. Lansing Hays and Carole Norton, who made the undertaking
a valuable and joy-filled experience; to Gene Tanke for his careful
and detailed editing; to Robert Cohen and Charles C. Hampton, whose
initial reading of the manuscript added immeasureably to its overall
shape; to friends, colleagues, and past and present students, all of whom

have helped to foster and sustain my own growth. Thanks of another kind are due to Katie Coffey and Glenda Back for their help in manuscript typing. Finally, grateful acknowledgement is made to the authors and publishers represented for their kind permission to reprint previously copyrighted materials.

THE DIRECTOR IN A CHANGING THEATRE

The Caterpillar and Alice looked at each other for some time in silence: at last the Caterpillar took the hookah out of its mouth, and addressed her in a languid, sleepy voice.

"Who are you?" said the Caterpillar.

This was not an encouraging opening for a conversation. Alice replied, rather shyly, "I—I hardly know, Sir, just at present—at least I know who I was when I got up this morning, but I think I must have been changed several times since then."

Lewis Carroll,
Alice's Adventures in Wonderland

INTRODUCTION

Directing for the theatre may be described as the process of transforming personal vision into public performance. In the words of a corporate advertising slogan, it demands "the mind to imagine, the skill to do." The director must first develop a capacity for creating vision, an ability to fuel his imagination from many sources; he must then be able to transform his vision into a theatrical reality, using his mastery of many theatre crafts. In order to meet this dual responsibility, he must also understand how the facts of performance relate to the moment of contact between actor and audience, merged together in a designated time/space architecture of action.

Such a description could prove misleadingly simple, however. The director's goal may have remained unchanged since the Greek *didaskolos* practiced his "teaching" with the chorus, but his methods, tools, and forms have changed significantly. His slow evolution, drawing most heavily on turn-of-the-century developments that led to a mid-century standardization of practice, has exploded in recent years, so the director now faces both problems and possibilities only dreamed of earlier.

Ours is a theatre nourished by long years of quiet innovation followed by a burst of experimentation during the 1960's and early 1970's. The theatre envisioned by Adolph Appia, Gordon Craig, and other theorists around the turn of the century has at last begun to blossom. More recent theorists like Antonin Artaud, Bertolt Brecht, Luigi Pirandello, Jerzy Grotowski, and Richard Schechner, have drawn heavily on that past history, assuring that current theatre practice is well grounded in historical precedent. Yet few would deny that change in our theatre, which proceeded gradually during the first sixty years of our century, accelerated at an unprecedented rate between 1960 and the early 1970's. In these years we witnessed the birth (and frequently also the death) of such forms as Theatre of Cruelty, Theatre of Fact, Rock Theatre, Multi-Media Theatre, Total Theatre, Poor Theatre, Environmental Theatre, Nude Theatre, Guerrilla Theatre, Street Theatre, Prison Theatre, Chance Theatre, Kinetic Theatre, Story Theatre, New Realism—and a host of others. Each of these, regardless of its quality or its staying power, has contributed to substantial change in theatre convention.

For a while, the result even enjoyed a commonly accepted name: New

Theatre.[1] The New Theatre has already become historical fact rather than current revolution, but the aesthetic it fostered—one which attempted to eliminate the arbitrary separation between art and its audience, and one which, because of its multiple options, demanded much more of its directors—seems less likely to disappear quickly. Perhaps, in fact, the most intriguing aspect of the entire New Theatre movement is the widespread accommodation of its attitudes, forms, principles, and techniques into the mainstream of theatrical activity. Consequently, it is now neither necessary nor possible to treat the new aesthetic as a thing apart from standard practice. What began as an alternative theatre, by and for a radical fringe, has become an intimate and integral part of our total theatre picture. It may have begun, geographically, with off-off Broadway. But it has now become an idea or an attitude without boundaries, which can be seen in the theatre's growing commitment to openness, to individuality, to playwrights, to companies, to experimentation, to economic sanity, to larger (different) audiences, and to a multitude of specific ideas for specific, even unique, theatres. Simply stated, theatre now is different from what it used to be, and will be more different still in the future.

The changes thus far have reshaped the face of theatre significantly, but they have not moved theatre far enough to make the new entirely comfortable. Ours is an age of transition, where theatre seems to stand teetering on the edge of a precipice, unable to fall, but unable also to return to the safety of level ground. The Third God in Bertolt Brecht's *The Good Woman of Setzuan* turns to his cohorts to say, "Good intentions bring people to the brink of the abyss, and good deeds push them over the edge. I'm afraid our book of rules is destined for the scrap heap."[2]

The awkwardness, the tenuousness, and the promise of our time is aptly expressed by Jean-Claude van Itallie in *The Serpent,* a ceremony first performed in 1968 and written with the collaboration of the Open Theatre and its director, Joseph Chaikin:

I no longer live in the beginning.
I've lost the beginning.
I'm in the middle,
Knowing
Neither the end

1 Michael Kirby discusses early elements of the New Theatre in "The New Theatre," *The Drama Review* (Winter 1965), T30, 23–43.

2 Bertolt Brecht, *The Good Woman of Setzuan,* in *Parables for the Theatre,* English version by Eric Bentley (New York: Grove Press, Inc., 1948), p. 86.

Nor the beginning.
I'm in the middle.
Coming from the beginning
And going toward the end.[3]

Because our transitional theatre is old enough not to be very new, but because it has, indeed, stretched past its beginnings, it has developed several recognizable traits.

First, new dramatic forms have exploded into existence. Although they express both a rejection of realism and the adoption of new communication principles, these new forms were created primarily out of a search for means to mirror effectively a world characterized by rapid change, social dysfunction, and moral disturbance. Such forms were heavily influenced by recent innovations in the theory of interpersonal relationships, game and play theory, social psychology, and the rediscovery of myth and ritual. Theatre also rediscovered the potential in distorting, rearranging, and exploring sequential order, information structure, and logically arranged dialogue. Non-rational, non-literal, non-verbal images can be effective. Plot and story can be replaced with intense bursts of directed energy and non-illusionary experience. The text, a raw material which provides one basis for performance, now joins with the performer and the audience in a designated space to create a total experience for everyone in the area of the activity. Sometimes the complete "play" cannot even be written down, because as the theatre began to assume its own language it stretched concepts of communication to include non-linguistic and non-verbal forms of visual and vocal behavior. The "word," for a while, was out, distrusted as overused and supplanted largely by action. Yet the "word" was also very much in, as playwrights, often working in collaboration with actors and directors, renewed the struggle to discover a way to use words meaningfully for our time. (The importance of this issue, however, has been exaggerated recently, for theatre has never really taken literature as an end in itself, and has always been more concerned with the problems of performance, even though it is true that the text as literature has played a more important role in the past than it does on occasion today.)

Second, audiences no longer simply watch plays. Instead, they are required to become involved in them. Initially, much of that involvement included actual participation in whatever action occurred; the distinction between spectator and performer frequently became obliterated. Increasingly today, however, it involves exploration between artist and audience of

3 Jean-Claude van Itallie, *The Serpent* (New York: Atheneum, 1970), pp.16–17.

new physical and psychological relationships in which each maintains a distinct if non-traditional role. Springing in part from Antonin Artaud's theory of theatre (and from a misunderstanding of that theory), audience participation in the act of art has become a fact of contemporary theatre. Though being part of the audience may not mean actually playing in the play, neither does it mean sitting passively in the dark while the play unfolds on stage. Theatre is no longer something done to an audience.

Third, the nature of acting is changing. Gone, probably forever, are the limiting ideas of acting only as psychological revelation or as undistorted transmission of an author's words. One can, in fact, argue that theatre development in the last hundred years has paralleled closely the developments in acting theory. Performers now frequently believe or live as much as they act. Like priests, they often become ceremonial leaders in a ritual act designed to lead the entire gathering into a communal celebration; the actor's vested interest here is larger than employment, ego-gratification, or elucidation of an author's thought. Actors frequently perform by moving into and around the group of spectators, rather than only in front of them. They are often asked to perform many roles in a single theatre event, and must rely on instantaneous transformation instead of gradual development. They are faced with a rediscovery of the body, with techniques such as improvisation, theatre games, collective creation, and rigorous physical and vocal training. A renewed focus on the actor as an instrument whose voice, body, and imagination know no bounds has led to an unprecedented eclecticism of performance possibilities.

Fourth, the proscenium stage, a sixteenth-century innovation which convinced almost everyone that watching a play was supposed to be like looking into an aquarium, has been augmented by architectural forms that offer new kinds of actor-audience contact. Some would even argue that every play demands a different kind of space and a different kind of theatre. Theatre has also begun again to explore the possibilities of non-theatre space: a return to the hillside, the street, the cathedral, the basement.

In short, the theatre in our age of transition looks, feels, sounds, and is different from the theatre of only a few years ago. The staleness of a century-old tradition has vanished, as has the shock and excitement of a theatrical revolution in progress. How can one recognize it? A. E. Housman claimed to recognize true poetry by the way it made his skin bristle.[4] In a real sense, our theatre is poetry.

4 A. E. Housman, *The Name and Nature of Poetry* (New York: The Macmillan Company, 1933), p. 46.

Alvin Toffler writes in *Future Shock* that "change, roaring through society, widens the gap between what we believe and what really is, between the existing images and the reality they are supposed to reflect."[5] Consequently, much of today's theatre involves ideas and actions still seen by some as distasteful, unartistic, unauthentic. And, in fact, at its worst it does contain mere gimmicks or kitsch, inarticulate substitutes for intellect, sensibility, and substance. At its best, however, it offers us sincere and effective efforts to make human contact in a world where human contact often seems beyond reach. At either extreme, as in all art, judgments about theatre are best made by referring to its individual works. But one can say that regardless of the function, form, or method of presentation they pursue, those productions which have real value will evoke depth and strength, and will make possible a vital contact between performer and spectator. The director's job is to make theatre happen— which happens more seldom than most will confess.

The emerging middle ground in theatre represents a radical shift—one that has occurred, one that is still occurring. Based on new modes of perception and on new attitudes toward what theatre can and should do, it has in both its positive and negative aspects a basis in the rejection of past assumptions, especially the assumptions about what constitutes effective communication of human experience.

It came about as a response to our changing collective perceptions of reality. The Newtonian world of fixed law has been largely supplanted by the Einsteinian world of relativity. The mechanical printing press—which helped reinforce perception as a sequential, linear, rational, one-thing-at-a-time phenomenon—has given way to electronic communication media— which reinforce perception as a multidimensional, compartmentalized, non-linear, all-at-once happening. Arthur Kubler in *The Shape of Time* suggests that the difference is like the difference between viewing reality as a biological science or seeing it as a physical science.[6] The biological pattern, expressed best in botany and characterized by the well-understood process of birth, growth, maturity, decline, death, and rebirth, has given way to the physical pattern, expressed best by electrodynamics and characterized by vast multidirectional transmissions of energy through relay points, transformers, and transistors. One process moves slowly, the other with amazing speed. One evolves in a straight line; the other explodes in all directions, as in an electric grid.

Although it is a vast oversimplification, one may say that any change in perception seems to cause dramatic changes in almost everything. The

5 Alvin Toffler, *Future Shock* (New York: Bantam Books, Inc., 1970), p. 179.
6 Arthur Kubler, *The Shape of Time* (New Haven: Yale University Press, 1962), p. 9.

theatre, quite naturally, has not been exempt, and it has responded to change elsewhere by changing itself.

A second aspect of the radical shift which blossomed in the 1960's involved dissatisfaction with existing theatre, an attitude that mingled easily, especially among the young, with dissatisfaction with the existing world: each seemed fragmented, disjointed, less-than-honest, having lost usefulness even as it gained complacency. A non-selective list of factors which have influenced recent changes in theatre, all of them responses to our changing perceptions of reality, might begin as follows.[7]

External	Internal
increasing skill in manipulating nature	breakdown of distinctions between the arts
diverse lifestyles	random selectivity vs.
consumerism	mathematical precision
war	idea: art is not something
the information explosion	that is done to you
rock music	compartmentalization
increased educational levels	technology
computer uses	architectural flexibility
emphasis on youth	the return of writers and poets
global awareness	passion to follow ideas
anti-materialism	to their extremes
the communications revolution	movement toward the concrete
rebellion, against family,	mixing media
educational systems,	anonymity of change
the organized church,	spectator creativity
government, society	increasing gap between serious
technology	and non-serious
increased leisure time	retreat from escapism
transience, impermanence	increasing experimentation
mobility	available money
television, film	decentralization

The rejection implied by these factors is sweeping, and the change implied by them extremely radical. Yet it must also be understood, as Lee Baxandall points out in his *Radical Perspective in the Arts,* that the word "radical" is frequently misused today.[8] It is too often used to mean

7 A slightly different version of this list first appeared in my article titled "Anyone Who Knows He Is God Go Up On Stage," *The Lutheran Quarterly* (May 1973), 115–23.

8 Lee Baxandall, ed., *Radical Perspectives in the Arts* (Baltimore: Penguin Books, Inc., 1972), p. 9.

extremist, marginal, or far-out. In fact, its more accurate root is "fundamental" and it means change that goes to the roots—either to destroy
them or to nourish them. For theatre, it has often meant a rejection of
recent conventions in favor of a return to once-central concerns: ritual,
myth, communal celebration, symbols, dreams, ceremonies, language that
towers beyond meaning and even words, action that strives to make
vibrant connections with the heart and mind of the spectator. Consequently, what was called the New Theatre involved a rediscovery of
theatre history, and especially of those periods where theatre proved most
direct, least formal, and overwhelmingly popular for large masses of
people. Particularly strong influences can be seen in primitive rituals, the
commedia dell'arte, the Elizabethan public theatre, romanticism, the
mid-nineteenth century popular stage and expressionism.

One impulse behind both the rejection and the rediscovery has been
the compulsion to experiment. Someone has suggested that developments
in art proceed in three stages: an initial stage that involves breaking new
ground, a middle stage that permits exploration of the new territory as
completely as possible, and a final stage during which artists create works
of enduring quality. One can argue that current theatre has lumbered
through the first stage for almost a hundred years, and that the recent
explosion in experimentation was an accelerating development of the
second stage. If so, we can see some reason for optimism: our current
awkwardness can be seen as merely a hesitation necessary before we
enter the third stage. However, it can also be seen as expressing a
yearning to return to the first stage. This process of experimentation in
theatre follows no neatly defined patterns.

If a desire for more experimentation has been one underlying impulse
for change in theatre, a second one has been a rediscovered sense of
play. When Peter Brook concluded *The Empty Space* by suggesting that
"a play is play," he both reflected and influenced much of current theatre.[9]
While he was not the first person to suggest such an idea, he may well
have been the first to popularize it, and his words express a philosophy
that has begun to dominate much dramatic activity. Luckily, the idea of a
play as play can be rather easily accepted. It has the ring of truth. It even
sounds like fun. Certainly it implies an attitude to be wished for.

Perhaps not surprisingly, play seems to be the gauntlet these days
through which artistic and intellectual concerns must run. Play-theory and
game-theory abound, and have found a place in such diverse fields as
psychology, anthropology, sociology, economics, literary criticism, philosophy, theology, and mathematics. Certainly theatre has not been exempt.

9 Peter Brook, *The Empty Space* (New York: Atheneum, 1969), p. 141.

Theatre games now enjoy widespread popularity and application. Transactional analysis provides one current tool for dramatic analysis. Role-playing, game logic, and other play-theory ramifications are beginning to be known.

Perhaps the most compelling reason for theatre's ready adoption of the play metaphor has been a desire to bring back to theatre a sense of joy. The modern theatre of realism, like modern education, has long been associated with the glum and the joyless. Alexander Tairov deplored this loss more than forty years ago: "Joy and youth have renounced the theatre," he said, "because, instead of wonderful flights into the fantastic region of the impossible, it struggles weakly in the snares of naturalistic banality or, wingless, drags itself about among the anemic, decadent conventions of formalism."[10]

Joy has its roots in play, and this whole idea is especially important for directors. Approaching theatre as play can create a coherent attitude toward one's work while also providing a practical approach for actually doing the work. Futhermore, it can offer an atmosphere conducive to rehearsal and performance. In other words, the idea of play as play can govern both the process and the product of the director's work. Consequently, it is important to see play for what it is, if only to remove from its image the sense of frivolity it enjoys in the minds of some.

In *Homo Ludens,* the earliest and still among the most significant writings on play, Johan Huizinga defines play as "a voluntary activity or occupation executed within certain fixed limits of time and place, according to rules freely accepted but absolutely binding, having its aim in itself and accompanied by a feeling of tension, joy, and the consciousness that is 'different' from 'ordinary life'."[11] As such, it has many recognizable attributes that can have direct relationships to theatre. (1) Play is voluntary. One enters into it freely, without obligation. No one forces participation. When it is not free, it ceases to be play. (2) Play is intense. It has genuine tension, and can be totally absorbing. It operates on the principles of involuntary attention, absorbing players totally. (3) Play is significant. It has serious consequences, and can even be deadly. Certainly "play" and "serious" are not opposites. Huizinga suggests that play is of a higher order because "seriousness seeks to exclude play, whereas play can very well include seriousness." (4) Play is superfluous. Its only purpose is the joy of playing. Necessary because it becomes culture, play exists for

---

10 Alexander Tairov, *Notes of a Director* (Miami: University of Miami Press, 1969), p. 41.
11 Johan Huizinga, *Homo Ludens* (Boston: Beacon Press, 1955), p. 28.

itself. (5) Play is irrational. It operates best beyond the realm of rationality, moving from frivolity to ecstasy in non-logical patterns that defy mere normality. (6) Play is uncertain. Impartial, unbiased, and disinterested, it keeps the outcome in question until play is finished. Its essence is risk and daring. (7) Play is out of the ordinary. It is separate from "real" life, proceeding in its own confined time and space, a temporary state with a definite beginning and end. (8) Play is ordered. It is governed by rules which suspend ordinary laws and establish a framework of expectation and regulation for the playing.

The parallels between play and theatre make "play as play" not only possible but necessary. Approached another way, concepts of Theatrum Mundi mix with Homo Ludens to make possible a Theatrum Ludens. Directors should play at making plays—with all the discipline, concentration, endurance, skill, and joy that play demands.

A revolution in communication principles, dissatisfaction with what seemed an inadequate theatre response to a changing world, the widespread adoption of practices drawn from theatre history, increasing quantities of experimentation, and the establishment of theatre as a playground for process and product—all have led to a theatre of unlimited possibilities. In our time one cannot point with certainty to central tendencies or single long-term trends. Instead, we operate within a continuum bound by extremes and limited only by imagination.

The resulting eclecticism quite naturally affects all theatre artists, including the director, and perhaps the easiest way to visualize the current situation is to list some obvious differences between the extremes of nineteenth-century realism and the now equally historic New Theatre, for these two movements form, in essence, the boundaries of current activity. In doing so, however, one must remember that these "opposites" can no longer be considered individually. The director or playwright need not choose between the two. Rather, the range of possibility falls between or beyond them. One must also remember that large generalizations contain limited detail, making for easily recognizable exceptions. The columns below are labeled Traditional and New, not because they hold that relationship today, but because during the 1960's and early 1970's, the time of their greatest interaction, they frequently appeared that way. Today, of course, neither one is either traditional *or* new.[12]

---

12 A list that details similar parallels for the actor can be found in Charles Marowitz, "Notes on the Theatre of Cruelty," in Part Two of this book.

Traditional

1 Actors play a scene or scenes, then exit out of audience sight, participating in the on-stage action only when personally involved.

2 Actors have an extended period of time, often two or three hours, to reveal a single character in all its depth and complexity.

3 Scripts are abstract, representational, realistic.

4 Performance presents an illusion of reality.

5 Single-focus dominates, enhanced by the formal picture-frame proscenium stage.

6 Performance preparation begins with a written script.

7 Language emerges as verbal dialogue between two or more characters arranged in logical (or illogical), linear fashion, designed to advance plot, story, characterization, atmosphere.

8 Performance is something done for or to an audience, while it sits more or less passively, watching.

New

1 Actors remain visible all the time. They stay on stage from start to finish of the performance, even for periods when they are not actively involved in what seems to be going on.

2 Actors play several roles in a single performance, facing an absence of exposition and the necessity for immediate wholeness, quick transformations, and the substitution of action for motivation.

3 Scripts, texts, or whatever comprises the performance score are concrete, presentational, non-realistic.

4 Performance presents only the reality of the performance itself.

5 Multiple-focus dominates, enhanced by informal, environmental, architectural arrangements in which audiences perceive performances from various flexible points of view.

6 Performance preparation begins with collective work, which may or may not involve a playwright; a text evolves as the result of, rather than the cause for, preparation.

7 Language emerges as sound, as pre-verbal or non-verbal outburst, as poetry arranged in non-logical, non-linear fashion, often struggling in the search for meaning rather than in the revelation of it.

8 Performance is offered as a shared event, inviting its audience to active or inactive participation.

9 Directors serve as a unifying artistic and pragmatic force, applying vision and craft to a textual property.

10 Movement gains importance as related to such things as motivation, composition, character development.

11 Time and space are fixed.

12 The performance event happens as a formalized occasion involving an invited audience using tickets for admission.

13 Audiences sit in ordered rows of seats facing the stage.

14 Audiences are in the dark during performance, helping to focus attention on the lighted stage.

15 Preparation for performance and performance itself have roots directly related to Konstantin Stanislavsky.

16 The actor-audience relationship is defined by the physical separation integral to the proscenium stage.

9 Directors serve as priests or celebrants, guiding through conviction and belief as well as through craft.

10 Movement erupts into a kinetic celebration either of the body as body or of the body as an instrument capable of its own spatial, non-verbal language.

11 Time and space are not established at all. Action takes place "on stage," with more emphasis on what than on when or where.

12 The performance event happens informally, often free of charge.

13 Audiences group randomly, unordered and unorganized, often on the floor, or standing, in bleachers or in small clusters.

14 Audiences are not in the dark during performance, helping to divide attention between the stage and audience.

15 Preparation, and performance itself, have roots in the ideas of Bertolt Brecht, Antonin Artaud, Jerzy Grotowski, and many other innovators, and also in fields once considered outside the realm of theatre—such as transactional analysis, structuralism, play and game theory, the organization of myth and ritual.

16 The actor-audience relationship is defined according to the needs of individual productions.

17 Plays are performed in theatres, where convention is determined by architecture.

17 Plays are performed in found space, created space, non-theatre space, where convention is determined by intent.

18 Technical elements of production play a strongly supportive, enhancing role.

18 Technical elements of production explore two extremes: "total" theatre, in which all elements—sometimes especially technical ones—are combined in often extravagant manner; and 'poor' theatre, in which technical elements—at least to the casual observer—seem to be extremely limited or nonexistent.

19 Verbal and vocal effectiveness are determined by transmission of meaning and emotion through words.

19 Verbal and vocal effectiveness are determined by gymnastic flexibility and control, with communication by sound and sound patterns. Language use is often like music—measured more by rhythm, intonation, intensity, melody, and harmony than by linguistic meaning.

The confrontation between these extremes led to the theatre revolution in the Vietnam era. That era having receded into history, we are left in the mid-1970's (and for the foreseeable future) with a question posed by playwright Benjamin Bradford late in 1973: "What do you do when the revolution is over?"[13] Revolutions, of course, can end in at least three ways: in victory, where their causes become the basis for a new regime; in defeat, where their concerns are obliterated or return underground; or, as in our age, in almost total absorption into the establishment system. What the director does, in this case, is work in a field of expanded possibility, where neither the old rules nor the new rules alone work effectively, because each limits him to a historical perspective that tends to conceal the central problem of theatre.

Peter Brook, in his Introduction to Marat/Sade, a play now more than a decade old but still perhaps the single theatre piece that best combines the two continuum extremes, describes the central problem for theatre

13 Benjamin Bradford, lecture at the University of Kentucky, April 1973.

as a search for density of experience. "What's the difference," he asks, "between a poor play and a good one? I think there is a very simple way of comparing them. A play in performance is a series of impressions; little dabs, one after another, fragments of information of reeling in a sequence which stir the audience's perceptions. A good play sends many such messages, often several at a time, often crowding, jostling, overlapping one another. The intelligence, the feelings, the memory, the imaginations are all stirred. In a poor play, the impressions are well spaced out, they lope along in single file, and in the gaps the heart can sleep while the mind wanders to the day's annoyances and thoughts of dinner. The whole problem of the theatre today is just this: how can we make plays dense in experience?"[14] Our current theatre, like theatre of any age, is suggesting new answers to Brook's question, answers that are firmly grounded in our changing perception of reality. Perhaps not surprisingly, many of the answers have been discovered in earlier theatre convention. None of the directions are yet fixed; most are surprisingly fluid, sometimes frustratingly so. But our current situation, having spawned a changed and changeable theatre, demands that its directors have more options available than once might have been necessary. The range of choices must be wider. It also suggests that directors need to be even more imaginative, more skilled in their craft, more knowledgeable and more discerning, for the very variety of options available makes the job more difficult and more challenging. Since, as Robert Edmund Jones suggested, we must all "work in the theatre of our own time with the tools of our own time,"[15] no good director will eliminate materials, forms, plays, or techniques from the past, present, or future as he works toward developing ever greater insight and skill. He will draw upon both the old and the new, while inventing the not-yet-known, in order to transform his own unique vision into the facts of theatre performance.

This book is designed to explore some of the possibilities currently useful for the director, and in its organization the material has been divided into two Parts and two Appendixes.

Part One, Contemporary Approaches to Directing, presents a smorgasbord of twentieth-century directors, each, with the exception of Bertolt Brecht, speaking for himself. They range in time from Edward Gordon Craig, whose ideas about theatre and directing are only now beginning

14 Peter Brook, "Introduction" to Peter Weiss, *Marat/Sade* (New York: Atheneum, 1966), p. v.
15 Robert Edmund Jones, *The Dramatic Imagination* (New York: Theatre Arts Books, 1941), p. 64.

to be realized, to very recent practitioners. Their thoughts collide in a cacaphony representative of our own time. They could be sorted out, arranged so as to contradict or support each other, argued for or against. Perhaps they could even be explained. Yet they speak well for themselves, and have been chosen not for their differences, which are frequently significant, but for their similarities. For although they are diverse in chronology, geography, and philosophy, these directors do share considerable common ground. Each expresses a deep and searching commitment to the overall effectiveness of theatre, and is as much concerned with discovering the nature of theatre art as with staging performances; each searches for an effective process that can produce the envisioned results; each encourages an approach that is open, flexible, and committed to continuing experimentation; and each feels more secure in erring, if at all, on the side of daring rather than timidity. Each, also, has enjoyed considerable influence, both on directing and on the theatre in general. Becoming familiar with a small portion of their work may serve in lieu of an apprenticeship with them. All directors can benefit from watching other directors at work, not to copy but to learn.

There are, of course, many directors not included. Names like Piscator, Copeau, Clurman, Chaikin, Gregory, and Papp are obvious ones. Those who are included, however, seem best to develop an implied if not a stated proposition that directing is a search for process as well as product. Furthermore, each points to the special tenuousness that now characterizes our own theatre.

A word of caution, however, must be said on their behalf. Because the written word gives the appearance of permanence, it may be easy to assume that the writing collected here represents the definitive and most recent thought of each writer. Such is not the case, especially for those directors still actively at work. Ideas change, as do methods, and the ideas represented here should be seen as moments of growth at a given time rather than as final answers.

That admonition has even more validity for the writings in Part Two, Contemporary Directing Practice: Some Possibilities. Many of the ideas on guerrilla theatre, street theatre, improvisation, and new staging techniques, for example, have recent roots in the political anger and frustration of the 1960's. But they have also become widely used for non-radical, non-political purposes as well. As a whole, they point to ways for providing less formal and more direct theatre opportunities than would have been possible fifteen years ago, and the critical reader will judge each of them accordingly.

Approached this way, the individual articles become a collage of practical and philosophical suggestions for directors in the current theatre—
specific plans, tools, techniques and ideas for working. Exposure to such
ideas grows increasingly important for directors as the diversity of our
changing theatre expands: the more he knows, the wiser his decisions
can be. The overlap among articles suggests how completely any one
aspect of our theatre is influenced by others. The tool most useful for
discovering specific topics will be the Table of Contents, rather than any
organizational progression, although Part Two begins with attention to
new or rediscovered forms of theatre, and then moves to an exploration of
some currently useful techniques and architectural considerations. This is
followed by three brief articles about the creative person and the creative
process, included because most available information about directing
sidesteps these issues, which are in the end most central to a director's
possibilities. Too often we treat creativity as a mystery, denying ourselves
knowledge of it in the mistaken assumption that knowing will confine the
creative impulse. On the contrary, though studying creativity and reading
about it may be less exciting than the act of creation itself, understanding
the process will enable directors to practice it—and to recognize it when it
presents itself. The section ends with Edmund Carpenter's analysis of the
artist's use of communication and playwright Jean-Claude van Itallie's
musing about a possible future for theatre.

One large area of recent activity, which is often implied but not directly
discussed in Part Two, is group collaboration, which has become a frequent method for creating theatre performance. In collective creation the
director's role changes considerably from that in rehearsing and performing the normal scripted production. Some groups function without a
director, each member sharing responsibility equally for all aspects of
production. Others function with the director as one member inside the
group, sharing in the collaboration but also providing leadership in the
creation, selection, organization, and presentation of performance material.
Still others function with the director as a non-performer outside the
group, assuming more closely a role usually associated with directing. In
any case, the skills involved rely less on creative vision translated into
performance technique and more on ability to generate, respond to, and
organize creativity in others. Both the process and the product of the work
differ from usual practice.

Theodore Shank has discussed some of the primary differences, while
suggesting the principal techniques of creating a performance collectively,
by relating the process to changes in society:

The group, rather than the individual, is the typical focus of the alternative society, and this is reflected in the structure of the new theatre organizations, their manner of working, and their theatre pieces. The collective creation of theatre pieces has become the method of conceiving and developing works in the alternative theatre. Society has become increasingly specialized and competitive. This is reflected in an established theatre based on competition and a theatrical method that focuses on individual specialists, such as playwright, director, and star actor. In reaction to the fragmentation of the established society, which for many has become disorienting, the alternative society has sought wholeness. This is evident in many ways, including its focus on group living and group activities, and in its theatre which is based on the cooperation of a creative collective.

Instead of the two-process method of the traditional theatre—a playwright writing a script in isolation and other artists staging it—the new theatre practices a one-process method, wherein the group itself develops the piece from initial conception to finished performance. The typical member of a new theatre group is not merely a performer, but a person with broader creative responsibilities, who may not distinguish between the work of performer, director, designer, and playwright, but who applies his creative energies to the making of a theatre piece, whatever that might involve. While some in the group will provide more leadership than others, the works that result are truly the expression of the group, not simply of a playwright or director.

Improvisation is the principal technique. It is used to train members of the group to work creatively and collectively, and to suggest initial conceptions for new pieces. It is the means by which embryonic conceptions are developed into finished productions. Sometimes, the improvisational exercises themselves become the performance. Despite the use of improvisations by nearly every group, each develops its own unique method that may change somewhat from work to work as they experiment with new conceptions and new means of expressing them. One of the chief ways their methods differ is in the source of or the means of discovering an inceptive idea for a piece: (1) from exercises; (2) from a social, political, or aesthetic problem; (3) from a text or painting; (4) from working with an object or materials; or (5) from a script by someone within the group. The groups may also vary in their means of developing the piece—through discussion, research, improvisation. And they are also distinguished by the circumstances of performance, which may be completely determined in rehearsal and set before performances, may be improvised within a scenario, and may involve spectators. . . .[16]

16 From Theodore Shank, "Collective Creation," first published in The Drama Review, vol. 16, no. 2 (T54) [June 1972, pp. 3–4]. Copyright © 1972 by The Drama Review. Reprinted by permission. All Rights Reserved.

Collective creation has several other recognizable characteristics and has expanded to involve more than just alternative theatre projects. (1) Most group efforts, whether flexible or rigid in performance, result in kinetic, non-verbal emphasis. Verbal language, especially dialogue, is relegated to a supporting role, perhaps because words are difficult to create collectively. (2) Much of it is problem-oriented, focused on concerns central to members of the group. Social, political, even artistic, questions are explored in a search for "meaningful" answers as well as worthwhile methods in presentation. (3) Group creativity usually develops in an open-ended manner, without the early pressure of a preestablished performance date. (4) Not infrequently, and especially when a writer is part of the group, the result is highly scripted. (5) It always seems to function with process being of equal importance to product. (6) It concentrates on the exploration of alternatives.

One major difference for the director or leader lies in the group itself, especially when it is formed primarily for the purpose of collective creation in theatre, which is and probably will continue to be an increasingly popular method for initiating production. The director's first job, then, is to help in the formation of the group itself, sometimes in the actual choosing of persons to participate, but always in the shaping of cohesiveness and unity. His role is shaped by the differences between groups and by the unique way of approaching process, as Shank points out:

The most significant differences between the working methods of the new theatre and traditional methods is that the pieces are created through a single process from inception to completion somewhat as in the visual arts. This change demands broader creative responsibility than is required of those in the established theatre, who are more narrowly specialized. Each participant contributes to the development of the conception for a piece and takes part in the search for materials and techniques to express the conception. Often each member of a group combines the specialized traditional functions of playwright, director, designer, etc. The leader of such a group, rather than possessing the specialized abilities of a director in the established theatre, must possess the same creative skills as the other members and in addition be able to stimulate and focus their creative energy. This might be accomplished by providing structures within which the group can improvise, by leading and directing discussion, or by providing objects and environments with which the group can work. Nearly always the leader has no official recognition; sometimes the leadership rotates from one member to another; often the leader is also a performer. Moreover, it is frequently necessary for the leader to become a kind of teacher because the members of the group usually come from schools and universities, where they have been trained in the methods of the traditional theatre, or from established theatre companies, and they have had little opportunity to develop the broad skills necessary in a creative collective. They may be skillful performers or technicians, but they often lack the conceptual ability that is requisite to their participation in the making of a work without the aid of a script. . . .[17]

One exception to the usual role of director or leader in the theatre collective can be found in women's theatre groups, many of which have been organized recently, as Charlotte Rea suggests, "as a means of exploring and expressing women's identity, potentialities, and the nature of oppression." Rea also explores the difference:

While the collective structure has been adopted by many feminists, their groups differ in one important aspect from their male-dominated counterparts. This difference is the absence of a leader or director. Almost without exception, heterosexual groups evolve into a leader-followers political structure. The leader is the person acknowledged, even if only implicitly, by the other members to be the most insightful, most creative, most objective, most powerful person in the group. Since women for centuries have felt themselves to be less creative in the arts, less important, and less powerful than men, feminists feel that to allow their groups to evolve into the accepted power structure would be to perpetuate the thinking that has kept women from realizing their own potentialities for creative expression. It is better to develop each member's idea to a limited degree, they reason, than to pursue fully one person's vision, while the other performers exist only as tools for the transmittal of the director's ideas. If every member must depend on her own creative output instead of relying passively on the leader-director for inspiration and guidance, then the theatrical forms that the group produces must convey to the women in the audience that they, too, possess untapped potential for artistic creativity. . . .[18]

Approaching collective creation involves renewed emphasis on process. Results still count: performance excellence is still a major goal, even if the ways of measuring such excellence change. But the means to this end, the process, becomes crucial both for itself and for the way it influences results. Furthermore, the results of collective creation are usually more ephemeral even than usual theatre performance. Even when scripted, performance is indigenous to the group and cannot easily be

17 Shank, p. 30. Reprinted by permission.
18 Charlotte Rea, "Women's Theatre Groups," first published in *The Drama Review,* vol. 16. no. 2 (T54), [June 1972, pp. 79–80]. Copyright © 1972 by *The Drama Review.* Reprinted by permission. All Rights Reserved.

duplicated or repeated. In fact, Alvin Toffler's forecast that "the future of art seems no longer to lie with the creation of enduring masterworks" has special relevance to group-created theatre.[19]

Whereas the first two Parts of this book attempt to provide insight into directing techniques and principles that will be useful in the contemporary theatre, the two Appendixes offer tools for the director who wishes to engage in actual production—first by offering a variety of plays for directing practice, and then by presenting a possible form for evaluating directing growth.

The first Appendix, Plays for Playing, may prove to be the most problematical section of the book, primarily because the plays presented there, as one potential director said prior to publication, can scare the hell out of anyone who contemplates producing them. Many of them seem on the surface to be without action; most seem to be without plot or story; some have no characters; at least two have no words at all, and one has nothing but words. Yet they need not be frightening, and will not prove so if one guards against the impulse to feel stymied after a first reading.

Each of the plays is eminently approachable, even though most dispense with the elements a director usually looks to first. That they require a high degree of director creativity, that they do not provide the director with his usual points of security, that they demand careful preparation—all are reasons for their inclusion. They afford opportunity to expand directorial approach and technique by providing freedom from the usual strictures that a director must contend with. In addition, each of the plays is open, flexible, and short, suitable for both classroom exercise and public performance.

None of the plays included are tied directly to the New Theatre movement, but all do rely on increasingly non-realistic attempts to create a theatre moment in performance that can be exciting, vibrant, and worthwhile. They represent, in short, a theatre for our time. If they appear unusual or difficult, it is because they share the common ground of dispensing with expected content, form, and development. Each creates an information envelope that must be transmitted for an audience as a totality. Segmented, slowly developing, expositional performance practices will be of little use. All are easily adaptable for a wide variety of performing spaces.

Benjamin Bradford's *Rehearsal* is perhaps the most accessible of the scripts. A one-actor monologue, it develops a style recently called the "new realism," and it draws heavily on traditional aspects of character

19 Toffler, p. 175, quoting John McHale in "The Plastic Parthenon," *Lineastruttura* (June 1966).

and story mixed with a highly sympathetic, almost old-fashioned, attitude toward adolescence. Yet the literary aspects of the play are overshadowed by the implied action necessary for its performance and by the clarity of purpose suggested in the title. The director's primary concern, and the actor's, will need to be character revelation, continuity, and inventiveness—rather usual concerns expressed in a fresh way.

The Tiger, The Man and the Mouse and *Master of All Masters* are short, typical story theatre pieces involving narration, spoken action, quick change from narration to action, and mime. Each is propelled by its story, brought to life by its characters, and given freshness by its imaginative demands on both performer and audience. A sense of play should pervade the performance of either script, but the variety of possibilities for character and action are virtually unlimited.

The next five plays may seem somewhat more confining. *Mathematics, Good Question,* and *9 Parts in 7 Circumstances* all share a specificity of author intention that would seem to limit a director to carrying out instructions. His freedom is limited by the stated requirements of the physical action and by the minimal or non-existent use of spoken language. *Love Lace* and *Self-Accusation* lie at the other extreme. Confined by a concreteness of language that seems to reduce the theatre experience to words alone, the plays leave entirely open their physical action and their method of presentation. *Self-Accusation,* for example, can be performed by two actors on stools before microphones, as Handke suggests; or by eight actors in a tightly confined space; or by almost any other number of actors in almost any other manner. The idea of the play, once discovered, can be revealed in a great variety of equally useful ways—which is also true of the plays that precede it.

The remaining plays may seem to be most problematical. The short poem plays by Ruth Krauss and Paul Reps, not unlike the older work of Gertrude Stein, each provide a strong central image that needs to be translated into theatrical convention so that both the image and the sense of play are recognized by the audience; they need directness in presentation. They are not obscure in meaning, but can be envisioned in many, many ways. A single piece, for example, has on one occasion been performed in several different ways as part of a single evening of theatre.

The director who reads *Help, Bo,* or *'', or REQ* for the first time may be struck with a single thought: it would be impossible to stage them for the theatre. Each presents problems that on first glance appear insurmountable. Yet each also provides an openness that is completely unconfined, and the director must rely almost completely on his own rather than the playwright's creativity for staging ideas. Even more than in

Self-Accusation and *Love Lace,* the work of the playwright "infringes" little upon the director, permitting him freedom to explore the work for performance effectiveness. The scripts, in a pure sense, are performance pieces rather than plays, and their authors provide only scant guidelines for directorial decisions, which should be a welcome opportunity instead of a puzzling obstacle.

These comments provide little in the way of specific suggestions for how to approach each of the plays included but that is deliberate. Suggested ideas have a strange way of limiting thought and creativity by unconsciously forcing the creative process into established patterns. The plays require an individual approach, unfettered by confines not established by the director. In fact, most can be produced effectively in many ways, and a useful exercise, especially for the shorter works, might be to present fifteen different versions of the same piece, each prepared by a different director. Each different director could also prepare several different versions of the same script.

Directors at any stage of development, from beginners to the truly accomplished, can gain from a confrontation with scripts that offer the kinds of demands represented by the variety of plays included here. The plays themselves, however, are included not because they are different or unusual or even new (which they most certainly are not), but because they have already proved themselves capable of offering exciting and worthwhile experiences in the theatre. In the end, of course, that is the criterion for any work of theatre.

The second Appendix, Evaluating Process and Product, offers two forms that may prove useful for measuring growth in directing. These need no comment here.

This Introduction began as an exploration of our changing theatre in the mid-1970's and has ended with a brief explanation of the individual selections which follow, in order to permit the collected material to propel itself without further interruption.

One further note needs to be added. Students of theatre, and of directing in particular, are more important to this book than they may recognize. I am convinced that we can all learn, that we can all grow more proficient, that the Gryphon doesn't have to be correct in saying, "That's the reason they're called lessons; they lessen from day to day." I am also convinced that directing, for individuals and for our art as a whole, is an ever-evolving process that expands with exposure to new ideas, and that even now we suffer unduly from our disregard for what others have already learned. Roy Mitchell spoke of the problem in *Creative Theatre* almost fifty years ago:

Our present theatre does not educate. Every director, actor, and designer starts anew, groping from one costly mistake to another in things which in any other art he could learn from a primer. We have no repositories of accumulated experience, no recapitulations of method, no handbooks of technic, no collections of axioms, no precise records of achievement.

We say of a director, "Ah, he is a great artist," and potentially he may be, but in all his greatness he attains little more than what is taught in the schools of the other arts. His achievement represents scarcely more than he could have learned from a good book. "It is a great art, too great an art for one man to learn," we say, and shake our heads. So would botany be too great to learn if everybody had to start away back where Linnaeus did, and modern building too great to learn if every builder had to discover for himself the processes of making structural steel. Botanists and builders set things down for the sake of those to come after them. Botany is a science that has learned to thrive by teaching, and building is a trade that has learned that ignorance is waste.[20]

This collection is offered as another step toward eliminating such problems. Here, then, are some people worth listening to, some ideas worth arguing about, some plays worth performing—in short, some sources for directors in these years when our theatre is evolving in many directions.

20 Roy Mitchell, *Creative Theatre* (Westwood, New Jersey: The Kindle Press, 1969), p. 197.

"What is a Caucus-race?" said Alice; not that she much wanted to know, but the Dodo had paused as if it thought that somebody ought to speak, and no one else seemed inclined to say anything.

"Why," said the Dodo, "the best way to explain it is to do it." (And, as you might like to try the thing yourself some winter-day, I will tell you how the Dodo managed it.)

First it marked out a race-course, in a sort of circle ("the exact shape doesn't matter," it said), and then all the party were placed along the course, here and there. There was no "One, two, three, and away!" but they began running when they liked, and left off when they liked, so that it was not easy to know when the race was over. However, when they had been running half an

PART I
CONTEMPORARY APPROACHES TO DIRECTING

hour or so, and were quite dry again, the Dodo
suddenly called out "The race is over!" and
they all crowded around it, panting, and asking
"But who has won?"

This question the Dodo could not answer
without a great deal of thought, and it stood
for a long time with one finger pressed upon its
forehead (the position in which you usually
see Shakespeare, in the pictures of him), while
the rest waited in silence. At last the Dodo said
"Everybody has won, and all must have prizes."

Lewis Carroll,
Alice's Adventures in Wonderland

The art of the theatre
Edward Gordon Craig

Edward Gordon Craig (1872–1966) was perhaps the earliest of modern theatre theorists to envision the director as the master craftsman and artist who had total responsibility for unity of performance. Opposed to realism, he laid the foundation for much theatre that has followed. Dr. Alexander Hevesi wrote in his Introduction to Craig's *On the Art of the Theatre,* "I think Mr. Craig is the truest revolutionist I have ever known, because he demands a return to the most ancient traditions of which we can dream." This essay was first published in 1905, then revised in 1911. In it Craig explores the overall role of the director, a role vastly different from the standard of his day, in a way that has proven to be prophetic.

"The Art of the Theatre (1st Dialogue)," from Edward Gordon Craig, *On the Art of the Theatre* (London: Richard Clay J. Sons, Limited, 1911).

STAGE DIRECTOR   You have now been over the theatre with me, and have seen its general construction, together with the stage, the machinery for manipulating the scenes, the apparatus for lighting, and the hundred other things, and have also heard what I have had to say of the theatre as a machine; let us rest here in the auditorium, and talk a while of the theatre and of its art. Tell me, do you know what is the Art of the Theatre?

PLAYGOER   To me it seems that Acting is the Art of the Theatre.

STAGE DIRECTOR   Is a part, then, equal to a whole?

PLAYGOER   No, of course not. Do you, then, mean that the play is the Art of the Theatre?

STAGE-DIRECTOR   A play is a work of literature, is it not? Tell me, then, how one art can possibly be another.

PLAYGOER   Well, then if you tell me that the Art of the Theatre is neither the acting nor the play, then I must come to the conclusion that it is the scenery and the dancing. Yet I cannot think you will tell me this is so.

STAGE-DIRECTOR   No; the Art of the Theatre is neither acting nor the play, it is not scene nor dance, but it consists of all the elements of which these things are composed: action, which is the very spirit of acting; words which are the body of the play; line and color, which are the very heart of the scene; rhythm, which is the very essence of dance.

PLAYGOER   Action, words, line, color, rhythm! And which of these is all-important to the art?

STAGE-DIRECTOR   One is no more important than the other, no more than one color is more important to a painter than another, or one note more important than another to a musician. In one respect, perhaps, action is the most valuable part. Action bears the same relation to the Art of the Theatre as drawing does to painting, and melody does to music. The Art of the Theatre has sprung from action-movement-dance.

PLAYGOER   I always was led to suppose that it had sprung from speech, and that the poet was the father of the theatre.

STAGE-DIRECTOR   This is the common belief, but consider it for a moment. The poet's imagination finds voice in words, beautifully chosen; he then either recites or sings these words to us, and all is done. That poetry, sung or recited, is for our ears, and, through them, for our imagination. It will not help the matter if the poet shall add gesture to his recitation or to his song; in fact, it will spoil all.

PLAYGOER   Yes, that is clear to me. I quite understand that the addition of gesture to a perfect lyric poem can but produce an inharmonious result. But would you apply the same argument to dramatic poetry?

STAGE-DIRECTOR   Certainly I would. Remember I speak of a dramatic poem. not of a drama. The two things are separate things. A dramatic poem is to be read. A drama is not to be read, but to be seen upon the stage. Therefore gesture is a necessity to a drama, and it is useless to a dramatic poem. It is absurd to talk of these two things, gesture and poetry, as having anything to do with one another. And now, just as you must not confound the dramatic poem with the drama, neither must you confound the dramatic poet with the dramatist. The first writes for the reader, or listener, the second writes for the audience of a theatre. Do you know who was the father of the dramatist?

PLAYGOER   No, I do not know, but I suppose he was the dramatic poet.

STAGE-DIRECTOR   You are wrong. The father of the dramatist was the dancer. And now tell me from what material the dramatist made his first piece?

PLAYGOER   I suppose he used words in the same way as the lyric poet.

STAGE-DIRECTOR   Again you are wrong, and that is what everyone else supposes who has not learnt the nature of dramatic art. No; the dramatist made his first piece by using action, words, line, color, and rhythm, and making his appeal to our eyes and ears by a dexterous use of these five factors.

PLAYGOER   And what is the difference between this work of the first dramatists and that of the modern dramatists?

STAGE-DIRECTOR   The first dramatists were children of the theatre. The modern dramatists are not. The first dramatist understood what the modern dramatist does not yet understand. He knew that when he and his fellows appeared in front of them the audience would be more eager to see what he would do than to hear what he might say. He knew that the eye is more swiftly and powerfully appealed to than any other sense; that it is without question the keenest sense of the body of man. The first thing which he encountered on appearing before them was many pairs of eyes, eager and hungry. Even the men and women sitting so far from him that they would not always be able to hear what he might say, seemed quite close to him by reason of the piercing keenness of their questioning eyes. To these, and all, he spoke either in poetry or prose, but always in action: in poetic action which is dance, or in prose action which is gesture.

PLAYGOER   I am very interested, go on, go on.

STAGE-DIRECTOR   No—rather let us pull up and examine our ground. I have said that the first dramatist was the dancer's son, that is to say, the child of the theatre, not the child of the poet. And I have just said that the modern dramatic poet is the child of the poet, and knows only how to reach the ears of his listeners, nothing else. And yet in spite of this does not the modern audience still go to the theatre as of old to see things, and not to hear things? Indeed, modern audiences insist on looking and having their eyes satisfied in spite of the call from the poet that they shall use their ears only. And now do not misunderstand me. I am not saying or hinting that the poet is a bad writer of plays, or that he has a bad influence upon the theatre. I only wish you to understand that the poet is not of the theatre, has never come from the theatre, and cannot be of the theatre, and that only the dramatist among writers has any birth-claim to the theatre—and that a very slight one. But to continue. My point is this, that the people still flock to see, not to hear plays. But what does that prove? Only that the audiences have not altered. They are there with their thousand pairs of eyes, just the same as of old. And this is all the more extraordinary because the playwrights and the plays have altered. No longer is a play a balance of actions, words, dance, and scene, but it is either all words or all scene. Shakespeare's plays, for instance, are a very different thing to the less modern miracle and mystery plays, which were made entirely for the theatre. *Hamlet* has not the nature of a stage representation. *Hamlet* and the other plays of Shakespeare have so vast and so complete a form when read, that they can but lose heavily when presented to us after having undergone stage treatment. That they were acted in Shakespeare's day proves nothing. I will tell you, on the other hand, what at that period was made for the theatre—the Masques, the Pageants—these were light and beautiful examples of the Art of the Theatre. Had the plays been made to be seen, we should find them incomplete when we read them. Now, no one will say that they find *Hamlet* dull or incomplete when they read it, yet there are many who will feel sorry after witnessing a performance of the play, saying, "No, that is not Shakespeare's *Hamlet*." When no further addition can be made so as to better a work of art, it can be spoken of as "finished"—it is complete. *Hamlet* was finished—was complete—when Shakespeare wrote the last word of his blank verse, and for us to add to it by gesture, scene, costume, or dance, is to hint that it is incomplete and needs these additions.

PLAYGOER   Then do you mean to say *Hamlet* should never be performed?

STAGE-DIRECTOR   To what purpose would it be if I replied "Yes?" *Hamlet* will go on being performed for some time yet, and the duty of the interpreters is to put their best work at its service. But, as I have said, the theatre must not forever rely upon having a play to perform, but must in time perform pieces of its own art.

PLAYGOER   And a piece for the theatre, is that, then, incomplete when printed in a book or recited?

STAGE-DIRECTOR   Yes—and incomplete anywhere except on the boards of a theatre. It must needs be unsatisfying, artless, when read or merely heard, because it is incomplete without its action, its color, its line, and its rhythm in movement and in scene.

PLAYGOER   This interests me, but it dazzles me at the same time.

STAGE-DIRECTOR   Is that, perhaps, because it is a little new? Tell me what it is especially that dazzles you.

PLAYGOER   Well, first of all, the fact that I have never stopped to consider of what the art of the theatre consisted—to many of us it is just an amusement.

STAGE-DIRECTOR   And to you?

PLAYGOER   Oh, to me it has always been a fascination, half amusement and half intellectual exercise. The show has always amused me; the playing of the players has often instructed me.

STAGE-DIRECTOR   In fact, a sort of incomplete satisfaction. That is the natural result of seeing and hearing something imperfect.

PLAYGOER   But I have seen some few plays which seemed to satisfy me.

STAGE-DIRECTOR   If you have been entirely satisfied by something obviously mediocre, may it not be that you were searching for something less than mediocre, and you found that which was just a little better than you expected? Some people go to the theatre, nowadays, expecting to be bored. This is natural, for they have been taught to look for tiresome things. When you tell me you have been satisfied at a modern theatre, you prove that it is not only the art which has degenerated, but that a proportion of the audience has degenerated also. But do not let this depress you. I once knew a man whose life was so occupied, he never heard music other than that of the street organ. It was to him the ideal of what music should be. Still, as you know, there is better music in the world—in fact, barrel-organ music is very bad music; and if you were for once to see an actual piece of theatrical art, you would never again tolerate what is to-day being thrust upon you in place of theatrical art. The reason why you are not given a work of art on the stage is not because the public does not want it, not because there are not excellent craftsmen in the theatre who could prepare it for you, but because the theatre lacks the artist—the artist of the theatre, mind you, not the painter, poet, musician. The many excellent craftsmen whom I have mentioned are, all of them, more or less helpless to change the situation. They are forced to supply what the managers of the theatre demand, but they do so most willingly. The advent of the artist in the theatre world will change all this. He will slowly but surely gather around him these better craftsmen of whom I speak, and together they will give new life to the art of the theatre.

PLAYGOER   But for the others?

STAGE-DIRECTOR   The others? The modern theatre is full of these others, these untrained and untalented craftsmen. But I will say one thing for them. I believe they are unconscious of their inability. It is not ignorance on their part, it is innocence. Yet if these same men once realized that they were craftsmen, and would train as such—I do not speak only of the stage-carpenters, electricians, wigmakers, costumers, scene-painters, and actors (indeed, these are in many ways the best and most willing craftsmen)—I speak chiefly of the stage-director. If the stage-director was to technically train himself for his task of interpreting the plays of the dramatist—in time, and by a gradual development he would again recover the ground lost to the theatre, and finally would restore the Art of the Theatre to its home by means of his own creative genius.

PLAYGOER   Then you place the stage-director before the actors?

STAGE-DIRECTOR   Yes; the relation of the stage-director to the actor is precisely the same as that of the conductor to his orchestra, or of the publisher to his printer.

PLAYGOER   And you consider that the stage-director is a craftsman and not
an artist?

STAGE-DIRECTOR   When he interprets the plays of the dramatist by means
of his actors, his scene-painters, and his other craftsmen, then he is a craftsman—a master craftsman; when he will have mastered the uses of actions,
words, line, color, and rhythm, then he may become an artist. Then we
shall no longer need the assistance of the playwright—for our art will then
be self-reliant.

PLAYGOER   Is your belief in a Renaissance of the art based on your belief in
the Renaissance of the stage-director?

STAGE-DIRECTOR   Yes, certainly, most certainly. Did you for an instant think
that I have a contempt for the stage-director? Rather have I a contempt
for any man who fails in the whole duty of the stage-director.

PLAYGOER   What are his duties?

STAGE-DIRECTOR   What is his craft? I will tell you. His work as interpreter
of the play of the dramatist is something like this: he takes the copy of the
play from the hands of the dramatist and promises faithfully to interpret
it as indicated in the text (remember I am speaking only of the very best
of stage-directors). He then reads the play, and during the first reading the
entire color, tone, movement, and rhythm that the work must assume
comes clearly before him. As for the stage directions, descriptions of the
scenes, etc., with which the author may interlard his copy, these are not
to be considered by him, for if he is master of his craft he can learn nothing
from them.

PLAYGOER   I do not quite understand you. Do you mean that when a playwright has taken the trouble to describe the scene in which his men and
women are to move and talk, that the stage-director is to take no notice
of such directions—in fact, to disregard them?

STAGE-DIRECTOR   It makes no difference whether he regards or disregards
them. What he must see to is that he makes his action and scene match
the verse or the prose, the beauty of it, the sense of it. Whatever picture
the dramatist may wish us to know of, he will describe his scene during
the progress of the conversation between the characters. Take, for instance, the first scene in *Hamlet*. It begins:—

Ber.   Who's there?
Fran.   Nay, answer me; stand and unfold yourself.
Ber.   Long live the king!
Fran.   Bernardo?
Ber.   He.
Fran.   You come most carefully upon your hour.
Ber.   'Tis now struck twelve; get thee to bed, Francisco.
Fran.   For this relief much thanks, 'tis bitter cold,
      And I am sick at heart.
Ber.   Have you had quiet guard?
Fran.   Not a mouse stirring.
Ber.   Well, good night.
      If you do meet Horatio and Marcellus,
      The rivals of my watch, bid them make haste.

That is enough to guide the stage-director. He gathers from it that it is twelve o'clock at night, that it is in the open air, that the guard of some castle is being changed, that it is very cold, very quiet, and very dark. Any additional "stage directions" by the dramatist are trivialities.

PLAYGOER   Then you do not think that an author should write any stage directions whatever, and you seem to consider it an offense on his part if he does so?

STAGE-DIRECTOR   Well, is it not an offense to the men of the theatre?

PLAYGOER   In what way?

STAGE-DIRECTOR   First tell me the greatest offense an actor can give to a dramatist.

PLAYGOER   To play his part badly?

STAGE-DIRECTOR   No, that may merely prove the actor to be a bad craftsman.

PLAYGOER   Tell me, then.

STAGE-DIRECTOR   The greatest offense an actor can give to a dramatist is to cut out words or lines in his play, or to insert what is known as a "gag." It is an offense to poach on what is the sole property of the playwright. It is not usual to "gag" in Shakespeare, and when it is done it does not go uncensured.

PLAYGOER   But what has this to do with the stage directions of the playwright, and in what way does the playwright offend the theatre when he dictates these stage directions?

STAGE-DIRECTOR   He offends in that he poaches on their preserves. If to gag or cut the poet's lines is an offense, so is it an offense to tamper with the art of the stage-director.

PLAYGOER   Then is all the stage direction of the world's plays worthless?

STAGE-DIRECTOR   Not to the reader, but to the stage-director, and to the actor—yes.

PLAYGOER   But Shakespeare . . .

STAGE-DIRECTOR   Shakespeare seldom directs the stage-manager. Go through *Hamlet, Romeo and Juliet, King Lear, Othello,* any of the masterpieces, and except in some of the historical plays which contain descriptions of possessions, etc., what do you find? How are the scenes described in *Hamlet?*

PLAYGOER   My copy shows a clear description. It has "Act I., scene i. Elsinore. A platform before the Castle."

STAGE-DIRECTOR   You are looking at a late edition with additions by a certain Mr. Malone, but Shakespeare wrote nothing of the kind. His words are "Actus primus. Scaena prima." And now let us look at *Romeo and Juliet.* What does your book say?

PLAYGOER   It says: "Act I., scene i. Verona. A public place."

STAGE-DIRECTOR   And the second scene?

PLAYGOER   It says: "Scene ii. A street."

STAGE-DIRECTOR   And the third scene?

PLAYGOER   It says: "Scene iii. A room in Capulet's house."

STAGE-DIRECTOR   And now, would you like to hear what scene directions Shakespeare actually wrote for this play?

PLAYGOER   Yes.

STAGE-DIRECTOR   He wrote: "Actus primus. Scaena prima." And not another word as to act or scene throughout the whole play. And now for *King Lear.*

PLAYGOER   No, it is enough. I see now. Evidently Shakespeare relied upon the intelligence of the stage-men to complete their scene from his indication. But is this the same in regard to the actions? Does not Shakespeare place some descriptions through *Hamlet,* such as "Hamlet leaps into Ophelia's grave," "Laertes grapples with him," and later, "The attendants part them, and they come out of the grave"?

STAGE-DIRECTOR   No, not one word. All the stage directions, from the first to the last, are the tame inventions of sundry editors, Mr. Malone, Mr. Capell, Theobald, and others, and they have committed an indiscretion in tampering with the play, for which we, the men of the theatre, have to suffer.

PLAYGOER   How is that?

STAGE-DIRECTOR   Why, supposing any of us reading Shakespeare shall see in our mind's eye some other combination of movements contrary to the "instructions" of these gentlemen, and suppose we represent our ideas on the stage, we are instantly taken to task by some knowing one, who accuses us of altering the directions of Shakespeare—nay more, of altering his very intentions.

PLAYGOER   But do not the "knowing ones," as you call them, know that Shakespeare wrote no stage directions?

STAGE-DIRECTOR   One can only guess that to be the case, to judge from their indiscrete criticisms. Anyhow, what I wanted to show you was that our greatest modern poet realized that to add stage directions was first of all unnecessary, and secondly, tasteless. We can therefore be sure that Shakespeare at any rate realized what was the work of the theatre craftsman— the stage-manager, and that it was part of the stage-manager's task to invent the scenes in which the play was to be set.

PLAYGOER   Yes, and you were telling me what each part consisted of.

STAGE-DIRECTOR   Quite so. And now that we have disposed of the error that the author's directions are of any use, we can continue to speak of the way the stage-manager sets to work to interpret faithfully the play of the dramatist. I have said that he swears to follow the text faithfully, and that his first work is to read the play through and get the great impression; and in reading, as I have said, he begins to see the whole color, rhythm, and action of the thing. He then puts the play aside for some time, and in his mind's eye mixes his palette (to use a painter's expression) with the colors which the impression of the play has called up. Therefore, on sitting down a second time to read through the play, he is surrounded by an atmosphere which he proposes to test. At the end of the second reading he will find that his more definite impressions have received clear and unmistakable corroboration, and that some of his impressions which were less positive have disappeared. He will then make a note of these. It is possible that he will even now commence to suggest, in line and color, some of the scenes and ideas which are filling his head, but this is more likely to be delayed until he has re-read the play at least a dozen times.

PLAYGOER   But I thought the stage-manager always left that part of the play—the scene designing—to the scene painter?

STAGE-DIRECTOR   So he does, generally. First blunder of the modern theatre.

PLAYGOER   How is it a blunder?

STAGE-DIRECTOR   This way: A has written a play which B promises to interpret faithfully. In so delicate a matter as the interpretation of so elusive a thing as the spirit of a play, which, do you think, will be the surest way to preserve the unity of that spirit? Will it be best if B does all the work by himself? Or will it do to give the work into the hands of C, D, and E, each of whom sees or thinks differently to B or A?

PLAYGOER   Of course the former would be best. But is it possible for one man to do the work of three men?

STAGE-DIRECTOR   That is the only way the work can be done, if unity, the one thing vital to a work of art, is to be obtained.

PLAYGOER   So, then, the stage-manager does not call in a scene painter and ask him to design a scene, but he designs one himself?

STAGE-DIRECTOR   Certainly. And remember he does not merely sit down and draw a pretty or historically accurate design, with enough doors and windows in picturesque places, but he first of all chooses certain colors which seem to him to be in harmony with the spirit of the play, rejecting other colors as out of tune. He then weaves into a pattern certain objects—an arch, a fountain, a balcony, a bed—using the chosen object as the center of his design. Then he adds to this all the objects which are mentioned in the play, and which are necessary to be seen. To these he adds, one by one, each character which appears in the play, and gradually each movement of each character, and each costume. He is as likely as not to make several mistakes in his pattern. If so, he must, as it were, unpick the design, and rectify the blunder even if he has to go right back to the beginning and start the pattern all over again—or he may even have to begin a new pattern. At any rate, slowly, harmoniously, must the whole design develop, so that the eye of the beholder shall be satisfied. While this pattern for the eye is being devised, the designer is being guided as much by the sound of the verse or prose as by the sense or spirit. And shortly all is prepared, and the actual work can be commenced.

PLAYGOER   What actual work? It seems to me that the stage-manager has already been doing a good deal of what may be called actual work.

STAGE-DIRECTOR   Well, perhaps; but the difficulties have but commenced. By the actual work I mean the work which needs skilled labor, such as the actual painting of the huge spaces of canvas for the scenes, and the actual making of the costumes.

PLAYGOER   You are not going to tell me that the stage-manager actually paints his own scenes and cuts his own costumes, and sews them together?

STAGE-DIRECTOR   No, I will not say that he does so in every case and for every play, but he must have done so at one time or another during his apprenticeship, or must have closely studied all the technical points of these complicated crafts. Then will he be able to guide the skilled craftsmen in their different departments. And when the actual making of the scenes and costumes has commenced, the parts are distributed to the different actors, who learn the words before a single rehearsal takes place. (This, as you may guess, is not the custom, but it is what should be seen to by a stage-director such as I describe.) Meantime, the scenes and costumes are almost ready. I will not tell you the amount of interesting but laborious work it entails to prepare the play up to this point. But even when once the scenes are placed upon the stage, and the costumes upon the actors, the difficulty of the work is still great.

PLAYGOER   The stage-director's work is not finished then?

STAGE-DIRECTOR   Finished! What do you mean?

PLAYGOER   Well, I thought now that the scenes and costumes were all seen to, the actors and actresses would do the rest.

STAGE-DIRECTOR   No, the stage-manager's most interesting work is now beginning. His scene is set and his characters are clothed. He has, in short, a kind of dream picture in front of him. He clears the stage of all but the one, two, or more characters who are to commence the play, and he begins the scheme of lighting these figures and the scene.

PLAYGOER   What, is not this branch left to the discretion of the master electrician and his men?

STAGE-DIRECTOR   The doing of it is left to them, but the manner of doing it is the business of the stage-manager. Being, as I have said, a man of some intelligence and training, he has devised a special way of lighting his scene for this play, just as he has devised a special way of painting the scene and costuming the figures. If the word "harmony" held no significance for him, he would of course leave to it the first comer.

PLAYGOER   Then do you actually mean that he has made so close a study of nature that he can direct his electricians how to make it appear as if the sun were shining at such and such an altitude, or as if the moonlight were flooding the interior of the room with such and such an intensity?

STAGE-DIRECTOR   No, I should not like to suggest that, because the reproduction of nature's lights is not what my stage-manager ever attempts. Neither should he attempt such an impossibility. Not to reproduce nature, but to suggest some of her most beautiful and most living ways—that is what my stage-manager shall attempt. The other thing proclaims an overbearing assumption of omnipotence. A stage-manager may well aim to be an artist, but it ill becomes him to attempt celestial honours. This attitude he can avoid by never trying to imprison or copy nature, for nature will be neither imprisoned nor allow any man to copy her with any success.

PLAYGOER   Then in what way does he set to work? What guides him in his task of lighting the scene and costumes which we are speaking about?

STAGE-DIRECTOR   What guides him? Why, the scene and the costumes, and the verse and the prose, and the sense of the play. All these things, as I told you, have now been brought into harmony, the one with the other—all goes smoothly—what simpler, then, that it should so continue, and that the manager should be the only one to know how to preserve this harmony which he has commenced to create?

PLAYGOER   Will you tell me some more about the actual way of lighting the scene and the actors?

STAGE-DIRECTOR   Certainly. What do you want to know?

PLAYGOER   Well, will you tell me why they put lights all along the floor of the stage—footlights they call them, I believe?

STAGE-DIRECTOR   Yes, footlights.

PLAYGOER   Well, why are they put on the ground?

STAGE-DIRECTOR   It is one of the questions which has puzzled all the theatre reform gentlemen, and none have been able to find an answer, for the simple reason that there is no answer. There never was an answer, there never will be an answer. The only thing to do is to remove all the footlights out of all the theatres as quickly as possible and say nothing about it. It is one of those queer things which nobody can explain, and at which children are always surprised. Little Nancy Lake, in 1812, went to Drury Lane Theatre, and her father tells us that she also was astonished at the footlights. Said she:—

> "And there's a row of lamps, my eye!
> How they do blaze—I wonder why
> They keep them on the ground."

That was in 1812! and we are still wondering.

PLAYGOER   A friend of mine—an actor—once told me that if there were no footlights all the faces of the actors would look dirty.

STAGE-DIRECTOR   That was the remark of a man who did not understand that in place of the footlights another method of lighting the faces and figures could be adopted. It is this simple kind of thing which never occurs to those people who will not devote a little time to even a slight study of the other branches of the craft.

PLAYGOER   Do not the actors study the other crafts of the theatre?

STAGE-DIRECTOR   As a rule—no, and in some ways it is opposed to the very life of an actor. If an actor of intelligence were to devote much time to the study of all the branches of the theatrical art he would gradually cease to act, and would end by becoming a stage-manager—so absorbing is the whole art in comparison with the single craft of acting.

PLAYGOER   My friend the actor also added that if the footlights were removed the audience would not be able to see the expression of his face.

STAGE-DIRECTOR   Had Henry Irving or Elenora Duse said so, the remark would have had some meaning. The ordinary actor's face is either so violently expressive or violently inexpressive, that it would be a blessing if the theatres were not only without footlights but without any lights at all. By the way, and excellent theory of the origin of the footlights is advanced by M. Ludovic Celler in *Les Decors, les costumes et al. mise en-scène au XVII. siecle*. The usual way of lighting the stage was by means of large chandeliers, circular or triangular, which were suspended above the heads of the actors and the audience; and M. Celler is of the opinion that the system of footlights owes its origin to the small plain theatres which could not afford to have chandeliers, and therefore placed tallow candles on the floor in front of the stage. I believe this theory to be correct, for common sense could not have dictated such an artistic blunder; whereas the box-office receipts may easily have done so. Remember how little artistic virtue is in the box-office! When we have time I will tell you some things about this same powerful usurper of the theatrical throne—the box-office. But let us return to a more serious and a more interesting topic than this lack of expression and this footlight matter. We had passed in review the different tasks of the stage-manager—scene, costume, lighting—and we had come to the most interesting part, that of the manipulation of the figures in all their movements and speeches. You expressed astonishment that the acting—that is to say, the speaking and actions of the actors—was not left to the actors to arrange for themselves. But consider for an instant the nature of this work. Would you have that which has already grown into a certain unified pattern, suddenly spoiled by the addition of something accidental?

PLAYGOER   How do you mean? I understand what you suggest, but will you not show me more exactly how the actor can spoil the pattern?

STAGE-DIRECTOR   Unconsciously spoil it, mind you! I do not for an instant mean that it is his wish to be out of harmony with his surroundings, but he does so through innocence. Some actors have the right instincts in this matter, and some have none whatever. But even those whose instincts are most keen cannot remain in the pattern, cannot be harmonious, without following the directions of the stage-manager.

PLAYGOER   Then you do not even permit the leading actor and actress to move and act as their instincts and reason dictate?

STAGE-DIRECTOR   No, rather must they be the very first to follow the direction of the stage-manager, so often do they become the very center of the pattern—the very heart of the emotional design.

PLAYGOER   And is that understood and appreciated by them?

STAGE-DIRECTOR   Yes, but only when they realize and appreciate at the same time that the play, and the right and just interpretation of the play, is the all-important thing in the modern theatre. Let me illustrate this point to you. The play to be presented is *Romeo and Juliet*. We have studied the play, prepared scene and costume, lighted both, and now our rehearsals for the actors commence. The first movement of the great crowd of unruly citizens of Verona, fighting, swearing, killing each other, appalls us. It horrifies us that in this white little city of roses and song and love there should dwell this amazing and detestable hate which is ready to burst out at the very church doors, or in the middle of the May festival, or under the windows of the house of a newly born girl. Quickly following on this picture, and even while we remember the ugliness which larded both faces of Capulet and Montague, there comes strolling down the road the son of Montague, our Romeo, who is soon to be the lover and the loved of his Juliet. Therefore, whoever is chosen to move and speak as Romeo must move and speak as part and parcel of the design—this design which I have already pointed out to you as having a definite form. He must move across our sight in a certain way, passing to a certain point, in a certain light, his head at a certain angle, his eyes, his feet, his whole body in tune with the play, and not (as is often the case) in tune with his own thoughts only, and these out of harmony with the play. For his thoughts (beautiful as they may chance to be) may not match the spirit or the pattern which has been so carefully prepared by the director.

PLAYGOER   Would you have the stage-manager control the movements of whoever might be impersonating the character of Romeo, even if he were a fine actor?

STAGE-DIRECTOR   Most certainly; and the finer the actor the finer his intelligence and taste, and therefore the more easily controlled. In fact, I am speaking in particular of a theatre wherein all the actors are men of refinement and the manager a man of peculiar accomplishments.

PLAYGOER   But are you not asking these intelligent actors almost to become puppets?

STAGE-DIRECTOR   A sensitive question! which one could expect from an actor who felt uncertain about his powers. A puppet is at present only a doll, delightful enough for a puppet show. But for a theatre we need more than a doll. Yet that is the feeling which some actors have about their relationship with the stage-manager. They feel they are having their strings pulled, and resent it, and show they feel hurt—insulted.

PLAYGOER   I can understand that.

STAGE-DIRECTOR   And cannot you also understand that they should be willing to be controlled? Consider for a moment the relationship of the men on a ship, and you will understand what I consider to be the relationship of men in a theatre. Who are the workers on a ship?

PLAYGOER   A ship? Why, there is the captain, the commander, the first, second, and third lieutenants, the navigation officer, and so on, and the crew.

STAGE-DIRECTOR   Well, and what is it that guides the ship?

PLAYGOER   The rudder?

STAGE-DIRECTOR   Yes, and what else?

PLAYGOER   The steersman who holds the wheel of the rudder.

STAGE-DIRECTOR   And who else?

PLAYGOER   The man who controls the steersman.

STAGE-DIRECTOR   And who is that?

PLAYGOER   The navigation officer.

STAGE-DIRECTOR   And who controls the navigation officer?

PLAYGOER   The captain.

STAGE-DIRECTOR   And are any orders which do not come from the captain, or by his authority, obeyed?

PLAYGOER   No, they should not be.

STAGE-DIRECTOR   And can the ship steer its course in safety without the captain?

PLAYGOER   It is not usual.

STAGE-DIRECTOR   And do the crew obey the captain and his officers?

PLAYGOER   Yes, as a rule.

STAGE-DIRECTOR   Willingly?

PLAYGOER   Yes.

STAGE-DIRECTOR   And is that not called discipline?

PLAYGOER   Yes.

STAGE-DIRECTOR   And discipline—what is that the result of?

PLAYGOER   The proper and willing subjection to rules and principles.

STAGE-DIRECTOR   And the first of those principles is obedience, is it not?

PLAYGOER   It is.

STAGE-DIRECTOR   Very well, then. It will not be difficult for you to understand that a theatre in which so many hundred persons are engaged at work is in many respects like a ship, and demands like management. And it will not be difficult for you to see how the slightest sign of disobedience would be disastrous. Mutiny has been well anticipated in the navy, but not in the theatre. The navy has taken care to define, in clear and unmistakable voice, that the captain of the vessel is the king, and a despotic ruler into the bargain. Mutiny on a ship is dealt with by a court-martial, and is put down by very severe punishment, by imprisonment, or by dismissal from the service.

PLAYGOER   But are you not going to suggest such a possibility for the theatre?

STAGE-DIRECTOR   The theatre, unlike the ship, is not made for purposes of war, and so for some unaccountable reason discipline is not held to be of such vital importance, whereas it is of as much importance as in any branch of service. But what I wish to show you is that until discipline is understood in a theatre to be willing and reliant obedience to the manager or captain no supreme achievement can be accomplished.

PLAYGOER   But are not the actors, scene-men, and the rest all willing workers?

STAGE-DIRECTOR   Why, my dear friend, there never were such glorious-natured people as these men and women of the theatre. They are enthusiastically willing, but sometimes their judgment is at fault, and they become as willing to be unruly as to be obedient, and as willing to lower the standard as to raise it. As for nailing the flag to the mast—this is seldom dreamed of—for compromise and the vicious doctrine of compromise with the enemy is preached by the officers of the theatrical navy. Our enemies are vulgar display, the lower public opinion, and ignorance. To these our "officers" wish us to knuckle under. What the theatre people have not yet quite comprehended is the value of a high standard and the value of a director who abides by it.

PLAYGOER   And that director, why should he not be an actor or a scene-painter?

STAGE-DIRECTOR   Do you pick your leader from the ranks, exalt him to be captain, and then let him handle the guns and the ropes? No; the director of a theatre must be a man apart from any of the crafts. He must be a man who knows but no longer handles the ropes.

PLAYGOER   But I believe it is a fact that many well-known leaders in the theatres have been actors and stage-managers at the same time?

STAGE-DIRECTOR   Yes, that is so. But you will not find it easy to assure me that no mutiny was heard of under their rule. Right away from all this question of positions there is the question of the art, the work. If an actor assumes the management of the stage, and if he is a better actor than his fellows, a natural instinct will lead him to make himself the center of everything. He will feel that unless he does so the work will appear thin and unsatisfying. He will pay less heed to the play than he will to his own part, and he will, in fact, gradually cease to look upon the work as a whole. And this is not good for the work. This is not the way a work of art is to be produced in the theatre.

PLAYGOER   But might it not be possible to find a great actor who would be so great an artist that as manager he would never do as you say, but who would always handle himself as actor, just the same as he handles the rest of the material?

STAGE-DIRECTOR   All things are possible, but firstly, it is against the nature of an actor to do as you suggest; secondly, it is against the nature of the stage-manager to perform; and thirdly, it is against all nature that a man can be in two places at once. Now, the place of the actor is on the stage, in a certain position, ready by means of his brains to give suggestions of certain emotions, surrounded by certain scenes and people; and it is the place of the stage-manager to be in front of this, that he may view it as a whole. So that you see even if we found our perfect actor who was our perfect stage-manager, he could not be in two places at the same time. Of course we have sometimes seen the conductor of a small orchestra playing the part of the first violin, but not from choice, and not to a satisfactory issue; neither is it the practice in large orchestras.

PLAYGOER   I understand, then, that you would allow no one to rule on the stage except the stage-manager?

STAGE-DIRECTOR   The nature of the work permits nothing else.

PLAYGOER   Not even the playwright?

STAGE-DIRECTOR   Only when the playwright has practised and studied the crafts of acting, scene-painting, costume, lighting, and dance, not otherwise. But playwrights, who have not been cradled in the theatre, generally know little of these crafts. Goethe, whose love for the theatre remained ever fresh and beautiful, was in many ways one of the greatest stage-directors. But, when he linked himself to the Weimar theatre, he forgot to do what the great musician who followed him remembered. Goethe permitted an authority in the theatre higher than himself, that is to say, the owner of the theatre. Wagner was careful to possess himself of his theatre, and become a sort of feudal baron in his castle.

PLAYGOER   Was Goethe's failure as a theatre director due to this fact?

STAGE-DIRECTOR   Obviously, for had Goethe held the keys of the doors that impudent little poodle would never have got as far as its dressing-room; the leading lady would never have made the theatre and herself immortally ridiculous; and Weimar would have been saved the tradition of having perpetrated the most shocking blunder which ever occurred inside a theatre.

PLAYGOER   The traditions of most theatres certainly do not seem to show that the artist is held in much respect on the stage.

STAGE-DIRECTOR   Well, it would be easy to say a number of hard things about the theatre and its ignorance of art. But one does not hit a thing which is down, unless, perhaps, with the hope that the shock may cause it to leap to its feet again. And our Western theatre is very much down. The East still boasts a theatre. Ours here in the West is on its last legs. But I look for a Renaissance.

PLAYGOER   How will that come?

STAGE-DIRECTOR   Through the advent of a man who shall contain in him all the qualities which go to make up a master of the theatre, and through the reform of the theatre as an instrument. When that is accomplished, when the theatre has become a masterpiece of mechanism, when it has invented a technique, it will without any effort develop a creative art of its own. But the whole question of the development of the craft into a self-reliant and creative art would take too long to go thoroughly into at

present. There are already some theatre men at work on the building of
the theatres; some are reforming the acting, some the scenery. And all of
this must be of some small value. But the very first thing to be realized is
that little or no result can come from the reforming of a single craft of the
theatre without at the same time, in the same theatre, reforming all the
other crafts. The whole Renaissance of the Art of the Theatre depends
upon the extent that this is realized. The Art of the Theatre, as I have
already told you, is divided up into so many crafts: acting, scene, costume,
lighting, carpentering, singing, dancing, etc., that it must be realized at
the commencement that *entire,* not *part* reform is needed; and it must be
realized that one part, one craft, has a direct bearing upon each of the
other crafts in the theatre, and that no result can come from fitful, uneven
reform, but only from a systematic progression. Therefore, the reform of
the Art of the Theatre is possible to those men alone who have studied
and practised all the crafts of the theatre.

PLAYGOER   That is to say, your ideal stage-manager.

STAGE-DIRECTOR   Yes. You will remember that at the commencement of
our conversation I told you my belief in the Renaissance of the Art of the
Theatre was based in my belief in the Renaissance of the stage-director,
and that when he had understood the right use of actors, scene, costume,
lighting, and dance, and by means of these had mastered the crafts of interpretation, he would then gradually acquire the mastery of action, line,
color, rhythm, and words, this last strength developing out of all the rest.
Then I said the Art of the Theatre would have won back its rights, and its
work would stand self-reliant as a creative art, and no longer as an interpretative craft.

PLAYGOER   Yes, and at the time I did not quite understand what you meant,
and though I can now understand your drift, I do not quite in my mind's
eye see the stage without its poet.

STAGE-DIRECTOR   What? Shall anything be lacking when the poet shall no
longer write for the theatre?

PLAYGOER   The play will be lacking.

STAGE-DIRECTOR   Are you sure of that?

PLAYGOER   Well, the play will certainly not exist if the poet or playwright
is not there to write it.

STAGE-DIRECTOR   There will not be any play in the sense in which you use
the word.

PLAYGOER   But you propose to present something to the audience, and I presume before you are able to present them with that something you must have it in your possession.

STAGE-DIRECTOR   Certainly; you could not have made a surer remark. Where you are at fault is to take for granted, as if it were a law for the Medes and Persians, that that something must be made of words.

PLAYGOER   Well, what is this something which is not words, but for presentation to the audience?

STAGE-DIRECTOR   First tell me, is not an idea something?

PLAYGOER   Yes, but it lacks form.

STAGE-DIRECTOR   Well, but is it not permissible to give an idea whatever form the artist chooses?

PLAYGOER   Yes.

STAGE-DIRECTOR   And is it an unpardonable crime for the theatrical artist to use some different material to the poet's?

PLAYGOER   No.

STAGE-DIRECTOR   Then we are permitted to attempt to give form to an idea in whatever material we can find or invent, provided it is not a material which should be put to a better use?

PLAYGOER   Yes.

STAGE-DIRECTOR   Very good; follow what I have to say for the next few minutes, and then go home and think about it for a while. Since you have granted all I asked you to permit, I am now going to tell you out of what material an artist of the theatre of the future will create his masterpieces. Out of *action, scene,* and *voice.* Is it not very simple?

And when I say *action,* I mean both gesture and dancing, the prose and poetry of action.

When I say *scene,* I mean all which comes before the eye, such as the lighting, and costume, as well as the scenery.

When I say *voice,* I mean the spoken word or the word which is sung, in contradiction to the word which is read, for the word written to be spoken and the word written to be read are two entirely different things. And now, though I have but repeated what I told you at the beginning of our conversation, I am delighted to see that you no longer look so puzzled.

Excerpt from
First attempts at a stylized theatre
Vsevelod Meyerhold

Vsevelod Meyerhold (1874–1942) was an actor with the Moscow Art Theatre who left it in 1902 to direct his own company, only to return at Stanislavski's suggestion to guide an experimental studio group. His concepts of constructivism and biomechanics have become widely known, exerting renewed influence during the 1960's. In this brief section from his collected work as translated by Edward Braun, *Meyerhold on Theatre*, one can begin to see Meyerhold's belief that all elements of a production must adhere to a director's overall concept, and that a director's concept must be expressed primarily in visual terms.

I should like to mention two distinct methods of establishing contact between the director and his actors: one deprives not only the actor but also the spectator of creative freedom; the other leaves them both free, and forces the spectator to create instead of merely looking on (for a start, by stimulating his imagination).

The two methods may be explained by illustrating the four basic theatrical elements (author, director, actor and spectator) as follows:

1 A triangle, in which the apex is the director and the two remaining corners, the author and the actor. The spectator comprehends the creation of the latter two through the creation of the director. This is method one, which we shall call the Theatre-Triangle.

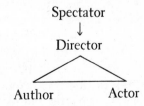

Spectator
↓
Director

Author   Actor

2 A straight, horizontal line with the four theatrical elements (author, director, actor, spectator) marked from left to right represents the other method, which we shall call the Theatre of the Straight Line. The

actor reveals his soul freely to the spectator, having assimilated the creation of the director, who, in his turn, has assimilated the creation of the author.

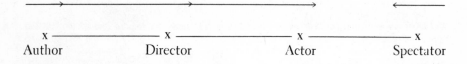

x	x	x	x
Author	Director	Actor	Spectator

1 In the Theatre-Triangle the director explains his *mise en scène* in detail, describes the characters as he sees them, prescribes every pause, and then rehearses the play until his personal conception of it is exactly reproduced in performance. This Theatre-Triangle may be likened to a symphony orchestra with the director acting as the conductor.

However, the very architecture of the theatre, lacking any provision for a conductor's rostrum, points to the difference between the two.

People will say that there are occasions when a symphony orchestra plays without a conductor. Let us consider Nikisch[1] and the symphony orchestra which has been playing under him for years with scarcely a change in its personnel; take a composition which it has played several times a year over a period of ten years. If Nikisch were absent from the conductor's rostrum on one occasion, would the orchestra play the composition according to his interpretation? Yes, it is possible that the listener would recognize it as Nikisch's interpretation. But would the performance sound exactly as though Nikisch were conducting? Obviously, it would be worse, although we should still be hearing Nikisch's interpretation.

So I contend this: true, a symphony orchestra without a conductor is possible, but nevertheless it is impossible to draw a parallel between it and the theatre, where the actors invariably perform on the stage without a director. A symphony orchestra without a conductor is possible, but no matter how well rehearsed, it could never stir the public, only acquaint the listener with the interpretation of this or that conductor, and could blend into an ensemble only to the extent that an artist can recreate a conception which is not his own.

1 Arthur Nikisch (1855-1922), celebrated conductor of the Leipzig Gewandhaus Orchestra.

The actor's art consists in far more than merely acquainting the spectator with the director's conception. The actor will grip the spectator only if he assimilates both the director and the author and then gives of himself from the stage.

By contrast, an orchestral musician is distinguished by his ability to carry out the conductor's directions precisely, by dint of his virtuoso technique and *by depersonalizing himself.*

In common with the symphony orchestra, the Theatre-Triangle must employ actors with virtuoso technique, but at all costs lacking in individuality, so that they are able to convey the director's exact concept.

2 In the Theatre of the Straight Line, the director, having absorbed the author's conception, conveys his own creation (now a blend of the author and the director) to the actor. The actor, having assimilated the author's conception via the director, stands face to face with the spectator (with director and author behind him), and *freely* reveals his soul to him, thus intensifying the fundamental theatrical relationship of performer and spectator.

In order for the straight line not to bend,[2] the director must remain the sole arbiter of the mood and style of the production, but nevertheless, the actor's art remains free in the Theatre of the Straight Line.

The director describes his plan during the discussion of the play. The entire production is colored by his view of it. He inspires the actors with his devotion to the work, and imbues them with the spirit of the author and with his own interpretation. But after the discussion all the performers remain completely independent. Then the director calls a further general meeting to create harmony from all the separate pieces. How does he set about this? Simply by balancing all the parts which have been freely created by the various individuals involved in the collective enterprise. In establishing the harmony vital to the production, he does not insist on the exact representation of his own conception, which was intended only to ensure

2 Alexander Blok (*Pereval*, Moscow, 1906, no. 2) fears that the actors "might set fire to the ship of the play," but to my mind, discord and disaster could occur only if the straight line were allowed to become crooked. This danger is eliminated if the director accurately interprets the author, accurately transmits him to the actors, and if they accurately understand him. [Meyerhold's note.]

unanimity and to prevent the work created collectively from disintegrating. Instead he retires behind the scenes at the earliest possible moment and leaves the stage to the actors. Then, either they are out of accord with the director or the author (if, say they are not of the new school)[3] and set fire to the ship, or they reveal their souls through almost improvisatory additions, not to the text but to the mere suggestions of the director. In this way the spectator is made to comprehend the author and the director through the prism of the actor's art. *Above all, drama is the art of the actor.*

3 The Theatre-Triangle requires non-individualistic actors who none the less are outstanding virtuosi, regardless of their school. In the "Theatre of the Straight Line" individual flair is most important, for without it free creativity is inconceivable. It needs a new school of acting, which must not be a school where new techniques are taught, but rather one which will arise just once to give birth to a free theatre and then die.

The Theatre of the Straight Line will grow from a single school as one plant grows from one seed. As each succeeding plant needs a new seed to be sown, so a new theatre must grow every time from a new school.

The Theatre-Triangle tolerates schools attached to theatres which provide a regular stream of graduates, who imitate the great actors who founded the theatre, and fill vacancies in the company as they occur. I am convinced that it is these schools which are to blame for the absence of genuine, fresh talent in our theatres. [Meyerhold's note.]

The director
Alexander Tairov

Alexander Tairov (1885–1950), founder of the Moscow Kamerny Theatre in 1914, ran the theatre until 1949, during which time he worked toward a non-realistic, ritualistic theatre that could offer a synthesis of all production elements. His book, *Notes of a Director,* first published in Russian in 1921, was translated into English by William Kuhlke in 1969. In this section Tairov discusses the director as the coordinator of a collective art.

"The Director," by Alexander Tairov, from *Notes of a Director* by Alexander Tairov, translated by William Kuhlke (Coral Gables, Florida, University of Miami Press), pp. 90–95. Reprinted by permission of University of Miami Press.

The art of the theatre is the art of action. It is realized on the stage by "one who performs an action," i.e., an actor, who is thus the sole and sovereign bearer of theatrical art.

This being the case, what is the role of the director in the theatre? What need is there of him? What do his duties consist of?

The art of the theatre is a collective art. Scenic action appears as a result of the very collisions that occur in its process; it is a result of the interrelations and conflicts which take place between individual "ones who act" or groups of them. In order that these conflicts not be governed by chance, in order that the scenic action be not chaotic but flow in orderly fashion, that it be cast not in separate and uncoordinated but in harmonious forms which follow one after another in a unified work of theatrical art, it is obvious that *someone* is needed. There must be someone who, creatively striving for this result, regulates and directs the conflicts that arise—softening, strengthening, eliminating, creating—in order to lead all the action to its harmonious completion.

This "someone" is the *director.*

Insofar as the theatre is a product of collective creativity, it requires a director, whose intrinsic role is the coordination and ultimate harmonization of the creativity of the separate individualities.

So it is, always has been, and always will be.

Under various guises, under various names, the director has invariably existed in the theatre; and he will continue to exist because he was engendered by the very essence of theatre art—its basis in action and the collective nature of its creativity. The director is the helmsman of the theatre; he pilots the ship of the theatrical production, avoiding shoals and reefs, surmounting unexpected obstacles, wrestling with storms and gales, unfurling and trimming the sails, and all the time guiding the ship toward a predetermined creative goal.

Insofar as the director is the pilot of the theatre, he undoubtedly limits to some degree the freedom of all the separate "ones who perform an action" in it.

Having proclaimed the invariable primacy of the actor, his hegemony in the theatre, having accounted him the sole and sovereign bearer of theatrical art, it would seem that now I am contradicting myself. But this is only a seeming contradiction. We need only look more carefully into the relationship between the director and actor to be convinced that in this case the dependence of the actor is in essence the strongest possible affirmation of his creative freedom.

I have no wish to play with words, and I am not inclined to paradox, but the structure of the theatre is such that there cannot be freedom for the actor outside this dependence.

You see, the theatre is indeed a collective art. The completely unrestrained creative freedom of a given individual will of necessity either neutralize the freedom of other individuals who come in contact with him during the action, or will transform the generated conflict from a factor which creates action to one which destroys it. In order that the individual freedom of every "one who performs an action" may be realized to the maximum—without detriment to the creatively directed wills of those other individuals who come in contact with him in the course of the action—it is necessary that there be some voluntary self-restraint and subjugation to the director. All concerned must depend on his talent and creative sensitivity to turn this act of voluntary self-restraint into a new assertion of the actor's freedom.

Naturally it is necessary that the director who takes unto himself such a tremendous and responsible mission be worthy of it, that he be a genuine master of the stage. In this new theatre about which I speak it may not be otherwise. Is it likely that a genuine master-actor, an actor who commands all the means and secrets of his art, would permit an untrustworthy pilot to stand at the helm of his ship?

So, I maintain that the art of the director is an integral part of the art of the theatre, and that in his intended capacity he not only does not restrict but rather assures the freedom of the individual actor's creativity.

Why, then, is the life of the contemporary theatre full of censures and complaints against the suppression of the actor's creativity by the director? Why do we hear that the director has turned the theatre into some kind of Procrustean bed, where the actor's creative ego is hemmed in, and where the actor cannot find for himself a full and joyful means of expression? These reproaches are made and in large measure justified not because the role of the director is in its essence that of suppressor of the actor's creative ideas, talent, and freedom, nor even because the majority of contemporary directors are so incompetent that they really have no right even to get near a theatre—but because *those scenic trends which have been cultivated by the most prominent directors of our time have placed them in a position where, like it or not, they must suppress the actor.*

I have already had occasion to say more than once that the contemporary theatre has developed along the lines of naturalism and stylization. Owing to separate causes inherent in each of these trends, the directors of both schools were deprived of the possibility to give free rein to the actor's creativity.

You know that the naturalistic theatre regards the principle of verisimilitude as of paramount importance; a play must evoke in the spectator the illusion of real life and not a stage production. Guided by this principle, the director had of necessity to secure from the actor a performance which would give the audience the impression that he was Ivan Ivanovich, Maria Ivanovna—a person taken as it were right out of life. In achieving this, he was forced to restrain the actor and to deprive his creativity of its color. In order not to destroy the illusion of life, he had to curtail the actor's gesture, muffle his voice, make his speech a-rhythmic, etc., that is, he had to deprive the actor of the possibility of using those means of expression, that material by means of which only he could create his art. For as soon as the actor was given the possibility of using his material, then his first genuine gesture, the first freely born sound of his voice, would at once smash to smithereens the whole structure of verisimilitude being constructed with such difficulty, and the spectator's illusion would come tumbling down.

Therefore, the director of the naturalistic theatre, however gifted and skillful, had *of necessity to stifle* genuine acting creativity. The evil in this case was inevitable; it arose as a logical and inexorable consequence. For once the director let himself be guided by a false principle, one fundamentally alien to theatre art, he had also to subjugate the actor to this false principle, thereby entering into actual conflict with genuine acting creativity and suppressing it.

From this point of view, and within the limits of this particular school of theatre, the resultant criticisms concerning the dominance of the director were undoubtedly well-founded.

The director of the stylized theatre fell into the same situation, albeit in a different way. Having given the position of utmost prominence in his work to style, and striving accordingly to suppress the actor's real being, which serves as his material, trying to force the real forms of the actor's creativity into a stylized design—trying to stylize his emotions, as it were—the director of the stylized theatre, just as the director of the naturalistic one, was faced with the necessity of denying the actor creative use of his own material. For if by using his material in the naturalistic theatre the actor would destroy the illusory structure of life, in the stylized theatre he would by the same token destroy the just as illusory structure of non-life—that whole mechanized structure to which, as we have seen, that theatre inevitably came.

Thus here too, in the stylized theatre, the director subjugated the actor to a false principle, fundamentally alien to art, and therefore had of *necessity to suppress* him—thereby justifying the widespread opinion that the director was dominant, and he was inevitably so.

As a matter of fact, this dominance is not at all an organic part of the role played by the director in the theatre; it is only a consequence of the indicated schools, for which certain directors have acted as champions. The falsity of the director's position was brought about not by the falsity of the phenomenon of the director in general, but by the falsity of the trends these directors set in motion.

Therefore, it is of course absurd to infer that the director generally is an abnormal phenomenon in the theatre, that he will inevitably suppress the actor's creativity, that with the renaissance and development of the theatre he is doomed to degenerate or even disappear. And of course Valery Briusov is just as wrong when he says that the director in the theatre is no more, as it were, than the editor of a journal.

No. The role of the director in the theatre is a tremendous one, and the more the theatre follows the path of its own perfection and self-expression, the more significant that role will become, for then the director will embody in himself the playwright as well, creating and bringing to life a given scenario with the help of the acting collective.

However, there is at present a theatre in which we do not hear the fashionable criticism of directorial dominance,* in spite of the fact that the role of the director is most active there, so active that it almost approaches the degree I have just mentioned. I am speaking of the ballet.

If you look closely into the art of the ballet and into the sort of role the ballet master plays in it, at first glance it seems as though the director is much more despotic here than in any other theatre, that he oppresses the actor to a much greater degree than any of the others. In fact, the ballet master, in his work with the actors, determines the entire pattern of the role down to the smallest details. It is not just that this or the other basic movement of the ballerina is provided for, nor even her every *pas*, but every turn of her head, every movement of her arms and hands, sometimes even her little finger—and nevertheless, I have never had occasion to hear complaints about the "domination" of the director.

This comes about because in the ballet the essence of its art is less obstructed by attendant elements than in any other theatre; because here the action-essence of the theatre has been preserved in its most pure form; because having been trained in the same school—which gives to acting mastery the tremendous significance it deserves—the ballet master and the actor understand each other to the fullest.

The actors and actresses of the ballet know that the pattern established together with the ballet master not only does not deprive them of the opportunity to express their own individual creativity, but on the contrary opens to them this very possibility. This is true because the final form which is the result of all the bits of work imposed or approved by the ballet master is based on a strict accounting of all the individual capacities of the given actor, in connection with the general creative plan of the whole production. Constructed in this fashion, the form not only does not restrict him, but on the contrary gives him indispensable confidence that the emotion he develops will not overwhelm him but will be cast in precisely those shapes which will communicate his art to the audience with the greatest strength, precision, and joy.

Unfortunately, formalism and some other phenomena which I have already mentioned are now destroying this interdependence of actors and

---

*If the director is talented, of course.

the director in ballet. But this is essentially how it must be on every stage which sets its foot upon the true path to theatrical art.

If the theatre stands firmly on a base of scenic action, if it does not subjugate itself either to naturalism or to stylization, if it does not fall under the influence of either literature or painting, if its whole and only intent is the maximum expression of the actor's creative will and the full-valued sounding of all his material, if by these means, that is, by his own independent art, the actor seeks to attract and win over his audience—in such a theatre there can be no question of any kind of directorial despotism. In such a theatre the director's whole task will be to help the actor find that scenic form, to give him that firm base, upon which, having become a full-fledged master, he can with ease display all the wealth of his creative potential. For it is only in the play of creativity's jewel-like facets that one may see all the charm, all the joy, and all the power of genuine theatrical action.

The art of the director is expressed primarily in the production process. This process may be broken down into several basic periods, the first of which, in my view, is the creative design of the production.

Genuine theatrical action hovers invariably between two basic poles—the *mystery* and the *harlequinade*. But between these poles it assumes special, original, and unique forms in every play, in every production. The first task of the director is to find a form for the production, taking into account the creative collective of the theatre, its strengths and needs, and that urge to action which lies in its path at that moment. Only when one has become aware of this urge and converted it to use may he set about the creation or interpretation of a scenario or play.

The theater of cruelty (first manifesto)
Antonin Artaud

Antonin Artaud (1896–1948), the French poet-playwright who with Brecht shares the major influence on mid-century theatre theory, first published *The Theatre and Its Double* in 1938. When translated into English twenty years later, the book became an instant rallying point for his envisioned Theatre of Cruelty. Influenced by Eastern mysticism and primitive ritual, devoted to a non-realistic and highly stylized total theatre, Artaud became a primary influence on experimental theatre in the 1960's. His vision of a unified theatre transcending realistic theatre technique allied him with Craig and with Adolph Appia, but his seeming emphasis on violence, his insistence on emotional and participatory values in production, and his ability to create poetry from madness set him apart from all other twentieth-century theoreticians.

We cannot go on prostituting the idea of theatre whose only value is in its excruciating, magical relation to reality and danger.

Put in this way, the question of the theatre ought to arouse general attention, the implication being that theatre, through its physical aspect, since it requires *expression in space* (the only real expression, in fact), allows the magical means of art and speech to be exercised organically and altogether, like renewed exorcisms. The upshot of all this is that theatre will not be given its specific powers of action until it is given its language.

That is to say: instead of continuing to rely upon texts considered definitive and sacred, it is essential to put an end to the subjugation of the theater to the text, and to recover the notion of a kind of unique language half-way between gesture and thought.

This language cannot be defined except by its possibilities for dynamic expression in space as opposed to the expressive possibilities of spoken dialogue. And what the theater can still take over from speech are its possibilities for extension beyond words, for development in space, for dissociative and vibratory action upon the sensibility. This is the hour of intonations, of a word's particular pronunciation. Here too intervenes (besides the auditory language of sounds) the visual language of objects, movements, attitudes, and gestures, but on condition that their meanings, their physiognomies, their combinations be carried to the point of becoming signs, making a kind

59

of alphabet out of these signs. Once aware of this language in space, language of sounds, cries, lights, onomatopoeia, the theater must organize it into veritable hieroglyphs, with the help of characters and objects, and make use of their symbolism and interconnections in relation to all organs and on all levels.

The question, then, for the theater, is to create a metaphysics of speech, gesture, and expression, in order to rescue it from its servitude to psychology and "human interest." But all this can be of no use unless behind such an effort there is some kind of real metaphysical inclination, an appeal to certain unhabitual ideas, which by their very nature cannot be limited or ever formally depicted. These ideas which touch on Creation, Becoming, and Chaos, are all of a cosmic order and furnish a primary notion of a domain from which the theater is now entirely alien. They are able to create a kind of passionate equation between Man, Society, Nature, and Objects.

It is not, moreover, a question of bringing metaphysical ideas directly onto the stage, but of creating what you might call temptations, indraughts of air around these ideas. And humor with its anarchy, poetry with its symbolism and its images, furnish a basic notion of ways to channel the temptation of these ideas.

We must speak now about the uniquely material side of this language— that is, about all the ways and means it has of acting upon the sensibility.

It would be meaningless to say that it includes music, dance, pantomime, or mimicry. Obviously it uses movement, harmonies, rhythms, but only to the point that they can concur in a sort of central expression without advantage for any one particular art. This does not at all mean that it does not use ordinary actions, ordinary passions, but like a springboard uses them in the same way that *humor as destruction* can serve to reconcile the corrosive nature of laughter to the habits of reason.

But by an altogether Oriental means of expression, this objective and concrete language of the theater can fascinate and ensnare the organs. It flows into the sensibility. Abandoning Occidental usages of speech, it turns words into incantations. It extends the voice. It utilizes the vibrations and qualities of the voice. It wildly tramples rhythms underfoot. It pile-drives sounds. It seeks to exalt, to benumb, to charm, to arrest the sensibility. It liberates a new lyricism of gesture which, by its precipitation or its amplitude in the air, ends by surpassing the lyricism of words. It ultimately breaks away from the intellectual subjugation of the language, by conveying the sense of a new and deeper intellectuality which hides itself beneath the gestures and signs, raised to the dignity of particular exorcisms.

For all this magnetism, all this poetry, and all these direct means of spell-binding would be nothing if they were not used to put the spirit physically on the track of something else, if the true theater could not give us the sense of a creation of which we possess only one face, but which is completed on other levels.

And it is of little importance whether these other levels are really conquered by the mind or not, i.e., by the intelligence; it would diminish them, and that has neither interest nor sense. What is important is that, by positive means, the sensitivity is put in a state of deepened and keener perception, and this is the very object of the magic and the rites of which the theater is only a reflection.

TECHNIQUE

It is a question then of making the theater, in the proper sense of the word, a function; something as localized and as precise as the circulation of the blood in the arteries or the apparently chaotic development of dream images in the brain, and this is to be accomplished by a thorough involvement, a genuine enslavement of the attention.

The theater will never find itself again—i.e., constitute a means of true illusion—except by furnishing the spectator with the truthful precipitates of dreams, in which his taste for crime, his erotic obsessions, his savagery, his chimeras, his utopian sense of life and matter, even his cannibalism, pour out, on a level not counterfeit and illusory, but interior.

In other terms, the theater must pursue by all its means a reassertion not only of all the aspects of the objective and descriptive external world, but on the internal world, that is, of man considered metaphysically. It is only thus, we believe, that we shall be able to speak again in the theater about the rights of the imagination. Neither humor, nor poetry, nor imagination means anything unless, by an anarchistic destruction generating a prodigious flight of forms which will constitute the whole spectacle, they succeed in organically reinvolving man, his ideas about reality, and his poetic place in reality.

To consider the theater as a second-hand psychological or moral function, and to believe that dreams themselves have only a substitute function, is to diminish the profound poetic bearing of dreams as well as of the theater. If the theater, like dreams, is bloody and inhuman, it is, more than just that, to manifest and unforgettably root within us the idea of a perpetual conflict, a spasm in which life is continually lacerated, in which everything in creation rises up and exerts itself against our appointed rank; it is in order to perpetuate in a concrete and immediate way the metaphysical ideas of certain Fables whose very atrocity and energy suffice to show their origin and continuity in essential principles.

This being so, one sees that, by its proximity to principles which transfer their energy to it poetically, this naked language of the theater (not a virtual but a real language) must permit, by its use of man's nervous magnetism, the transgression of the ordinary limits of art and speech, in order to realize actively, that is to say magically, *in real terms*, a kind of total creation in which man must reassume his place between dream and events.

THE THEMES

It is not a matter of boring the public to death with transcendent cosmic preoccupations. That there may be profound keys to thought and action with which to interpret the whole spectacle does not in general concern the spectator, who is simply not interested. But still they must be there; and that concerns us.

The spectacle   Every spectacle will contain a physical and objective element, perceptible to all. Cries, groans, apparitions, surprises, theatricalities of all kinds, magic beauty of costumes taken from certain ritual models; resplendent lighting, incantational beauty of voices, the charms of harmony, rare notes of music, colors of objects, physical rhythm of movements whose crescendo and decrescendo will accord exactly with the pulsation of movements familiar to everyone, concrete appearances of new and surprising objects, masks, effigies yards high, sudden changes of light, the physical action of light which arouses sensations of heat and cold, etc.

The mise en scène   The typical language of the theater will be constituted around the mise en scène considered not simply as the degree of refraction of a text upon the stage, but as the point of departure for all theatrical creation. And it is in the use and handling of this language that the old duality between author and director will be dissolved, replaced by a sort of unique Creator upon whom will devolve the double responsibility of the spectacle and the plot.

The language of the stage   It is not a question of suppressing the spoken language, but of giving words approximately the importance they have in dreams.

Meanwhile new means of recording this language must be found, whether these means belong to musical transcription or to some kind of code.

As for ordinary objects, or even the human body, raised to the dignity of signs, it is evident that one can draw one's inspiration from hieroglyphic characters, not only in order to record these signs in a readable fashion which permits them to be reproduced at will, but in order to compose on the stage precise and immediately readable symbols.

On the other hand, this code language and musical transcription will be valuable as a means of transcribing voices.

Since it is fundamental to this language to make a particular use of intonations, these intonations will constitute a kind of harmonic balance, a secondary deformation of speech which must be reproducible at will.

Similarly the ten thousand and one expressions of the face caught in the form of masks can be labeled and catalogued, so they may eventually participate directly and symbolically in this concrete language of the stage, independently of their particular psychological use.

Moreover, these symbolical gestures, masks, and attitudes, these individual or group movements whose innumerable meanings constitute an important part of the concrete language of the theater, evocative gestures, emotive or arbitrary attitudes, excited pounding out of rhythms and sounds, will be doubled, will be multiplied by reflections, as it were, of the gestures and attitudes consisting of the mass of all the impulsive gestures, all the abortive attitudes, all the lapses of mind and tongue, by which are revealed what might be called the impotences of speech, and in which is a prodigious wealth of expressions, to which we shall not fail to have recourse on occasion.

There is, besides, a concrete idea of music in which the sounds make their entrance like characters, where harmonies are coupled together and lose themselves in the precise entrances of words.

From one means of expression to another, correspondences and levels of development are created—even light can have a precise intellectual meaning.

Musical instruments They will be treated as objects and as part of the set.

Also, the need to act directly and profoundly upon the sensibility through the organs invites research, from the point of view of sound, into qualities and vibrations of absolutely new sounds, qualities which present-day musical instruments do not possess and which require the revival of ancient and forgotten instruments or the invention of new ones. Research is also required, apart from music, into instruments and appliances which, based upon special combinations or new alloys of metal, can attain a new range and compass, producing sounds or noises that are unbearably piercing.

Lights, lighting The lighting equipment now in use in theatres is no longer adequate. The particular action of light upon the mind, the effects of all kinds of luminous vibration must be investigated, along with new ways of spreading the light in waves, in sheets, in fusillades of fiery arrows. The color gamut of the equipment now in use is to be revised from beginning to end. In order to produce the qualities of thinness, density, and opaqueness, with a view to producing the sensations of heat, cold, anger, fear, etc.

Costumes Where costumes are concerned, modern dress will be avoided as much as possible without at the same time assuming a uniform theatrical costuming that would be the same for every play—not from a fetishist and superstitious reverence for the past, but because it seems absolutely evident that certain age-old costumes, of ritual intent, though they existed at a given moment of time, preserve a beauty and a revelational appearance from their closeness to the traditions that gave them birth.

The stage—the auditorium We abolish the stage and the auditorium and replace them by a single site, without partition or barrier of any kind, which will become the theater of the action. A direct communication will be reestablished between the spectator and the spectacle, between the actor and the spectator, from the fact that the spectator, placed in the middle of the action, is engulfed and physically affected by it. This envelopment results, in part, from the very configuration of the room itself.

Thus, abandoning the architecture of present-day theaters, we shall take some hangar or barn, which we shall have reconstructed according to processes which have culminated in the architecture of certain churches or holy places, and of certain temples in Tibet.

In the interior of this construction special proportions of height and depth will prevail. The hall will be enclosed by four walls, without any kind of ornament, and the public will be seated in the middle of the room, on the ground floor, on mobile chairs which will allow them to follow the spectacle which will take place all around them. In effect, the absence of a stage in the usual sense of the word will provide for the deployment of the action in the four corners of the room. Particular positions will be reserved for actors and action at the four cardinal points of the room. The scenes will be played in front of whitewashed wall-backgrounds designed to absorb the light. In addition, galleries overhead will run around the periphery of the hall as in certain primitive paintings. These galleries will permit the actors, whenever the action makes it necessary, to be pursued from one point in the room to another, and the action to be deployed on all levels and in all perspectives of height and depth. A cry uttered at one end of the room can be transmitted from mouth to mouth with amplifications and successive modulations all the way to the other. The action will unfold, will extend its trajectory from level to level, point to point; paroxysms will suddenly burst forth, will flare up like fires in different spots. And to speak of the spectacle's character as true illusion or of the direct and immediate influence of the action on the spectator will not be hollow words. For this diffusion of action over an immense space will oblige the lighting of a scene and the varied lighting of a performance to fall upon the public as much as upon the actors—and to the several simultaneous actions or several phases of an identical action in which the characters, swarming over each other like bees, will endure all the onslaughts of the situations and the external assaults of the tempestuous elements, will correspond the physical means of lighting, of producing thunder or wind, whose repercussions the spectator will undergo.

However, a central position will be reserved which, without serving, properly speaking, as a stage, will permit the bulk of the action to be concentrated and brought to a climax whenever necessary.

Objects, masks, accessories   Manikins, enormous masks, objects of strange proportions will appear with the same sanction as verbal images, will enforce the concrete aspect of every image and every expression—with the corollary that all objects requiring a stereotyped physical representation will be discarded or disguised.

The set   There will not be any set. This function will be sufficiently undertaken by hieroglyphic characters, ritual costumes, manikins ten feet high representing the beard of King Lear in the storm, musical instruments tall as men, objects of unknown shape and purpose.

Immediacy   But, people will say, a theater so divorced from life, from facts, from immediate interests. . . . From the present and its events, yes! From whatever preoccupations have any of that profundity which is the prerogative of some men, no! In the Zohar, the story of Rabbi Simeon who burns like fire is as immediate as fire itself.

Works   We shall not act a written play, but we shall make attempts at direct staging, around themes, facts, or known works. The very nature and disposition of the room suggest this treatment, and there is no theme, however vast, that can be denied us.

Spectacle   There is an idea of integral spectacles which must be regenerated. The problem is to make space speak, to feed and furnish it; like mines laid in a wall of rock which all of a sudden turns into geysers and bouquets of stone.

The actor   The actor is both an element of first importance, since it is upon the effectiveness of his work that the success of the spectacle depends, and a kind of passive and neutral element, since he is rigorously denied all personal initiative. It is a domain in which there is no precise rule; and between the actor of whom is required the mere quality of a sob and the actor who must deliver an oration with all his personal qualities of persuasiveness, there is the whole margin which separates a man from an instrument.

The interpretation   The spectacle will be calculated from one end to the other, like a code (*un langage*). Thus there will be no lost movements, all movements will obey a rhythm; and each character being merely a type, his gesticulation, physiognomy, and costume will appear like so many rays of light.

The cinema   To the crude visualization of what is, the theater through poetry opposes images of what is not. However, from the point of view of action, one cannot compare a cinematic image which, however poetic it may be, is limited by the film, to a theatrical image which obeys all the exigencies of life.

Cruelty   Without an element of cruelty at the root of every spectacle, the theater is not possible. In our present state of degeneration it is through the skin that metaphysics must be made to re-enter our minds.

The public   First of all this theater must exist.

The program   We shall stage, without regard for text:

1 An adaptation of a work from the time of Shakespeare, a work entirely consistent with our present troubled state of mind, whether one of the apocryphal plays of Shakespeare, such as *Arden of Feversham,* or an entirely different play from the same period.
2 A play of extreme poetic freedom by Leon-Paul Fargue.
3 An extract from the Zohar: The Story of Rabbi Simeon, which has the ever present violence and force of a conflagration.
4 The story of Bluebeard reconstructed according to the historical records and with a new idea of eroticism and cruelty.
5 The Fall of Jerusalem, according to the Bible and history; with the blood-red color that trickles from it and the people's feeling of abandon and panic visible even in the light; and on the other hand the metaphysical disputes of the prophets, the frightful intellectual agitation they create and the repercussions of which physically affect the King, the Temple, the People, and Events themselves.
6 A Tale by the Marquis de Sade, in which the eroticism will be transposed, allegorically mounted and figured, to create a violent exteriorization of cruelty, and a dissimulation of the remainder.
7 One or more romantic melodramas in which the improbability will become an active and concrete element of poetry.
8 Buchner's *Wozzek,* in a spirit of reaction against our principles and as

an example of what can be drawn from a formal text in terms of the stage.

9 Works from the Elizabethan theater stripped of their text and retaining only the accouterments of period, situations, characters, and action.

Brecht as director
Carl Weber

Bertolt Brecht (1898–1956), easily one of the most influential figures of twentieth-century theatre, left a large body of both plays and theoretical writings that are now widely available. His ideas about "alienation," " the Chinese effect in acting," the minimal use of scenery, and non-emotional audience involvement developed over a long period of time. In this particular article, Carl Weber, now the Chairman of Directing at New York University, described Brecht as a director, revealing in practice his theories of the theatre, now firmly identified as Epic Theatre. This article was first prepared as a lecture at Tulane University.

"Brecht as Director," by Carl Weber. First published in *The Drama Review*, Vol. 12, No. 1 (T37). Copyright © 1967 by *The Drama Review*. Reprinted by permission. All Rights Reserved.

Much has been written about Brecht in this country, some—though not enough—of his poetry has been translated, selections of his theoretical writings and most of his plays have been published in English. From all of this, people quite naturally assume that Brecht was primarily a poet and playwright. But, although this is true, in order to understand Brecht the playwright one ought to know Brecht as a man of practical theatre—as a director. Brecht's influence on the theatre of his time stems mainly from the productions he created at the Berliner Ensemble; Germany's theatre has been changed considerably by his exemplary work during the early and mid-fifties in East Berlin. The new movement in England—The Royal Court, Peter Brook and Peter Hall, Kenneth Tynan, to mention a few names only—would probably have been vastly different if the Berliner Ensemble had not presented his work in London in 1956, and again in the sixties, and Giorgio Strehler in Italy and Roger Planchon in France have been deeply influenced by what, and how, Brecht created in Berlin. Though Brecht had worked for the theatre nearly all his life, as a critic at first, then as a playwright and director, it was not until 1949 that he found a permanent place for his experiments, a company, and later a building, which he could form into the ideal instrument for his ideas, a theatre which was a laboratory, a place for investigation, analysis, and construction of models.

When Brecht returned to Europe after his wartime stay in the United States, the East German authorities offered to let him direct a production of

Mother Courage with his wife, Helene Weigel, in the lead; for the first time in fifteen years he had a chance to demonstrate the theories he had been fighting for all his life, in Germany and elsewhere. The production opened in 1949, at the Deutches Theatre, Berlin, and was a turning point of German theatre history. The critics—most of whom had almost unanimously condemned Brecht's directing efforts in the years before 1933—did a somersault, and the performance was hailed by many as the most important theatrical event in fifteen years. I went to see it as a young man coming from the university at Heidelberg; it remains the greatest theatre experience of my life. It is hard now to describe exactly what was so unique, since I have come to know the production so well, from acting in it and restaging it in 1954. One thing: it was the first time I had ever seen people on the stage behave like real human beings; there was not a trace of "acting" in that performance, though the technical brilliance and perfection of every moment was stunning. The economy of the set, of every prop used, was absolutely overwhelming to one who had seen until then only run-of-the-mill—and sometimes the best—German theatre. And it was astonishing how the idea of the play was brought across without pushing, without hammering it into the audience. All this was above and beyond the superb individual performances of Weigel and the rest of the company.

I decided that I had to work with Brecht, but it was not until 1952 that the Ensemble had a vacant position for an assistant director. I went to a dramaturge of the company, Peter Palitzsch, and asked how to apply to Brecht. He answered that Brecht didn't like to interview people and the best thing was to submit a piece about one of the Ensemble's productions— not a review, just a description of what the actors did, why, and whether it worked. I went to see *Puntila* several times, wrote about two of its scenes, and sent it to Brecht. After a while, I called Brecht's secretary and said, "Shall I come, or is it so bad there's no point?" The answer was, "How can you make him read anything? He doesn't read very much." But I convinced her to try again to bring the piece to Brecht's attention. I called after two weeks, and she said, "Well, we've lost it." Disaster! I didn't have a copy; but they found it again. Then three more weeks went by, and I phoned again, and she said that Brecht had read the piece and wanted to see me.

The next morning, there he was in his cap. I was very embarrassed and shy, and right away he became even shyer than I. He said, "Yes, you are . . . Yes, I have read. . . ." There was a long pause. I probably stammered something about why I would like to work in his theatre and he just looked at me.

Then finally he said, "I have to go to rehearsal. Why don't you go to our business office and talk to Weigel about your contract?" And off he went.

I asked at the office if I could watch a rehearsal, and they told me that anyone who had a legitimate interest could watch rehearsals unless Brecht, as happened rarely, thought an actor was extremely nervous—even then he would work with that actor separately, but the rest of the rehearsal would be kept open. He wanted actors to get used to spectators, to get laughs, to be in contact with the people down there as early in the processs as possible, to work with an audience. At that time they were rehearsing the *Urfaust*, which the young Goethe wrote decades before he did the final version of *Faust*. Brecht preferred the *Urfaust* for several reasons. It is mostly written in *Knittelvers*, a verse which is unrhythmic or of changeable rhythm, and rhymes often not at all or very forcefully. It was used in the farces and mystery plays of the late Middle Ages and early Renaissance; also, it is the language of German Punch and Judy shows. *Faust* itself, however great, is the play of an old man, with a detached view of society and of the individual—the *Urfaust* is a *Sturm und Drang* work with a young, aggressive approach to the world. In its treatment of the love story, it is remarkably close to Brecht's in *Baal* and *Drums in the Night*.

I walked into the rehearsal and it was obvious that they were taking a break. Brecht was sitting in a chair smoking a cigar, the director of the production, Egon Monk, and two or three assistants were sitting with him, some of the actors were on stage and some were standing around Brecht. Then one actor went on the stage and tried about thirty ways of falling from a table. They talked a little about the *Urfaust*-scene "In Auerbachs Keller" (Mephisto brings Faust into an inn where drunken students enjoy themselves with dirty jokes and silly songs). Another actor tried the table, the results were compared, with a lot of laughing and a lot more horse-play. This went on and on, and someone ate a sandwich, and I thought, my god this is a long break. So I sat naively and waited, and just before Monk announced a break, I realized that this was rehearsal. And it was typical of the loose way Brecht often worked, of his experimental approach and of the teamwork the Ensemble was used to. Whatever ideas he brought to rehearsal he tried out, threw away, tried something else; sometimes twenty versions of one scene were tried, once in a while only two. Even when a production had opened, and been reviewed, he reworked parts of it, re-rehearsed it, changed the blocking. The actors also took an experimental attitude. They would suggest a way of doing something, and if they started to explain it, Brecht would say that he wanted no discussions in rehearsal—it would have to be tried. Since his whole view of the world was that it was changeable and the people in it were changing, every solution discovered was tentative and regarded as the starting point for a new, better, different solution.

All this was—of course—not just for love of experiment. Brecht was mainly concerned with the play as the telling of a story to an audience, clearly, beautifully, and entertainingly. If he found that in an almost completed production one certain part was opaque or boring, he rewrote and reworked it or simply cut it. I have never seen anyone cut a script as mercilessly as Brecht cut his own. Brecht had another important ability: if he had worked at a scene, and then dropped it for a week, he could come back and look at it as if he had never seen it before. I remember a scene from the third act of *Caucasian Chalk Circle*, when Grusha, with her adopted child and her brother Lavrenti, arrives at the house of the dying peasant whom she is forced to marry. The scene hadn't been done for about three weeks (the play was rehearsed for eight months); he came back to it, and we all thought it was going rather well when suddenly Brecht yelled, "Stop!" He asked what the actor playing Lavrenti, who was walking across the room, was doing. Well, we answered, there's a good reason; he has to be over there for his next line, you blocked it this way. Brecht denied this angrily, saying there was no reason for such a move. "But his next line asks for it." "What line?" he barked. The actor said the line. "But that's impossible, I couldn't have written that!" We had to show him in the book that he had indeed written it, and he was furious—at us. But he rewrote the scene. He had looked at it as if it were by someone else, from a play he'd never heard of before, which he was judging as a spectator, and it failed.

The initial preparation of a play usually took about half a year, while it was discussed and adapted (if it was a translation). The set was developed on paper and as a model during that period, as were the costumes. Then, when Brecht went into rehearsal, it could take three to four months to block the play. This blocking involved the working out of a considerable number of details. To Brecht, blocking was the backbone of the production; ideally, he thought, the blocking should be able to tell the main story of the play—and its contradictions—by itself, so that a person watching through a glass wall, unable to hear what was being said, would be able to understand the main elements and conflicts of the story. To work out blocking this clear takes an enormous amount of time; he would try out every thinkable possibility—and if a scene didn't seem to work in dress rehearsal, the first thing reworked would be the blocking.

After the basic blocking was finished, he started to work on the acting detail; by this time the actors knew their lines completely, and could play around with them freely. The most meticulous attention was paid to the smallest gesture. Sometimes it took an hour to work out whether an actor should pick up a tool one way or another. Particular attention was devoted to all details of physical labor. A man's work forms his habits, his attitudes, his physical behavior down to the smallest movement, a fact usually neglected by the stage. Brecht spent hours in rehearsal exploring how Galileo would handle a telescope and an apple, how the kitchen-maid Grusha would pick up a waterbottle or a baby, how the young soldier Eilif would drink at his General's table, etc. Often paintings or other pictorial documents of the play's period were brought into rehearsal for the study of movements and gestures. Brecht's favorite painters were Breughel and Bosch: their paintings told "stories" (not in the sense of the veristic nineteenth-century school, of course), their people were stamped by their lives and occupations, their vices and beliefs. The influence of pictures he had seen often could be felt in Brecht's work; certain moments of the blocking, as well as character-images, were derived from paintings or photos.

Each moment had to be examined: for the characters' situation, for the story's situation, for the actions going on around the character. When all these details had been brought to a certain point, not of completion, but of diminished possibilities, Brecht would have the first run-through. This might be six months after the actors started work on the play, six months of working on blocking, single beats, and small units of scenes. The first run-through was usually a disaster—it was impossible for the actors to pull things together so fast. But this was just what Brecht was waiting for; in the second and third run-throughs, a rhythm began to appear, and all the mistakes made so far emerged clearly. So then Brecht broke the whole thing down again into short beats and small units, and reworked every detail that had not been satisfactory. After the second break-down of the play, the final period of rehearsal usually came. This included run-throughs—but interrupted by frequent reworking of scenes and details. A week or more was given to the technical rehearsals. Lighting a show sometimes took five days alone, and extras were used to walk through all the motions, so the actors wouldn't waste their time and energy. He always wanted a light which was very bright and yet very varied—a result not easily achieved. During dress rehearsals details were constantly changed or developed further, including the blocking and quite often even the text. I remember first nights, when actors would find a little note from Brecht on their dressing-room tables, wishing them good luck and asking them to say a new line in scene X instead of one Brecht had decided to cut, because audience reactions in dress rehearsals had indicated that the former line didn't work the way Brecht intended it.

After the last dress rehearsal Brecht always did an exercise, which he called the "marking" or "indicating" rehearsal: the actors, not in costumes, but on the set, had to walk quickly through all the actions of the show, quoting the text very rapidly, without any effort at acting, but keeping the rhythm, the pauses, etc., intact. The effect—if you were sitting far back in the house—was very much like an early silent movie: you saw people moving and gesturing very quickly, but you couldn't hear the words or get any kind of emotions, except the most obvious ones. This proved to be an extremely helpful device; it made the actors relax, helped them to memorize every physical detail and gave them a keen sense for the show's rhythmic pattern.

Finally first night came, which in fact was a preview with audience, after which rehearsals were used to change the production according to audience reactions. After five to eight previews, the official "opening" with press and invited guests took place. Brecht introduced these previews to Germany, probably drawing on his American and English experiences. In the beginning, the German critics strongly rejected this procedure; now other theatres have followed Brecht's example. After the opening, work on the production didn't stop. The director—or one of his assistants—watched every performance, and whenever changes or a reworking were felt necessary, rehearsals were scheduled.

This sounds like a monumentally laborious process, and to some extent it was. But it took place in an atmosphere of humor, ease with experimentation, relaxation. Actors (and directors) new at the Ensemble were usually very tense, and tried to get results right away—as they must when they have only a few weeks' rehearsal time. Brecht would tell them, "Fast results are always to be regarded with suspicion. The first solution is usually not a good solution. Not enough thinking goes into it. Instinct is a very dubious guide, especially for directors."

Brecht regarded design as of the highest importance, and had worked out his methods of handling it with his friend Caspar Neher. When Neher designed a play for him, he started with little sketches depicting the im-

portant moments of the story, the "turning points"—sometimes he arrived
at a kind of comic strip of the entire play. He began with people, sketching
the characters in relation to a given situation, and thus visualizing the
blocking. When he and Brecht were satisfied with the sketches, they started
to develop a set. For Brecht, for Neher when he worked with Brecht, for Otto
and von Appen, who worked with Brecht in the fifties, the set was primarily
a space where actors tell a certain story to the audience. The first step was
to give the actor the space and architectural elements he needed; the next
was to work out the set so it by itself would tell the audience enough about
the play's story and contradictions, its period, social relations, and the like;
the last step was to make it beautiful, light, "elegant"—as Brecht used to
say.

Whatever is called the "style" of Brechtian productions was always something arrived at during the last phase of production. Brecht never began
with a preconceived stylistic idea, even something so "basic" as whether
the production should be "period," "naturalistic," or whatever silly labels
theatre convention usually pins on plays. He began with a long exploration
of the intricate social relationships of the characters and the behavior resulting from them. Their psychology was not left out, but was developed from
their social contradictions. The designer watched, working out his ideas as
Brecht rehearsed. Twice I saw about 75 percent of a completed set—and the
finished costumes that went with it—thrown away after the first dress
rehearsal, because although it was beautiful it did not tell the audience what
Brecht and von Appen wanted. An enormous amount of money was poured
into these experiments, but certainly not wasted. One of Brecht's favorite
proverbs—"The proof of the pudding is in the eating"—was always applied
to his theatre work.

From the time Brecht began directing in Munich in the twenties, until
the end, he liked to have people around him when he directed. He asked
everyone he trusted to come to rehearsal and constantly asked their opinions;
he controlled his work through their reactions. In the fifties, his productions
were always team-work, and he constantly used all the people connected
with a production—assistants, designer, musicians (Eisler and Dessau were at
many rehearsals). Brecht asked the Ensemble's technicians to attend dress
rehearsals, and afterward sought their opinions. I remember the last rehearsals
of *Kratzgraben* (a play by the contemporary East German novelist and
playwright Erwin Strittmatter, which Brecht produced in 1953), to which

Brecht had invited a group of children between ten and fourteen. He spent two hours with them after rehearsal to find out what they understood and what not, trying to pin down the reasons. The discussion's result was a reworking of many scenes to achieve more clarity, a higher quality of "telling the story." Brecht believed strongly in the unspoiled and unprejudiced observation of children. They possessed the naive and poetic quality of thought he felt so important for the theatre.

In the Ensemble, Brecht decided that the young directors should co-direct —two or even three of them as directors of the same standing. This worked well. The directors would arrive at a basic concept on which they could agree before going into rehearsal. But in actual rehearsal, beautiful things would come out of the tension between different minds working on the same problems—better solutions than any one of the directors could have arrived at on his own. In fact, many productions before and most productions after his death were directed this way. For instance: *Playboy of the Western World* by Synge (Palitzsch/Wekwerth), *The Day of the Great Scholar Wu* (Palitzsch/Weber), *Optimistic Tragedy* by Vishnevski (Palitzsch/Wekwerth), *Private Life of the Master Race* by Brecht (Bellag/Palitzsch/Weber), *Arturo Ui* by Brecht (Palitzsch/Wekwerth), *Little Mahagonny* and *The Breadshop* by Brecht (Karge/Langhoff).

Brecht never cared how his actors worked. He didn't tell them to go home and do this or that, or to go behind the set and concentrate. He didn't give a damn about the mechanics they used, he just cared about results. Brecht respected actors and was extremely patient with them; he often used their suggestions. During breaks, he would listen sometimes to rather obvious nonsense from the actors, wanting them not to feel uncomfortable with him, wanting to gain their confidence in all matters. But he was extremely demanding and could become stern and very angry with actors who he felt were not trying to do their best. He himself could probably have become a great actor. Frequently he demonstrated specific details of movement or speech for the actors. Since he could be a marvelous clown, the actors liked to provoke him to demonstrate something, for the sheer joy of watching him. He did not prod the actors to ape what he had demonstrated, but rather would exaggerate enough so that while they saw exactly what he wanted, they were never tempted to copy him.

It is interesting to compare the way in which I saw Brecht direct actors with what's reported by Leon Feuchtwanger's wife (who was there) about his first directing. When Brecht was twenty-four and his play *Drums in the Night* was being rehearsed in Munich, the director found to his surprise that the young author was coming to rehearsals, interrupting him, yelling at the actors, and demonstrating how they should do things. Pretty soon Brecht had almost taken over the entire production, and the director—a mature man—was practically his assistant. As usual in the German theatre of that time, the rehearsal period was short, somewhat under three weeks, but by the last week the actors, some of whom were quite prominent, were trying very hard to do what Brecht wanted them to. Basically, he was attempting to wean them from the pompous, overambitious typical German manner of the time, to bring them back to a realistic treatment of the lines. Mrs. Feuchtwanger's report is of great interest: that very young man, who came to attend rehearsals of his first play, kept yelling at the actors that what they offered was shit. When I met him in his fifties, mellowed perhaps, but not the least weakened in his determination, he was still busy cleaning the stage (and all art) of the "sweet lies" which keep man from recognizing the world as it is.

Brecht tried to present in his theatre a realistic view of the world, no gold-plated images of false heroes, no "revealing" photos of rabbits, busy nibbling cabbage and humping their mates, of whatever sex. Doubt in man-made gods, doubt in man-made rules, doubt in whatever man is told to accept was proclaimed on his stage. And a profound insight into man's weakness and longing to conform, an insight, by the way, which was not without understanding, and even compassion.

Brecht used this theatre as a laboratory, to experiment with plays and players. Human behavior, human attitudes, human strength and weakness— everything was explored and investigated, to be exposed finally to a public which often enough refused to recognize its own image in this very clear, but sometimes perhaps too well-framed, mirror. The realistic treatment of the lines, which Brecht demanded from his first hour in the theatre to the last, was more than a theatreman's protest against the theatre's degraded conventions. For him, the stage was a place to construct models—models of the world man has created for himself.

Murder of the director
Jean Vilar

Jean Vilar (1912–1971), with Jean Louis Barrault a leader of French theatre following World War II, was appointed director of the Théâtre National Populaire in 1951. He resigned in 1963, having established the reputation for integrity toward the script while placing emphasis on the actor. Strict attention to detail and an attempt to appeal to a wide, popular audience were hallmarks of his work, as revealed in this translation by Christopher Kotschnig.

1

The following notes concern only a particular technique of theatrical art, that of transposing a written work from the imaginary realm of reading to the concrete realm of the stage. To look for anything more than "means of interpretation" in these often deliberately cryptic lines would be vain.

When so many theories, *ars poetica* and metaphysics have been made up about this art, it is perhaps necessary that one advance, as a preliminary, a few artisan's considerations.

2

One can never read the play often enough. Actors never read it often enough. They think they understand the play when they follow the plot more or less clearly—a fundamental error.

Sticking my neck out, I would point out that in general, directors underrate the professional intelligence of actors. They are asked to be bodies only, animated pawns on the director's chessboard. The play once read by the director, read a second time *à l'italienne*, the actors are thrust onto the stage. What is the result?

Subjected too early to the demands of physical presence and action, the actors fall back on their habitual, conventional reactions, and develop their characters conventionally and arbitrarily, before their professional intelligence and their sensibilities can grasp the director's intention. Hence, so many hack performances!

For there are hack performances in the most sensitive actor, just as a writer will produce hack work when he hurries, or is hurried. How many actors, including some of the best, have murmured to us for twenty years in the same voice, with the same bearing and gestures, with the same emotional quality, in the most diametrically opposed roles!

Hence the necessity for many reading rehearsals: about a third of the total number. At least. Manuscript in hand, seat firmly planted on a chair, body in repose. Thus the deepest sensibilities will gradually pitch themselves to the desired note, as the actor comes to understand, or feel, the new character that is to become himself.

3

All characters must be *composed.* All good actors are necessarily *composers.* All roles are the result of *composition.*

4

The composition of a character is the work of creation which, alone, asimilates the actor's craft to the artist's; for composing a character implies selection, observation, research, inspiration, and discipline.

5

The actor selects within and around himself.

Around himself, because nature presents to his eyes the most various and distinct models, for his observation; one might almost say, for his contemplation.

Within himself, because if, on the one hand, the actor cannot sufficiently observe the life teeming around him, neither can he sufficiently expose his sensibilities to contact with it.

In short, the actor must be able to retain in his visual memory the human types that strike his attention, as also the sympathetic (or sensory) memory of his own wounds and moral suffering. He must know how to use this memory and, better yet, cultivate it.

6

In blocking, the point is to simplify and pare down. Contrary to the usual practice, the idea is not to *exploit* space, but to forget or ignore it.

For a production to have its full power of suggestion, it is not necessary that a so-called scene of action should be "busy" (with acrobatics, fisticuffs, brawling and other "realistic" or "symbolic" activity). One or two gestures, and the text, suffice; provided both are "right."

7

The work of blocking and physical characterization should be fairly quickly completed by good professional actors: say fifteen rehearsals out of forty.

8

An actor's—or a director's—talent does not necessarily lie in the variety and strength of his powers (which are a relatively unimportant gift of Providence), but above all in the refining of his powers, the severity of his selectivity, in his voluntary self-impoverishment.

9

Music-hall theatre: a great actor, a splendid costume, a striking decor, music brimming with genius, strong-colored lighting.

10

No actor worthy of the name imposes himself on the text; he serves it. Humbly. Let the electrician, musician, and designer, accordingly, be even more humble than this "right interpreter."

11 CHARACTER AND ACTOR

The script carefully studied and the characters "felt" in all their ramifications, in the course of the fifteen or twenty reading rehearsals, the director begins the bland work of blocking, completes it, and finds himself at once in a renewed struggle with those slippery monsters, the characters. The actors know it well, for character and actor are two separate entities. For long days, the first eludes the second with infernal ease. The worst thing to do at this stage is to try to fight the demon, to force him to your will. If you wish him to come and meekly enter into your body and soul, forget him. The director's role, as expert observer of this pursuit by osmosis, is to inspire the actor with confidence, to convince him that he has, in the very expressive phrase, "found" or "rediscovered" his character. It is by no means naive to state that at a certain point in the development of a character, confidence is all. It is by non-violence, by confidence in his ultimate conquest of the elusive monster, that the actor finally triumphs.

12

The scenic artist must realize the designer's sketches. Alternatively, there should be a designer-carpenter, right hand of the director, with full powers over the stage: a man of taste, devoted to his work, cultured. A hard trade.

13 OF COSTUME

In theatre, the hood sometimes makes the monk.

14 WHAT MUST BE DONE?

The work of production must include a written analysis of the play. The director must write it, and not despise the thankless job. The drafting of such an analysis compels the director to a clear and exhaustive knowledge of the play.

15

Question: Can one interpret something one doesn't understand?

16 CODA TO "WHAT MUST BE DONE?"

How many playwrights would be incapable of giving you a precise analysis of their play! of its plot, even!

17

A director who cannot detach himself from his work during the final rehearsals is only a mediocre craftsman, however much it might seem that this is the very point at which he should be most intensely involved in it. Failing this detachment, the director blinds himself—the worst possible error. Such poor fools forget that the theatre is play, in which inspiration and childlike wonder are more important than sweat and tantrums.

It is true that such detachment is so difficult to achieve at the right time that it is not surprising to find that few directors either desire or achieve it.

18

A quality fully as important to the actor in the right practice of his art as sensitivity and instinct, is the spirit of *finesse* (for a definition, see Pascal, who opposes it to the spirit of geometry). Without this quality, his work will only present a riot of anarchic expressions.

19

The actor is not a machine. This is a truism that needs to be shouted in people's ears. The actor is neither pawn nor robot. The director must assume from the start that his players have all the necessary talent.

20 INTERMISSION

"The idleness of an artist is work, and his work, repose." Signed, Balzac.

21

There is no technique of interpretation, but only practices, *techniques* (plural). Personal experience is all, and personal empiricism.

22

For the director, every actor is a special case. From this follows the requirement that he know every member of his cast well. Know his work, of course, but even more his *person,* up to the threshold of his inner life, and perhaps even beyond.

23 DIRECTOR AND ACTOR

Where the actor is concerned, the director's art is one of suggestion. He does not impose, he suggests. Above all, he must not be brutal. The "soul of an actor" is not an idle phrase: even more than the "soul of a poet," it is a continuing necessity. One does not win a creature's soul by brutalizing it, and the actor's soul is more necessary to the work of theatre than his sensitivity.

24 OF SIMPLICITY

Three references:

(a) Shakespeare-Hamlet: "Speak the speech, I pray you, as I pronounced it to you, trippingly on the tongue; but if you mouth it . . . I had as lief the town-crier spoke my lines . . . Be not too tame neither, but let your own discretion be your tutor," etc., and all the rest of this famous passage.

(b) Moliere: *The Versailles Impromptu.*

(c) Talmá-Lekain: "Lekain guarded against that hunger for applause that torments most actors and leads them into frequent error; he wished to please only the discriminating members of the audience. He rejected all theatrical fakery, aiming to produce a genuine effect by avoiding all 'effects'. . . . He *practiced a right economy of movement and gesture, deeming this an essential part of the art, since their multiplication detracts from dignity of bearing.*" (Talmá)

25

A production must be reduced to its simplest—and most difficult—expression: the stage action or, more precisely, the acting. Hence, the stage must not be turned into a crossroads of all the arts, major and minor (painting, architecture, electromania, musicomania, mechanics, etc.).

The designer must be put in his place, which is to solve the sightline problems of masking and teasers and to see to the construction of such set and hand properties as are strictly necessary to the action on stage.[1]

---

1 His chief task being to find the single *keynote of the set,* if set there must be. [J. V.]

The immoderate use of projectors, floodlights, and arc lamps should be left to the music-hall and circus.

Music should be used only for overtures and scene bridges, and otherwise only when the script explicitly calls for music off, a song, or a musical interlude.

In short, all effects should be eliminated which are extraneous to the pure and Spartan laws of the stage, and the production reduced to the physical and moral action of the players.

Directing a play
Tyrone Guthrie

Tyrone Guthrie (1900–1971), a director known most widely for his unorthodox approach to classic plays, served as director for the Old Vic Theatre in London from 1937–1945. A founder of the Stratford Festival Theatre in Ontario, he also provided impetus for the American regional theatre movement by forming the Tyrone Guthrie Theatre in Minneapolis in 1963. This article is the transcript from a lecture he delivered at New York City's West Side YMCA while he was directing *Gideon.* In it he discusses his attitude toward the director's job, ranging from initial problems with a text to work with collaborators. The emphasis is on interpretation: the director's responsibility for script enhancement.

'm going to talk tonight about producing a play—well, directing a play. The terms—it's confusing—in Britain we speak of the producer where you say the director, and we don't have a director; and where you say producer we say manager or management, but it really doesn't matter, and in neither case, director nor producer, does the term, I think, give the slightest indication of what the fellow is expected to do.

I'm going to divide the job into two parts: first of all, your dealings with the author and the script, which is preliminary; secondly, the dealings with the actors and the other technicians in the preparation of the play for rehearsal. In point of fact, the director doesn't meet the public very much at all. The public, of course, is the final arbiter of whether they go or stay home, and we often think they make the oddest decisions, but by the time that's happened, the work of the director is over and the matter, although financially important, is in other respects comparatively negligible.

Perhaps some of you may wonder how plays get on the stage, and, indeed, I've often wondered myself. Of course, like everything else there is no hard and fast rule. In London the channels are more orthodox, and, on the whole, I think that the methods are more efficient. In New York it's more unorthodox; it's often wildly inefficient, but that has its own wild, strange charm and produces some excellent results. Now I think this is largely a matter of economics; in New York there's much more money knocking about. It's possible for a group of ten or twelve people who really are not any one of them wildly rich, to club together and to badger the life out of their friends to raise money and put on a play. And it constantly happens that they do so, and make all the mistakes that beginners make at everything. You know, it's like you're coming on and playing croquet for the first time, you just play terribly badly. And a lot of these amateur managements make just about every possible mistake you can make. They know nothing about it, and they make all the mistakes of ignorance and overexcitement and overenthusiasm, but it performs one inestimable service: it means that no play, really no play, can be nutty enough and boring enough and silly enough and wild enough not eventually to get on.

Now I think that's great. It does mean that there are some extraordinary evenings in the theatre, but also that's the only way that interesting innovations can take place. The weird things happen, and suddenly out of some weird little group of people who know nothing about anything really, they produce something that is splendid and memorable and influences the theatre, possibly for generations.

In London it's all more proper and more orthodox. There are fewer managements, and most of them have been in the game not just for years, but for generations. And they know a very, very great deal about it, but they tend to know about it in a very stereotyped way. And things certainly run on much more oiled wheels. It's easier for everybody: things happen more punctually; there's far less screaming and hollering and cursing and anxiety and panic; but it's all so dull.

In a bracket, the same thing precisely applies to the trades union situation. In New York, the theatre is artistically hampered at every turn by what I consider the gross tyrannies of the stage unions, who are entirely sectarian in their interests. They don't look at the things as a whole at all. They simply say "what's in it for our chaps; I propose to squeeze the last drop, the last fragment of blood out of the stone for my section"—be it the electricians, the musicians, the stage-hands, the actors, whoever else it may be. It's not only selfish, it's silly, but it's very well understood how it came about: it came about through gross oppression. In London at no time was the oppression as great as it was in New York fifty to sixty years ago—and the bitterness of the underdogs [in London] consequently is not now expressing itself in biting every hand that it can lay teeth into, and it's all a little easier; there are more concessions; the demands are not made in such a hostile spirit, and the demands themselves are not as extravagant. And there is a little more awareness all around that this is a common affair, that the stage-hands have as much to gain—no, not as much, but a great deal to gain from a prosperous and successful theatre—and a great deal to lose if they ruin the theatre by exorbitant demands just for their private members. But I didn't come here to talk politics, I only put that in a bracket.

Also I didn't come here to compare the New York to the London theatre. I've often been asked. I've worked a lot in both and I'm often asked what I think about it, and it's basically a silly question. The two things are so different and the differences depend upon such a complicated series of factors. What I'm here to discuss is the job of the director, and basically speaking, with differences of procedure and differences contingent on the climate of the two theatres, the thing is the same.

THE DIRECTOR AND THE SCRIPT

First of all, you get sent a play.

When you're young, you die of excitement if somebody sends a play and would you consider producing it and you write back simply before you've opened the envelope to say, "Yes of course, I think its the greatest play I've ever read; when do we start rehearsal?" When you get a little older, you get more choosey, because if you're successful at all, you're getting more scripts sent to you than you can deal with, and you space your time out according to whatever you think is the best way of doing so.

Again, when you're young, you're sent a script and you're told by the management who sends it that the leading part will be played by Mr. X, and the leading lady will be Mrs. Y, the designer will be Mr. Z, and so on and so forth, and you accept or refuse the package. As you get up in the world a bit, you get a bit more say in all that. When you're a kind of Methuselah like I am, you're in a position where you don't accept a package unless it's a very nice one; you say, "Well I would like to be consulted about the choice of these people, and I think the best designer for this would not be Mr. W at all but Mr. J," and so forth and so on. But I think that is precisely like any other business; as you get older and more experienced and they know you better, they entrust you with a little more responsibility. And I think even for a young director it's not wise for management to force them into a package, because the director—and I shall come to this in a moment, under the matter of his dealings with his collaborators—the director has to be the chairman of the proceedings. And it's rather easier to chair proceedings if you've packed the committee.

But the first thing you have to deal with is the script itself. And this may strike you as a very revolutionary statement, and certainly most of the directors I know would consider it such, but it always seems to me that the first thing to do with the script is to read it. Not once and again, but, like the young lady of Spain, again and again and again and again. And again. And at some stage of the game, to read it aloud, not necessarily to somebody, to your cat if you've got one. Reading the play aloud, in my experience, shows you all kinds of things that you hadn't found when you're reading to yourself.

Everybody reads a play differently and this is why I think a very, very great deal of dramatic criticism proceeds on a fallacy. Dramatic criticism of the classics, certainly, is nearly always conducted on the assumption that there exists, probably in the mind of the critic, an ideal performance which completely realizes the intention of Shakespeare or Molière or Eugene O'Neill or whoever else. What they see on the stage is judged in comparison with that imagined ideal performance. Now I think that is just nonsense, for the following reason. Every performance of a play, every contact with the play, is that person's comment on it. If you read a play, if you read a novel, if you look at a picture, you may not be aware of it but what you're seeing is only part of the author's intention, and you're also seeing things that the author never meant to put in. In other words, your contact with the work of art is your personal comment upon it. You go and look, say, at the Mona Lisa in the Louvre, and you must see something quite different from what I see. And I always think it would be a very amusing game to take a group of people who've never seen an important picture before, sit them down before it for ten minutes, then take them away and say, "Write down what you saw in the fullest detail." You know as well as I do that what they wrote down would differ in the wildest and most extravagant respect, as wildly as differs the police-court evidence of the five or six people who see a motor accident, who all see something totally different, and none of whom are probably lying. And what you see in that picture is what it's got to say to you. What I see is what it's got to say to me. When you read a play, you get out of it what you can, which may be pretty little or it may even be a great deal more than the author put into it. But if you're honest, that is what your interpretation is going to be based on.

All my life in the theatre I've been fairly severely criticized—much more in Britain than here, but somewhat here, and really punished in Britain—for what the critics have considered my impudence in daring to interpret Shakespeare. What else can you do? If you're asked to put a Shakespeare play upon the stage, you do two things. You either get the actors and try to make them help to make it what you think Shakespeare was after, which clearly is not precisely what Shakespeare was after, but it's the impression he's made on you; or you put something on that is like some other Shakespearean production that you've admired. You warm up cold pudding, and cold second-hand pudding at that. And of the two, I would prefer to risk the impertinence of trying my own thing. If it's consistently bad enough you won't be asked to do it again.

Now in the case of Shakespeare you may say that this is somewhat impertinent and I agree it is. There is a certain impertinence in relating yourself to a great master of anything and saying, "Well, now, I've got to interpret you and it's going to be done my way." But Shakespeare ain't here to defend himself. And what is the alternative? Of course, I'm not going to say that you don't mug up in the books and read what the critics have said and read all these notes, most of which I'm sure you'll agree are just ineffably dreary, the dull scribblings of ponderous, pompous dullards who've been well paid to be dull. But, now and again, something good comes up. But then, having read all that, having absorbed all that, you've got to get back to the fact that you read the text and it makes on you an impression of such a kind. And I think that the conscientious artist has no alternative but to take his courage in both hands, shut his eyes, hold his nose and jump in, and do it the best he knows. Because the only other thing is just to do it the stock way, and there really is no other stock way, you just do it as what you remember of Walter Hampton's production in mangy fur and purple velvet. And I don't think that's any good; its not a service to Walter Hampton, to the public, to Shakespeare, or to anybody else.

Now, this may seem a little impertinent when it's applied to Shakespeare, but I don't think it is, because when you come to think of the nature of a play, it is not a thing in itself. The dramatist writes down the script—and with the deference due, which in my opinion is not a very high deference, to all the professors of literature in all the universities of the world for the last 400 years—the printed script is not the end of the matter; it's the beginning. The printed script bears no more relation to the author's intention than the score of a symphony bears to the composer's intention. And it's generally accepted that the score of a symphony is merely there; it's merely the raw material waiting for a conductor and an orchestra to bring it to life. Similarly, the printed text in the play is the raw material of the dramatic performance. It seems to be more because any literate person can read the text, and very few literate people can read the score of a symphony. But there isn't one of us who can't put on our specs and read "To be or not to be, that is the question . . . whether 'tis nobler, etc., etc., etc." So then there goes out the erroneous idea that the reading of the play is enough, that everybody by reading that can extract the full meat of it. Well, of course they can't. Many people can, and many people justifiably find the reading of a speech like that a more satisfactory experience than listening to it spoken by anybody.

The best speaker of that speech that I've ever heard is John Gielgud, who makes of it, I think, a matchless piece of music. It's an operatic aria that in itself is a joy to the ear, but far more than that, he sets it in its context. He apprehends with his actor's intelligence that, through what has gone before and what is to come and what is inside himself, this is a young man at his wit's end, who is really out on the battlements of Elsinore in the dead of night, saying, "Shall I take my own life or shan't I?" And when in a dramatic performance he speaks that, that's as clear as mud.

But when you read it in the classroom or when you read it to yourself, I don't think most of us know enough about reading plays to apply all that imaginative context. And even if we can supply the facts of it, few of us are trained enough, imaginatively or in the techniques of the theatre, to be able to bodyforth the idea with the poignancy that a gifted actor can do. In other words, it's not at all an easy matter to read a play. It's not a question of just reading the words. You've got to supply—which is something that none of us to the ends of our lives can do fully—you've got to supply the architecture of the scene; you've got to see where the climaxes are, how the thing builds up to a certain point, which is the crisis of it, which leads to the next thing, and so on and so forth. Because a play is, in a way, a piece of architecture. Shakespearean plays are great complicated cathedrals. Great echoing cathedrals, filled with music, but the music itself is dependent upon the shape of the thing into which they're put. These scenes are all designed and they have some sort of a shape. Now there isn't a definitive shape, and this is my point: the critics say, "Yes there is: Shakespeare intended the play to be just precisely so" (only nobody quite knows precisely how), "and anything that doesn't realize that is no good." I say No! If a play is any good, any act of it, any scene of it, any character of it, can be interpreted fifteen different ways, each one as good as the other, or each one as bad as the other. And if you come to think of it, it must be so.

No playwright, except amateurs—of course I'm always getting plays from beginners, which begin with eleven pages of stage direction which say Cynthia is an exquisitely pretty girl of 19 and ¾, she was born in May, so and so, she has blue eyes; then they proceed to give her bust, waist, and hip measurements, her shoe size, what she has for breakfast, an amateur psychoanalysis of her character; then they proceed to do that for the rest of the characters in the play; then they describe in four pages, the set, which is just the ordinary usual drawing-room comedy set with the usual mistakes made, like placing the windows at the back so that the brightest light is in the audience's eyes; and so you go on from there. But that's the amateur. The professional, and the greater the professional, I think, the more terse are his stage directions. Shakespeare's stage directions are absolutely minimal, for two reasons: he knows that piles of stuff about what Cynthia had for breakfast on Tuesday last week, and all that kind of rubbish, is only inhibiting to the imaginations of the people who've got to interpret the play; it puts their backs up; it bores them, and prevents them from thinking the thing out freshly for themselves. Secondly, he knows very well that if the play is any good, it's going to be performed in a thousand different contexts.

Hamlet, we have reason to suppose, was written for Burbage, who was a big, fat man, a bit old for the part. But Hamlet can be played by a big man, a little man; a tenor, a bass; a manly man, an effeminate man; an aggressive man, a shy man: there are 15,000 different ways of playing Hamlet, all of which still add up and make the play interesting. Claudius is a little more limited because the script perfectly well tells us that he's a bloated king, that he drinks a good lot, that he smiles and smiles and is a villain. There are certain obligations under Claudius to conform to things in the text, but still it can be played in many, many dozens of ways. It is possible to cast Mr. A, B, C, D, E, F, or G. And on the casting of that, and of the five or six other main parts, of course, depends the interpretation of the whole play. If John Gielgud plays it with a certain group, it is one thing; if Maurice Evans plays it with another group, the play becomes something totally different. And any playwright who's setting out to do this thing seriously knows that the same thing holds true. That you don't just write that you think your play is going to be performed in the Longhurst Theatre by Ethel Barrymore, and X, Y, and Z, and that it's going to be precisely so; of course it isn't. If the play's any good, it's going to be performed all over the world by countless different people in the parts, by countless different directors throwing in their two-cents-worth. And if you're a playwright of any ambition at all, you hope that your play is going to go on long after you're dead—when theatrical fashions change, because theatrical fashions change just as often as dress fashions.

The performance of a play that is given now, let us suppose a new play, and is acclaimed a great masterpiece (if it's a great masterpiece it sure won't be, but let's just for fun suppose it is), the author naturally hopes that it will still be playing in Uzbekistan in 2061, when, you know, they'll all be in great beards and blowing horns and carrying on in the maddest way and the whole theatrical context will have changed. And things will be being done to that play that he could not possibly have envisioned. But if the play is any good, the meat of it will still be there. The general philosophy of the play will come through but the trappings will be totally different.

THE DIRECTOR AND THE PRODUCTION

Then there's another point: no author who's any good, I've come to the conclusion, has the faintest idea really of what he's written. This is my opinion and it's very hard to substantiate, but I haven't arrived at it lightly. Anything that distinguishes it from journalism, that really gives it a bit of earth-wisdom, has got in between the lines and over and above the conscious intention of the author. I didn't understand this at first; when I was much younger I was very friendly with James Bridey, the Scottish dramatist; I don't know if his work is familiar here to anybody; he's not as well known on this continent as I think he should be. And for years he used to send me drafts of his plays as he was writing them and ask what I thought. And for years I used to write back in very similar terms, you know, couched in this way and that way, but the gist of the letter was, "Well I think it's immensely amusing, there are some great jokes—it'll make a cat laugh—and there's some wisdom and splendid things in it—but what's it all about?" And always he would reply "Well, I don't know. I only wrote the thing." And I thought that was his kind of whimsical, ironical, Scot's way of making a fool of me and saying, "Well, don't you try to teach me my business." But as the years passed I learned that he meant it in literal, sober fact; that he considered that anything in his plays that was any good, had got in there without his knowing it. And I'm pretty sure of that.

Take this present play that I'm working on, which is *Gideon* by Paddy Chayevsky. Now, I don't want to sell it to you as the greatest play in the world. I think it's an important play, but that's not for me to say, but for you.

It's beautifully written, has all of Chayevsky's uncanny skill of setting up a sentence so that the laugh comes at the right moment; setting the poignant moments against the laughs so that they enhance one another; setting the important and weighty ideas in a sort of fluff of gay meringue so that they stick out like lighthouses in a stormy sea; it's a very big advance on *The Tenth Man* in seriousness and in topic and that kind of thing, and on the conscious level an enormous amount of artifice and know-how has gone into the construction of it. But again and again and again and again, we come on things, and the actors say the lines in a certain way and he says, "By God that's marvelous, I had no idea that was the way it was to be spoken." And the collective thing of the group sheds light on the things that he didn't know were there. They were in it all right, because they were in his unconscious. But what distinguishes the first-rate from the merely journalistic is that it somehow carries this load of dynamite of the over-and-above from the author's subconscious.

Do you really believe that when Shakespeare sat down to write *Hamlet* he said to himself, "I'm going to create a character so interesting that 600 years later, a public librarian will say, "The biographies of three people are in outstandingly greater demand than those of anybody else'." (This was said to me in England during the war by a public librarian. And the three people in order of preference were Jesus Christ, Napoleon Bonaparte, and pressing hard on the heels of Napoleon, Hamlet. This figment is of surpassing interest to all of us, down the generations, across the world.) Well now, do you think Shakespeare sat down and said, "I'm going to write something that is the mind of every man, that is every young man or young woman in torture in a certain situation?" No author can write a great part without drawing enormously on his own experience. And if you happen to be, as Shakespeare was, a tremendous poet, the subconscious bubbles rather quickly into the consciousness. It creeps up in the lines; and very soon this young man was speaking the innermost thoughts and intuitions of the human race. But he didn't mean to. Nor is the thing set down in such a form that anybody can possibly have the impudence to say, this is the definitive way of doing it.

And when you press people who take that point of view and really push them into a corner, you find that what they've got in mind is some performance that *they* saw when they were seventeen and were in a faint about, which left an immense—because you know, we're all in the same boat, there's no great acting after one's eighteen years of age. Great acting is one's memories of the great actors that one saw when one was very, very young and impressionable. And these people remember something as being wonderful, they will remember—well, when I was young, it was the performances of Irving and Ellen Terry in Britain that were the sort of standard, and things that departed from the way Irving and Ellen Terry played the parts were wrong. It wasn't just different, it was wrong. They were right, it was wrong, in the eyes of the senior critics. And I've noticed that—and this doesn't just apply to Shakespeare, it goes all the way down the line—there are certain ways of doing things which dramatic critics proclaim are right and are wrong. There is no right way of doing anything. There are a million wrong ways, and some of them are wronger than others, but there is no right way.

Therefore, I think when you're dealing with the script, you must not be humble. You must say, "This is what it seemed to mean to me." And if the author is there, that's fine, you can discuss the things as they come along. And I'm here to say that all the authors I've worked with—and I've worked with many live authors—have never been nuisances. If you ask them what they mean by something, they always say humbly, "Well I'm not really quite sure that I know, but I think it's something like this." The only place Paddy Chayevsky's ever dogmatic about his plays is in certain, nearly always quite unimportant, ways of getting a laugh. He says, " I think it would be much funnier if he delayed the take, instead of, you know, just snapping back on the answer, if he looked at the guy as if he didn't understand and then gave the reply very mildly after a pause," or something like that—little technical points like that, which is something that he has heard when he was writing it; and God knows that's something that he should know all about; and the ideal way of putting on a play is for the author himself to direct it. But authors are rarely good directors. They haven't got what it takes as a general rule in the other department, which is dealing with the collaborators.

I hope I haven't left the impudent impression that I think that directors know more about authors' scripts than the authors do themselves. Of course, I don't. I'm only saying that the author doesn't know everything about his script, and that the script itself is merely the raw material upon which a group of collaborators have got to work; it is not the finished article. That idea is merely the invention, for the most basely materialistic reasons, of literary professors.

I'm not going to go maundering on about the business with the script.

There is a good deal to be said. There's no script, however good—I didn't say this, Ezra Pound did—that isn't the better for cutting. Everybody writes too long. The Sermon on the Mount could take a bit of cutting.

Well now then, on to next thing: the collaborators department.

First of all, you've got to face it—you never get the people you want. If you're casting a play, everybody goes, for the leading part, for five or six leading actors who are hot at the time. And as every management in the world, including the films and including the television, is casting their crowns before them—and in the case of the films and the television, the crowns are much more heavily jewelled—your chances of getting the top five are slender. Then there are thousands of reasons why you can't get the people you want for the other parts—well, you can't get Miss So-and-So because she used to be married to the leading man and now she ain't. Or you didn't know it, but the stage-manager tells you that she's drinking fairly heavily right now, or she's gone away on vacation, or she's making a film. The popular supposition is that actors' lives are spent sitting at the telephone waiting for it to ring so they can say "yes!" to any offer that is made to them. It's not so. There are many thousands of actors like that at the bottom, but alas and alack, so unfair is life, that those are not the people you want for leading parts.

Then there is the further thing that the best actors are not always the best citizens. I won't say that they're the worst citizens, but the best citizens—the people who are never late, who never fluff a cue, who always know their lines, who're always helpful, tidy, sober, reliable, cooperative, and perfectly dear in every way—usually have no talent. And, alas, the converse is true: the bundles of talent are usually bloody nuisances. So that you can face it from the start, the collaboration will not be exactly what you've dreamed of.

Nevertheless, in my opinion, I think the most important function that the director performs is creating a certain atmosphere at rehearsals. And the first essential for that is to make the company feel that they are, in fact, a unit. Now, that's much harder in New York than it is in London because the theatre is so vast. The theatre here is almost the entire assemblage of professional talent from the whole continent. There are literally tens of thousands of actors, and a company is assembled, and you know that you perhaps won't see any one of those people again for ten or fifteen years. In London, it's quite different. The market is much smaller; we all know one another;

everybody is on first-name terms; most of them are Godparents of the other ones' children, and all that kind of thing; and it's much more chummy and much more a family affair.

And the same thing goes for the relation with the staff. Oddly enough, in this democracy, the people who do the manual work are considered lower than they are in London. In the London theatre there will be old stage-hands who have worked—and their fathers before them and their grandfathers before them—in the same theatre; and generations of actors have come, and, you know, when they're young kids, these old boys will have been kind of uncles and daddys to them. And they're not the lower classes at all; they're respected and liked friends; and the relation is infinitely more friendly and sort of mutually supporting between them.

The New York Theatre—not for any failing of the human thing, but simply because it's such a huge great, over-competitive, over-bustling, money-making machine—has extraordinarily little of that kind of humanity. Therefore, it is harder for the director to do what I think is his first duty, which is to make everybody feel that they are part of a oneness, that the company is a unity, to create a morale in which everybody wants to do well, not just for their own self-advantage, but for the forwarding of the cause for which we are met.

And allied to that but not quite the same thing, it's up to the director to create the atmosphere of a rehearsal. A director who is unpunctual or who is lazy will never have good rehearsals going. It's my experience that people have got to feel that they've got to arrive on time; it's a duty for them to be absolutely punctual, not because punctuality in itself is anything, but it's a nuisance if the others are kept waiting. And the proceedings have got to move at a certain speed. It's up to the director to see that the people, you know, who have to wait by for a long time and then come on and say, "My lord, the carriage waits," and then bugger off and not say anything again until the end of the play—that they don't have to wait for hours and hours and hours to do that, that they are called—you can't say precisely when—but maybe twenty minutes before their turn comes, and are allowed to go after it. And little things like that which make an immense difference to the morale of rehearsal and to the humanness and the pleasantness of going on.

Then, on a deeper level, it's the director's business to create an atmosphere in which people can do often quite embarrassing things—play love scenes with people whom you don't find in the least sexually attractive, or perhaps even more embarrassing, play love scenes with people whom you find overwhelmingly sexually attractive. Make confessions, show all sorts of strange things about themselves. It's an odd paradox of the stage that as soon as you start pretending to do something and enlarge it to the scale that is necessary to carry it to the back of the theatre, you not only portray what you're pretending to do, but you portray yourself, your innermost self, in capital letters, red ink and underscored three times. Homosexuality peeps out from the most butch men—gentlemen who carry on, you know, like they're great lechers and things, suddenly they have to do some kind of a revealing scene, and you see suddenly that inside all this facade of tweed and manliness is a terribly frightened little spinster lady. And not only in the sexual department: sweet-faced spinster women, pillars of the Presbyterian Church, have to get up and show something and suddenly you see that inside all this, there is a raging, voluptuous tigress. Well, that's not awfully funny; it can be very shaming for those who have to undergo it. And there is a sort of free-masonry of the stage that we accept that—you know, that is why the stage is often accused of being too tolerant of irregularity. But it is because we've learned that that has got to be taken, that people are not what they seem to be, that the world is just chock-full of homosexual clergymen and kleptomaniac ladies of the utmost respectability and all kinds of things like that.

I think the important thing is the creation of the atmosphere of rehearsal. And the most single important thing about that is that it must not become a bore. And I'm inclined to be pretty bored by the sort of rehearsals in which the director goes into long psychoanalytic huddles with certain members of the cast and they whisper and whisper and whisper and everybody else hangs about. And as often as not, all that sort of talk doesn't really show in the performance at all. If you want to do it, for God's sake, yes, but not in rehearsal hours. You go out and have a drink and do that in some dark corner. And similarly, the scales have got to be held—the powerful and rich and important actors must not oppress the small-part people. I don't think they're apt to, but you have to watch that. And, equally, the small-part people must not be allowed to bore and suck up to and vex the lives out of the big ones. Because in the desperate struggle—and again this applies particularly to New York—in the desperate struggle to get on, the small-part people with their way to make have no option but to try to make contact with people that they think are going to be useful—and to be dreadful nuisances. And the little people in the company very often feel that it's necessary for their self-advantage to get to know the big people and they rather push and hang around and make themselves nuisances in a not really very suitable way. And although it's not really the director's business, I think, as the sort of chairman of the meeting, you can protect them a bit from that, and you can suggest to the young people that there are better ways of getting on.

THE DIRECTOR AND STAGING

Well, then, it is not my view that a director is there to *instruct* actors how to do things. You have to set up a framework in which they can work; it's no use just saying, "Well, there's the stage and the door's going to be there, dear, and the window's there and the staircase there and the sofa here—now get on and act it." That's not a help. I've been an actor, and I know that you've got to be, to some extent, put into a framework. It's much more helpful to be told more or less—started off, anyway—with precise positions, and if the director is wise he will start that precisely, and he will say, "When you say the word 'spit' you stand up and you walk over to the sofa, and when you say the word 'teapot' you sit down and begin pouring out the tea." But if he's also sensible, he will say, "Now this is only a preliminary thing; when you've done it a few times and if you want to change this, let's discuss it: it's not a hard and fast drill. There are certainly six ways in which it could be done." But it's a help, I think, always, if only because it saves time, if somebody blocks it out absolutely autocratically at first, provided it's understood by everybody that no offense is going to be taken if they say, "I feel very uncomfortable here; do you mind if I cross later?"

And I think that certain decisions have to be taken by the director as to the general interpretation of a play, and, inside that, the particular interpretation of a scene. Of course, again, the wise director is not autocratic about this; if somebody disagrees, they should certainly be entitled to say so, but not in front of everybody and not in such a way that it wastes the time of the whole gang. They say, "I'm not happy about this; can we discuss it," and you say, "Yes," and at the end you discuss it, and they say, "I quite disagree with you because-because-because-because," and if you're sensible, you listen very carefully and probably they're right.

But any scene must be arranged so that the climax comes at a certain point. Dialogue must be arranged, must be to some extent orchestrated, because the dialogue of a play is its music upon which it lives; the pace of that music and the way one cue is given, the way one speech leads to another, is the music of the evening; and just as an orchestra cannot play a symphony without a conductor, for very obvious reasons, so a company cannot play a play without somebody who's going to regulate the music of the play; who says it's going to get steadily louder, faster, faster, faster, faster, mounting to that point—pause—and then begin. And then you start building again. All that's a very obvious instance, but there are many things that can be done with the music. The pattern of it must be agreed beforehand, and the actors must know the pattern into which they're expected to fit. And again, I don't think that this should be dogmatic. An actor can say, "Well, I think I can make that line much more effective if I didn't have to gabble it, and if the climax could come a little bit earlier so that my line is the beginning of the anti-. . . "—you can see that sort of talk which is very easy to have.

Well, the director of course is responsible for the mise-en-scène—the designer designs, and if the director is sensible he will let him design but only exercise some kind of an over-all control. No sensible director says, "Oh, I couldn't have the ribbons on that dress pink, they must be blue." But he does say, "Well, she's got to get up some very steep stairs, so there's no use giving her a skirt that's that tight; you'd better think again about that." Or, "She's got to get through a narrow doorway, so there's no use giving her a hat that sticks out to here." Or "She's got to be seen from the dress circle, so there's no use having a hat that does that." And common sense stuff like that. But overall, the style of a play, particularly in a classical play, has got to be determined; the director, I think, has got to be the chairman of this, but if he's wise he won't autocratically settle it; he will do it by discussion.

The designer with whom I've worked a very very great deal, and most of my classical productions have been done with, is Tanya Moisevyich, and we've worked so much together that we've developed almost a sort of shorthand. We discuss the thing and we have our own kind of abbreviations, and we refer back to other things that we've done and say, "If it were a little like this only not so black," and "If this was dark black," and drawings are made on the backs of envelopes and half-sheets of paper of a very rough nature, and we exchange these drawings, and then the drawings give place, before any finished drawings are done, to rough models cut out in cardboard and the thing is set up so that you can see what is happening not merely in the flat but in two dimensions. And if that is agreed, then the rough cardboard model gives place to a tidy one, which is painted, and the dress sketches go through a rather similar thing: very rough scribbles on the back of an envelope are replaced by samples of material, and then the samples of material are the basis for more careful painted drawings. But I don't think any director who's any good is taken in for very long by the elaborately finished drawings —you know, with sort of shaded backgrounds and immensely realistic imitations of texture and things, which many, particularly commercial designers, put in because they think that only so can they get the job. In fact, the design should show just, without any frills at all, how the thing is made, what it's going to be made of and why it's being made in that particular way.

And there's plenty more that might be said, but I hope I've given you an indication of my attitude to this job and some of the things that the job embraces. And again before I finish, may I say that if I've ever given a dogmatic impression, I really think I've belied myself. It was never my intention, either off the stage or on it, to be dogmatic. Direct, yes. And without frills, yes. But not to the extent of thinking that my point of view is right and that nobody else knows anything.

Sandra, holy whoopee and me
Norman D. Dietz

Norman D. Dietz, playwright and director, has also acted extensively, traveling in America with his wife, Sandra, and he describes their twosome as "kind of a mad Hansel and Gretel of the underground theatre." This article was written as an Introduction to his collection of plays titled *Fables and Vaudevilles and Plays: Theatre More-or-Less at Random*. His attitude toward theatre gives one an indication of just how completely a sense of joy can dominate theatre work.

After a performance once a teenager asked Sandra and me, "How did you get involved in all this jazz?"

The answer, I suppose, is that we happened to have an old instrument.

We happened, actually, to have a theatre.

Now, a lot of people think a theatre is a building, of course, probably because the sign on the building says so. And others think it is a group of people, undesirable people usually. I understand a few even think it is just a large television set.

They are *all* wrong. Even though it doesn't look anything like a clarinet or saxophone, a theatre is an instrument. A theatre is an instrument that people use to "make beautiful music together." Or something like that. It is an instrument that people use to bring a play into being.

All of which may strike you as just about the least important information you have encountered thus far in the twentieth century. And it probably is.

But unfortunately, unless one understands a theatre as an instrument (or something like an instrument), it is difficult to understand just what it is that a theatre brings into being; it is difficult to understand what a play is.

And understanding what a play is, *is* important, I happen to believe, even in an age when importance is calculated in light-years and megadeaths.

For understanding what a play is may help us to understand better what a person is, what it means to be a person; and understanding this may just help us to understand once and for all what human life is. And understanding *that* I *know* is important—especially since if we don't, we may just accidentally snuff it out one of these days.

So "the play's the thing" then, even today. Hamlet is still right.

Well, a lot of things are not a play. A book on a shelf is not a play. Lines of dialogue and directions for movement are not a play. The antics of actors on a stage and the noises they make are not a play. Nor are the scenery or properties or costumes they may fall over. Nothing that an audience sees or hears is a play. All this is just part of a theatre. It is just a part of the instrument.

A play is players playing. And if that sounds too obvious to be a distinction, then try it this way: a play is people pretending. For it is as simple as that.

A play is something that happens, that goes on in people. And it happens when the people—some of them actors and some of them audience—agree among themselves purposefully to regard certain things that are not true as if they were, while being very careful not to pretend that anything that really is true is not.

Which is an involved way of saying that a play is just a game of let's-pretend, just basic children's make-believe with an adult awareness, which all children share and only grown-ups seem to lose, that all of us are, after all, always and only very real persons in a very real world no matter what we pretend, and that we are engaged together in this momentary make-believe for a very real purpose directly related to that reality.

That purpose, of course, like the instrument, is an old one: celebration. For when we play together what we are really doing is celebrating. We are making holy whoopee about what it means, as we see it, to be human, to be alive together in a world full of strangers impossible to understand. And in our celebrating we are, almost inadvertently, providing, for ourselves and for one another, that occasion for community which is the theatre's chief, if infrequent, contribution to the common life of man.

The beautiful music occurs, occasionally at least, when, preoccupied with the instrument and our playing, we suddenly drop our guard and betray ourselves, momentarily revealing in honest confession to one another that we are indeed, underneath our strangenesses, all only real live human beings after all, condemned alike to face both life and death alone but for the saving company of one another.

Which is more than enough to make most people launch out into a good long love song.

And that jazz, as any good lover will tell you, is nothing if not important.

The director and the permanent company
Peter Hall

Peter Hall (1930–) proved a driving force in the rise of the Royal Shakespeare Company following its inception in 1961. He first directed professionally in 1953 and, in addition to the RSC, has directed for Theatre Royal Windsor, The International Playwrights Company, the Royal Opera and on Broadway. His directing style has changed considerably over the years, a factor he discusses in this 1966 interview with Charles Marowitz. He also explores the idea of directing actors in multiple roles over several seasons.

Has your style of directing changed in the past ten years?

I hope it has. I was fascinated initially in the theatre by sound, being a musician. I'd often get sound that was perhaps not very full of meaning. For instance, I could be fascinated by the production of a scene because tempo and pause and dynamic were arresting to my ears and my rhythmic sensibilities. I was blind as a bat when I started. I was also, I think, not aware of dramatic meaning in any intellectual sense. My responses were entirely instinctive. I was just seduced by the theatre. I don't know if I've changed for the better or the worse, but I'm quite certain I've changed. I'm now very obsessed by meaning. If I saw a production of ten years ago I would find it much more hateful than a production of a year ago. . . .

Lots of directors believe that casting is ninety percent of the job; that if you cast a play right you are three-quarters of the way there. Do you go along with that?

I think it's too easy a remark. If you don't cast people with enough complexity to examine the play, then it's boring; but if you cast the play by the textbook, it can also be very boring, because what you think about a play before you start working with the group can, by itself, be limiting. Good casting, in a West End sense, can be a very limiting factor. I think everybody has got to be balanced in relation to everybody else: if you have X, you may not need Y, but you must have Z. Good casting is impossible to define; it's like style.

What do you feel about the English actor today?

I think things have improved a lot in the last three or four years. A few years ago, the idea of instinctive challenges, improvisation, stretching the actor's psyche, or the application of very difficult technique, whether physical or verbal, were all considered unwarrantable intrusions on the holy actor's Ego. I think this is going a bit now—more and more work is being done in drama school which opens the actor to many different challenges. But basically I still think that the English actor out of drama school hasn't learned enough craft. As soon as you learn too much craft, you've got to feed the instinct so that you can fill out the craft. But I don't think, in the early stages of training, that you can learn too much craft. I mean, craft must inhibit, it must stop, and the time to learn it is when you're young. You can open up your personality as you mature and as you enrich. A painter can forget how to be a good draughtsman once he knows what he is. But too few actors have sufficient training—they haven't developed their voice to its full, for instance, which is one of the obvious things; and most English actors don't even know they've got a body. And the work we've been doing in Shakespeare at Stratford unfortunately encouraged that. One of the problems about Shakespearean acting is that people must think about the text and the rules that are written into the text, about how they should approach it formally. But the minute they start learning that, they become a walking head with a couple of legs and an intellect. We've done a great deal of damage in making actors even more intellectual. I think the future work at Stratford has got to concentrate on the body.

Do you think it's necessary for an actor to understand an intellectual concept in order to make that concept clear to an audience?

I think it is necessary for him to understand it sufficiently to believe it. That's not the same thing as being able to give a lecture on it, but he must instinctively believe it, he must be able to go along with it emotionally.

Do you think the director has to understand it?

Yes.

What are the main problems of working with a permanent company, as opposed to an ad hoc production set-up?

You may find that you get a less-than-ideal cast from a permanent company than if you are surveying the whole field. I don't personally find that very often, because I think you never are surveying the whole field if you're casting commercially; you can't get certain actors either for money reasons or because of other commitments. The disadvantages, I suppose, are the other side of the advantages. There is a danger in security. There is a danger in working with people you know: there is a danger in keeping inside one's range as an actor: there is a smugness: there is a laziness. But I think the group system can more readily be brought up to something worthwhile in the hands of the right director than the non-group system. But a company is no substitute for good playwriting, good directing, good acting. I think it is an environmental situation which helps. It saves time, it gives short cuts. It also creates an atmosphere in which we are more ready and open to learn from each other.

The ideal in companies has always been to develop a style, an acting style, and I think it's true to say that the Royal Shakespeare has now developed a style which is recognizable. If you accept the fact that a style has been developed, how has it developed? Can directors consciously and methodically develop a style, or is it something that just comes about?

It comes about by the work. A group with shared assumptions will unconsciously develop a style. I think any style which you consciously develop is phoney. Just as I would say, if you said, 'I will approach this play in such-and-such a way," that's phoney.

What would be unphoney? What would be the organic approach?

Well, the organic approach is to answer the following questions: Why are you doing the play in the first place, at this particular time, in this particular situation? Why do you want to do it? What does it mean? How can you clearly express that meaning? If the Royal Shakespeare has got a style, it comes out of the choice of repertoire and the way we approach what a play should say on the stage. Myself, I am not interested in plays that mean nothing. They must have some relevance to the problems of our lives. I think our job is to put on plays in order to convey such meanings and to take everything away which doesn't *mean*—one tries constantly to strip away things which are decorative.

Aren't you sometimes in the position of having to choose a play as an expedient?

Well, of course. Life is often less than ideal. . . .

. . . to what extent do you think directors should take liberties with the text?

I think we live in a free country. It's not a cultural state. When I or anybody else abuses a text, it's not abused forever, like painting out a chunk of the Mona Lisa. I think we're perfectly at liberty to do it. We must expect to be reviled and abused if we make a fool of Shakespeare; but we're not really making a fool of Shakespeare. We're making a fool of ourselves, because the text is still there when we've finished. I find that mature Shakespeare should be left alone, because he knows considerably more what he's at than any latter-day director. But with the *Henry VI,* so much of it's apprentice work, and so much of it is frankly padding (because he's set himself the task of covering an enormous canvas, and sometimes he's just bored with doing it) that I think one can be fairly radical. I think you must judge by the results.

Do you think there is such a thing as a Shakespearean masterpiece, in inverted commas, which no longer affects an audience because it is too well known, like an operatic aria, or a pop tune, for that matter, that gets so overplayed, people are inured to it?

When people know something so well it's almost dead, that is the moment when you can slant it into a new life.

When you say, "slant it" . . . ?

I mean interpret it. It's the idea of the Greek plays depending on known legend. If you know "To be or not to be" backwards, and the audience know it backwards, you can convey something very particular by a minutely defined interpretation of the soliloquy.

Do you find the problems in the plays of Pinter very different from those you encounter in Shakespeare?

The technical problems are very similar. The world is different, obviously; the personality is of a different time, different age; but they both depend on precise verbal form. When Pinter writes three dots, he means something different than when he writes "Silence." There is also an organic rhythm and shape about his prose, which has to be observed. In exactly the same way, you cannot ignore the ends of the lines of Shakespeare, the commas of Shakespeare, the full stops, the rhythmic regularities and irregularities. Although, perhaps, it's worth noting that in Shakespeare it's important to know that you're working on the earliest text and not one which some scholar has corrected.

What about the texture of feeling from actors in Shakespearean acting as opposed to modern acting: do these pose different problems?

I think our experience has been, with a number of actors, that the discipline and the selection needed to play Pinter or Beckett is the most wonderful training to do the same thing for Shakespeare, so that you don't generalize or varnish him with unnecessary emotion. But of course it must depend on the dramatist. There are many modern dramatists who explore areas which are not very useful for Shakespeare. But then, what is Shakespeare? Shakespeare is what we are doing at this particular moment (I hope with knowledge, and unselfconsciously) with a Shakespearean play. But interpretations change with the times. The new, cool, intellectual, rather formed, rather witty (in the eighteenth century sense) style of speaking Shakespeare which we adopt, which concentrates more on meaning than it does on emotion, will seem in ten years' time the most horrible cliché and affectation.

Would you say that's the main difference if we were to compare let's say, the Shakespearean tone of the 1920's, the 1930's, with that of the 1960's, this cool tone you've just described?

Yes, I would. We distrust pyrotechnics today, either in our statesmen or in our artists, unless it's fully conscious, and then we're in the area of "camp," which is another form of modern art. I think the idea of making a Shakespearean speech effective (which is the 20's and 30's idea: "Here is my aria, and I will show as much range as possible for me") is not what we do now at all. We do something which many people find limiting in emotional range, but I find meaningful. The main thing now is, "What is it about, conceptually, and how can I express that with intellectual clarity?"

Do you think it breaks the continuity of a permanent company for actors to go away to do commercial work?

My ideal dream would be the fully subsidized theatre with me and a couple of colleagues that I really respect as directors, only twenty actors, and the need to do one play each a year—three programmes a year. That will never happen. It costs too much money. The next step from that is to say, "Well, we must have a larger range of products in order to get this thing going at all, and we'll try to keep the actors by the range and amount of work." Then you get into a sort of puritanical attitude, so that if anybody wants to go away, they're selling out and losing their integrity and all that. . . . Six years of trying it makes me think that the only way you'll get actors to stay in a permanent company, in our western society, is by letting them go. Then they come back. It can sometimes be good for them; it opens them, it makes them feel that other people value them, they lose the parochialism which is inevitable in a permanent company. It can also be very bad, because they are encouraged to think of themselves in temporary commercial terms which are inaccurate or inflated, and then they don't come back, because they don't get the big parts with us. But I am convinced that only by letting them go will they really stay, and you've just got to face it. The big money and the acclaim of the outside would is something which is attractive to an actor's temperament. It measures his status and is part of his actor's vanity. And a necessary part of being an actor is vanity; and to repress it is dangerous.

But doesn't that destroy the healthy incestuous feeling that groups like The Living Theatre and the old Group Theatre bolstered? Are you saying that sort of tightly-knit small company can't make out today?

I don't think it can make out in our society, because the market pressures are so strong and the rewards are so enormous. And I think the way to run a permanent company is to admit these facts. Actually, over several years, I have lost very few actors that I wanted to keep, and the number of people who are actually part of the company who keep coming and going is now quite enormous. They are permanent, and yet to accept the offer of a film company is not now considered a major betrayal. This was the great trauma of the Group Theatre which you mentioned. I think also that if a company is to exist beyond a certain time limit, it needs probably to be impure, because you can have three, four, maybe five years of a group which is tight, but then it's going to be past its peak and something's going to go wrong.

Most permanent companies, with a few exceptions like the Moscow Arts, have lasted about ten years. Are you afraid that the Royal Shakespeare might have the same kind of lifespan?

I reckon ten years is about it. And on the present dispensation, I reckon there's probably another three or four years to run—and then something will happen. And the thing that I hope is going to happen is the new theatre, which will change our whole raison d'être in every single way. In a few years, we shall move into our specially designed theatre in the City of London's Barbican. This will change everything about us. I am praying we shall last until that cataclysm.

What was the original impulse that made you want to do Hamlet?

Ever since I went to Stratford I'd been looking for a young actor who, in the broadest sense, represented the young intellectual of today. David Warner seemed to be that, from the moment of his first audition for the company. I remember Peter Brook and I auditioning him, and saying, "Well, I reckon he can play *Henry VI*." And then I said, "And in two or three years, he'll be the Hamlet we want." And for me, he is. But what triggered it off was a particular feeling about the powerlessness of the intellectual in a political state. It's pompous to state it, but I always have a major preoccupation. From *Troilus and Cressida*, through *The War of the Roses*, through the other four Histories, through *Hamlet*, I was on a political kick. I was fascinated by power politics in Shakespeare. Now, if you ask, "What's your label now?" I am being metaphysical. That's why I want to do *Macbeth*. That's why I did Schoenberg's *Moses and Aaron*. I want to move into late plays of Shakespeare. I'd like now to examine *The Tempest* or *Winter's Tale*.

Can you say why you are on your metaphysical kick?

I've been very obsessed for the last two years by the idea of religion, in the broadest sense. I am an agnostic, and have always been, and a couple of years ago I started worrying about it.

That means that you were never a true agnostic!

Exactly. It's difficult to live and say I don't know about the major problems of living.

Has the director's relationship to actors changed in the past ten years?

As far as I'm concerned, it's changed considerably, because ten years ago I was a young whippersnapper saying, "Would you mind trying . . . ?" If I got above myself and said "Do this . . ." everybody got a bit tight, thin-lipped. Now I'm in the reverse situation. They think, "Well, if he says it, it must be good." Which is equally dangerous, because ninety percent of the time he's wrong. I find I'm treated much more as the sort of master-figure who's supposed to know, which absolutely horrifies me.

What do you think is the best sort of relationship?

I think a sort of open situation in which the actor can say to the director, "That's a bloody silly idea, and I'll show you why," without prejudice. And the director can treat it in the same way back.

Is there a danger that a director who is perhaps not too sure of himself will too often simply go along with the actor?

Oh, of course, of course.

To what extent do you think an actor is a good guide . . .

I think an actor is very often an extremely bad guide. Many actors, for their own self-preservation, stop at the point where things start getting dangerous or painful. When I do a play now I know the areas that I want, otherwise I don't do it. I have a subjective state of preparation that I am confident about, I know what I'm asking. I wasn't always like that. I used to wander in and try fourteen hundred different ways, and then say, "Which is the best?"

I don't think you really can direct like that. You've got to be drawing on something very positive, because the number of solutions for a scene are infinite, and if you're going to set down and examine infinity, you'll end up with nothing. So you must select very rigorously.

With Shakespeare, I believe you usually have about six or eight weeks' rehearsal.

Yes.

At what stage in the rehearsal process do you think one should batten down the hatches and say, "These are our final choices"?

I can never batten down the hatches.

Not even at dress rehearsals?

Well, yes, surely. But only because one has to be practical. But the way I work now is to daub it down in very rough, free but quite strong colors, as quickly as possible. I then try and explore how the actors can create in that broad sketch.

Do you plot in a premeditated way?

No, not at all.

You plot instinctively as you go along?

I have a rough idea, but it is very, very rough.

If you have an eight-week period, at what stage do you plot?

Well, I wouldn't plot with any firmness until we'd really examined what is needed. For the purposes of the early rehearsals, you can stand there, and he can stand there, and we'll see in this situation what physically is necessary, but don't write it in the book, and don't remember it as an external thing. Only do it if it is an actual thing: if it is needful for what we're actually finding. In the middle stages I like to give the actors an enormous amount of rope and then start stripping away. The modern production that, for myself, was nearest to what I mean in the theatre was *The Homecoming*. I took away from it every single thing that didn't mean something to the play. Everything went. It was a painful task of just stripping and stripping until one was left with "it."

How long do you spend building up before you start stripping?

Oh about a fortnight or three weeks.

Do you feel that there is a period in the rehearsal process where the director loses sight of what he's got?

Yes, I'm sure.

Where does that point usually come for you?

About halfway through, where I tend to confuse happiness with achievement. And that's where one has to step back, and say, such and such has got to be done.

Do you think the director himself can do this?

It's a great help if there's somebody who can help him do it. That's where I'm lucky in having colleagues who can talk very freely to me. I think that's very important, and that's why the commercial theatre holds no great appeal to me. Most of the people in the commercial theatre who tell the director what's right or wrong are not on the same wave length as him. They are not knowledgeable as directors.

Do you find that your own attitude to rehearsals is determined by each play, or do you start off with a kind of rehearsal principle, and stick to that in each case?

Each play requires a different rehearsal rhythm. If I was given all the time in the world on a Shakespearean text, I would spend a fortnight sitting down with the books not so much to talk technicalities, but to get the actors to freely associate with the imagery, to start getting responses to the imagery. I think actors—particularly in Shakespeare, where the language itself is almost a cliché to an actor—don't realize the burning illumination of metaphor, they just let it ride.

You said before that future work in the theatre has to concentrate on the body. Could you elaborate on that?

I think that, as a nation, the English tend to walk around pretending they don't have bodies. This is certainly true of the English actor. The fault of bad young American actors is a flaying of the body all over the place, an aggressive physicalness. The fault of a bad young English actor is a cool precision, a gentlemanly craft, which is intellectual and verbal. It is contained in his clothes without any movement or life whatsoever, no sweat or smell or bulge or anything. I am after the illumination of character by physical life, by physical propensity, but not in an illustrative way. This is what I admire most about the present work of the Berliner Ensemble, which I find verbally retrograde, and verbally boring—but physically, they have selected that aspect of a character which means. They don't tell you things about the character, which you don't need to know, but physically it is clear. And this is an area of work which we haven't even begun in our theatre.

Is that something which a director can impose, or is it something that an actor has to learn himself?

Just as a director can select and strip away and define verbal or emotional presentation, so he can do the same for an actor in his physical life. But the actor's got to be fully alive and creative in the first place. You can't say to an actor, "It seems to me that this character is best represented by this particular physical trait." That is an external imposition. With many English actors, it is very difficult to get hold of it at all, because he's not doing anything except standing in a neutral way. It's the neutrality of standing on stages which distresses me. I've just been spending six weeks working at Covent Garden Opera House—and I find something quite comforting in the lack of neutrality of opera singers' bodies. They're not trained to be modest, and they're abominable and they're messy, and they're often unmeaningful, not to say distracting. But they're not neutral. Physically, they are.

Is there some way in which this physical consciousness can be induced in the actor in training?

I think what one has to challenge young actors with is this: Tell this story, without words, but not in the formality of mime. I'm not talking about external mime, because mime is like asking you to improvise a sonnet, something formal, external. We're not asking for that.

That presupposes that there is a language of movement that the actor can find and the audience can understand.

There is a language of movement. But there are as many languages as there are people. You can see it all around you. Everybody's body works in totally different and unique ways. As we look at each other, we have certain physical apprehensions of each other's characters because of the way we're sitting, because of the way we are. This is part of the meaningful creation of character, not the decorative or illustrative presentation of character. I am not interested in saying, "This minor character here is a clerk all his life, so it would be very important to see the exact way in which he bites his nails, because he's been biting nails and pencils all his life." That's meaningless to me unless the play is actually dealing with that. What I am actually saying is: "Right, you are playing Gertrude. I don't want a generalized queenliness, a generalized good bearing, a physical cliché, but what is it about her, which, if one just looked at her, would help us to understand Gertrude?" And that is different for every single actor, because every single actor's body is working in a different way.

I find the theatre an obsession because it is always changing like life itself. This is why it is so difficult and undesirable to theorize about theatre practice like this. Immediately, dogma sets in, hard and unyielding, and the work automatically lacks the flexibility which keeps it really in touch with its times. In this interview I've been talking a lot about the physical life of the actor, because at this moment it is an obsession with me—a swing against the excessive intellectual and textual work which the Royal Shakespeare Company has been doing for the last six years. But in another few years I might feel quite differently. A well-balanced plan must take account of the whole of the actor's being.

This process of action and interaction must be remembered whenever any theories of the theatre are studied. Brecht's theories of alienation for actors only make sense in the heavily sentimental and excessive tradition of German acting before he began his work. People who elevate the first period of Stanislavsky's work (up till about 1915) as the ultimate truth in acting forget that he rejected nearly all his own findings and methods in his later and perhaps more mature period. So I study theories, and I even utter them, but I would beware of living or working by them. Only theorize after you have created. And creation is produced by the pressure of now.

For a total interpretation
Jerzy Grotowski

Jerzy Grotowski (1933–), founder and director of the Polish Laboratory Theatre, is perhaps the single most influential all-around theatre person of recent times. Author of *Towards a Poor Theatre* and director of plays like *Akropolis, The Constant Prince,* and *Apocalypsis cum figuris,* Grotowski in his work with the Lab Theatre placed primary emphasis on the actor and his relationship both to the audience and the script. He believed that theatre should be communal and ritualistic and that it should be stripped to its essential elements.

"For A Total Interpretation," by Jerzy Grotowski, *World Theatre,* Vol. XV, No. 1, 1966. Reprinted by permission of Ninon Tallon Karlweis.

1 What is "Total Theatre"? While the underlying concept has never been rigorously defined, the term itself has been repeatedly used by critics to designate productions—including my own up to 1960—involving a wide range of differing modes of expression. The productions concerned are those that utilize flexible architecture, an important musical score, lighting effects, technical tricks borrowed from the circus, the simple or multiple film screen, the contrast between actor and plastic forms and, in the interpretation, the conjunction of various conventions: that, for instance, of "straight acting" with ballet, clowning, pantomime, cabaret, and so forth. Another frequently encountered feature is the extension of the stage area by means, notably, of laterally projecting platforms.

The text, on the other hand, is often a mixing of, for instance, dramatic fiction and factual documentary. . . .

2 *By reason of the medley of styles, the theatre loses its specificity.* The theatre's particularity is to bring actor and spectator face to face, to establish a direct and tangible relationship between them. While this is universally admitted, the time has now come to see what it implies, to realize that the actor who struts across the stage with padded chest, false nose and delicately applied make-up has no bearing on the essence of the theatre.

This essence is approached by the actor who shows himself as he really is, who changes his appearance before the spectators' eyes, who forges himself a mask, suggests, transforms himself from thin to fat, from young to old, from character to character, from type to type solely by the play of his muscles and the force of his psychical impulsions.

The time has come for us to realize that extraneous music—i.e., recorded and amplified or even executed by musicians who are not the actual actors—is an element foreign to the performance, an attempt to exploit outside talent, a form of kleptomania. We should recognize that the true substance of theatrical music is constituted by the voices of the actors, by the sonorous rhythm of feet striking the stage or by the clash of hand prop against hand prop.

It is also time we realized that the costume which fails to reflect the changing moods of the actor and which the latter cannot transform, pertains to the plastic arts and not to the theatre, and that the same applies to the decors. If the actor merely serves as a dummy for displaying costumes or as a pretext for decors that act in his stead, we are up against a plastic creation that palliates the weakness of the here all but nonexistent theatre. Similarly, a literary text is made theatrical solely by the manner in which it is delivered: intonation, sonority, etc.

And now for the laws that govern scenic space. If the particularity of the theatre resides in the actor-spectator relationship, the role of scenic space is to modify this relationship in accordance with the structure of the play in hand. There is no need to build new theatres for this purpose: an empty hall in which the respective places of the actors and the spectators are distributed afresh for each new play is amply sufficient.

One can, for instance, separate the spectators from the actors by secluding them behind a neck-high partition; the sort of curved perspective thus provided enables them to follow the actors' interpretation of the play in the same way as one observes the behavior of animals at a zoo: they are fans at a bullfight, medical students watching the surgeon at work, Peeping Toms, in a word, who, for this reason, automatically invest the action with the traits of a moral transgression.

The actors can also interpret the play amidst the spectators without noticing them, erect an edifice amongst them and integrate them not into the action itself but into the setting of the action.

Or else the entire auditorium can be regarded as a concrete spatial unit: in our *Faustus* (Marlowe), the "last meal" takes place in a monastic refectory where Prior Faustus entertains his guests at huge baroque tables and then enacts episodes from his own life on these same tables right in the midst of the spectators.

There are, in fact, innumerable possibilities. The readaptation of the auditorium for each production is no doubt the simplest and cheapest solution for the smallish theatre.

3 I am not convinced that what the public wants today is more important than what it may want tomorrow. But, above all, the very existence of a regular and well-defined public strikes me as problematical in the extreme.

One can define "the public" as being the spectators who have collectively reacted in the same way to a specific "challenge." And it must be admitted that this type of joint reaction is now definitely a thing of the past. For my collaborator Flaszen, the existence of such a public must be regarded as an occasional phenomenon: the public exists at certain specific moments of history; apart from these moments, there is no public, there are only spectators.

Personally, I am awaiting a spectator who would really like to see himself, see the true aspect of his hidden nature. A spectator willing to be shocked into casting off the mask of life, a spectator ready to accept the attack, the transgression of common norms and representations, and who—thus denuded, thus disarmed, and moved by a sincerity bordering on the excessive —consents to contemplate his own personality.

This implies the rejection of accepted opinions and consists rather in an attack on the infra- or ultra-conscious regions of the psychism of the spectator than in an intellectual discussion. For the theatre, in its essence, is not an intellectual art. It operates through "the actor-spiritualized incarnation" (I would prefer to say "incarnate spirituality"), it operates tangibly through the dedication, psychic tension, physiology, rhythm, and vital spark of the actor.

In the ages of universal faith, of the more or less sacred theatre, the spectator virtually identified himself with the myth: he made no distinction between the truth of the myth and his personal truth. Today, there is no such thing as universal faith. This is why the spectator must be confronted with the collective complex, with the myth; he must try out the truth of it on himself, on his own present-day and experience-marked person. To transgress and transcend the taboo, to accede to the truth by a sacred blasphemy (in the Middle Ages: *parodia sacra*), the myth must be endowed with a universal vitality; the age in which we live is, however, marked by the decline of the traditional forms of myths if not of these themselves.

This is why the "transgression" is at present inseparable from the violation of the taboo of "corporality." The strictly corporal sense of the myth—that is to say its indubitable human literality—and violation, these are the occasion for the transgression. Even today, and provided he surrenders himself to the torments inflicted on his model in their full corporal literality, the actor playing the principal part in a production based on the myth of the Passion can achieve a *parodia sacra*, an act of transgression.

4 The theatre is perhaps obliged to be "total" but it must become so on its own ground, that is to say in the interpretation.

The seven imperatives of contemporary theatre
and
Notes toward a statement on anarchism and theatre
Julian Beck

Julian Beck (1925–) founded The Living Theatre in 1946 and with his wife, Judith Malina, molded it into the most enduring of all alternative theatres. Indeed, it became the symbol for theatre revolution itself. Although first dedicated to exploring the literary aspects of performance, The Living Theatre moved increasingly toward improvisation and flexibility, as epitomized perhaps by their performances of *Paradise Now*. Concerned with ritual, political anarchism, and the discovery of a new lifestyle (for the theatre and for the world), Beck's most complete philosophical statement is *The Life of the Theatre*. In these brief excerpts one can glimpse the scope of his concern and the poetic vision he propounded.

---

1 THE SEVEN IMPERATIVES OF CONTEMPORARY THEATRE

In the Street: outside of the cultural and economic limitations of institutional theatre.

2 Free: Performances for the proletariat, the *Lumpenproletariat*, the poor, the poorest of the poor, without admission charge.

3 Open Participation: Break through, Unification: Collective Creation.

4 Spontaneous Creation: Improvisation: Freedom.

5 Physical life: Body: Sexual Liberation.

6 Change: Increase of Conscious Awareness: Permanent Revolution: Unfixed (Flexible, Free) Ideology.

7 Acting as Action.

NOTES TOWARD A STATEMENT ON ANARCHISM AND THEATRE

The purpose of the theatre is to serve the needs of the people. The people have no servants. The people serve themselves.

The people need revolution, to change the world, life itself. Because the way we are living is too full of pain and dissatisfaction. Fatally painful for too many people. For all of us.

The seven imperatives of contemporary theatre   **119**
and Notes toward a statement on anarchism and theatre
Julian Beck

This is a period of emergency. Therefore emergency theatre is the theatre
of awareness.

The first thing is to feed everybody, to stop the violence, and free us all.
This is what anarchism means in our time.

The theatre of anarchism is the theatre of action.

The slavery to money has to end. Which means that the entire money system has to end. A society of free goods, freely produced, freely distributed. You take what you need, you give what you can. The world is
yours to love and work for. No state, no police, no money, no barter, no
borders, no property. Time and disposition to seek good, seek one
another, to take trips deep into the mind, and to feel, to find out what
it is to have a body, and to begin to use and make joy with it.

The theatre has to work with the people to destroy the systems of civilization
that prohibit the development of body and brain. In order to work in
most factories you have to stop the mind from working lest it die of
pain and injury. You have to stop the body from feeling lest it wince
consciously thru the day.

This is the work of the theatre.

Theatre has to stop being a product bought and paid for by the bourgeoisie.
The whole age of buying and selling has to end. Theatre has to stop
being the servant of a system in which the only people who go to the
theatre are those who can pay for it.

The poor are disinherited. Well, activist artists are going to play in the
streets,

we are going to tell what's going on, how bad it is,

and what the people can do to change things,

and what the destination—the objective of the revolution— is,

and ways to get there:

how to make the revolution, to bring it into being, and what to do when we
have it, and how to carry it further.

The revolutionary artist will seek ways to drench the people in such beauty
that they tear down the flags and subvert the armies, form communes
and cells and a society in which there is a possibility of being.

Because bourgeois society doesn't tell the people what beauty is. The secrets
have been appropriated by the rich with their exclusive education and
avidity, and the people are poisoned by the mercury in the mass media.

The working people are going to take over the means of production, occupy
    the places of industry and turn them all into factories of food clothing
    shelter heat love and the extended mind.
It is going to happen.
And we are going to do this by exorcising all violence, and the cause of
    violence, the need for violence, violence in all its forms, violence of
    hands, teeth, bombs, police, army, state, law, land, real estate, prop-
    erty, education, social, political, moral and sexual.
This is the work of the world.
And this work of the world is the only work of the theatre:
because the theatre principally is the dancing place of the people.
and therefore the dancing place of the gods who dance in ecstasy only amid
    the people
And therefore we aim this theatre at God
and the people
who are the destination of the most holy
holy holy revolution.

Excerpts from
The immediate theatre
Peter Brook

Peter Brook (1925–) joined the Royal Shakespeare Company in 1962 and the International Center for Theatre Research (Paris) in 1971. During the interim he became perhaps the most influential theatre director in the Enslish-speaking world. Popular and eclectic, he directed such productions as *Marat/Sade, The Tempest,* and *A Midsummer Night's Dream,* as well as *King Lear* and Sophocles' *Oedipus Rex*—all productions, according to critic Albert Bermel, "that bumped the theatre out of its old decorum while winning over a general public." His book *The Empty Space* explores the approach to theatre which brought him international acclaim. In this section he discusses his actual practice as a director in rehearsal.

A t the beginning of rehearsals the actors are the opposite of the ideally relaxed creatures they would like to be. They bring with them a heavy baggage of tensions. So varied are these tensions that we can find some very unexpected phenomena. For instance, a young actor playing with a group of inexperienced friends may reveal a talent and a technique that put professionals to shame. Yet take the very same actor who has, as it were, proved his worth and surround him with the older actors he most respects, and often he becomes not only awkward and stiff, but even his talent goes. Put him then amongst actors he despises and he will come into his own again. For talent is not static, it ebbs and flows according to many circumstances. Not all actors of the same age are at the same stage of their professional work. Some have a blend of enthusiasm and knowledge that is supported by a confidence based on previous small successes and is not undermined by fear of imminent total failure. They start rehearsals from a different position from the perhaps equally young actor who has made a slightly greater name and who is already beginning to wonder how much farther he can go—has he really got anywhere yet, what is his status, is he recognized, what does the future hold? The actor who believes he may one day play Hamlet has endless energy: the one who sees that the outside world is not convinced he will ever play a lead is already tying himself into painful knots of introspection with a consequent need for self-assertion.

In the group that gathers for a first rehearsal, whether a scratch cast or a permanent company, an infinite number of personal questions and worries hang unspoken in the air. Of course, these are all enhanced by the presence of the director: if he were in a God-sent state of total relaxation he could greatly help, but more of the time he too is tense and involved with the problems of his production and here too the need publicly to deliver the goods is fuel to his own vanity and his self-absorption. In fact, a director can never afford to begin with his first production. I remember hearing that a budding hypnotist never confesses to a subject that he is hypnotizing for the first time. He has "done it successfully many times." I began with my second production, because when at seventeen I faced my first group of sharp and critical amateurs, I was forced to invent a non-existent just completed triumph to give them and myself the confidence we both required.

The first rehearsal is always to a degree the blind leading the blind. On the first day a director may sometimes make a formal speech explaining the basic ideas behind the coming work. Or else he may show models or costume sketches, or books or photographs, or he may make jokes, or else get the actors to read the play. Having drinks or playing a game together or marching round the theatre or building a wall all work in the same way: no one is in a state to absorb what is said—the purpose of anything you do on the first day is to get you through to the second one. The second day is already different—a process is now at work, and after twenty-four hours every single factor and relationship has subtly changed. Everything you do in rehearsal affects this process: playing games together is a process that has certain results, like a greater feeling of confidence, friendliness, and informality. One can play games at auditions just to bring about an easier atmosphere. The goal is never in the game alone—in the short time available for rehearsing a play, social ease is not enough. A harrowing collective experience—like the improvisations on madness we had to do for the *Marat/Sade* brings about another result; the actors having shared difficulties are open to one another and to the play in a different way.

A director learns that the growth of rehearsals is a developing process; he sees that there is a right time for everything, and his art is the art of recognizing these moments. He learns that he has no power to transmit certain ideas in the early days. He will come to recognize the look on the face of an apparently relaxed but innerly anxious actor who cannot follow what he is being told. He will then discover that all he needs is to wait, not push too hard. In the third week all will have changed, and a word or a nod will make instant communication. And the director will see that he too does not stay still. However much homework he does, he cannot fully understand a play by himself. Whatever ideas he brings on the first day must evolve continually, thanks to the process he is going through with the actors, so that in the third week he will find that he is understanding everything differently. The actors' sensibilities turn searchlights on to his own—and he will either know more, or at least see more vividly that he has so far discovered nothing valid.

In fact, the director who comes to the first rehearsal with his script prepared with the moves and business, etc., noted down, is a real deadly theatre man.

When Sir Barry Jackson asked me to direct *Love's Labour's Lost* at Stratford in 1945, it was my first big production and I had already done enough work in smaller theatres to know that actors, and above all stage managers, had the greatest contempt for anyone who, as they always put it, did not know what he wanted. So the night before the first rehearsal I sat agonized in front of a model of the set, aware that further hesitation would soon be fatal, fingering folded pieces of cardboard—forty pieces representing the forty actors to whom the following morning I would have to give orders, definite and clear. Again and again, I staged the very first entry of the Court, recognizing that this was when all would be lost or won, numbering the figures, drawing charts, maneuvering the scraps of cardboard to and fro, on and off the set, trying them in big batches, then in small, from the side, from the back, over grass mounds, down steps, knocking them all over with my sleeve, cursing and starting again. As I did so, I noted the moves, and with no one to notice my indecision, crossed them out, then made fresh notes. The next morning I arrived at rehearsal, a fat prompt book under my arm, and the stage management brought me a table, reacting to my volume, I observed, with respect.

I divided the cast into groups, gave them numbers and sent them to their starting places, then, reading out my orders in a loud confident way I let loose the first stage of the mass entrance. As the actors began to move I knew it was no good. These were not remotely like my cardboard figures, these large human beings thrusting themselves forward, some too fast with lively steps I had not foreseen, bringing them suddenly on top of me—not stopping, but wanting to go on, staring me in the face: or else lingering, pausing, even turning back with elegant affectations that took me by surprise—we had only done the first stage of the movement, letter A on my chart, but already no one was rightly placed and movement B could not follow—my heart sank and, despite all my preparation, I felt quite lost. Was I to start again, drilling these actors so that they conformed to my notes? One inner voice prompted me to do so, but another pointed out that my pattern was much less interesting than this new pattern that was unfolding in front of me—rich in energy, full of personal variations, shaped by individual enthusiasms and lazinesses, promising such different rhythms, opening so many unexpected possibilities. It was a moment of panic. I think, looking back, that my whole future work hung in the balance. I stopped, and walked away from my book, in amongst the actors, and I have never looked at a written plan since. I recognized once and for all the presumption and the folly of thinking that an inanimate model can stand for a man.

Of course, all work involves thinking: this means comparing, brooding, making mistakes, going back, hesitating, starting again. The painter naturally does this, so does the writer, but in secret. The theatre director has to expose his uncertainties to his cast, but in reward he has a medium which evolves as it responds: a sculptor says that the choice of material continually amends his creation: the living material of actors is talking, feeling and exploring all the time—rehearsing is a visible thinking-aloud.

Let me quote a strange paradox. There is only one person as effective as a very good director—and that is a rotten one. It sometimes happens that a director is so bad, so completely without direction, so incapable of imposing his will, that his lack of ability becomes a positive virtue. It drives the actors to despair. Gradually his incompetence makes a gulf that yawns in front of the cast, and as the first night approaches insecurity gives way to terror, which becomes a force. It has happened that in the last moments a company found a strength and a unity as though by magic—and they gave a first night performance for which the director got high praise. Equally, when a director is fired, the new man taking over often has an easy job: I once entirely re-staged someone else's production in the course of one night—and got unfair credit for the result. Despair had so prepared the ground that a touch from one finger was all that was required.

However, when the director is plausible enough, stern enough, articulate enough to get the actors' partial trust, then the result can misfire easiest of all. Even if the actor ends by disagreeing with some of what he is told, he still passes some of the load on to the director feeling that "he may be right," or at least that the director is vaguely "responsible" and will somehow "save the day." This spares the actor the final personal responsibility and prevents the conditions for the spontaneous combustion of a company coming into being. It is the modest director, the honorable unassuming one, often the nicest man, who should be trusted least.

What I am saying can very easily be misunderstood—and directors who do not wish to be despots are sometimes tempted to the fatal course of doing nothing, cultivating non-intervention in the belief that this is the only way of respecting the actor. This is a wretched fallacy—without leadership a group cannot reach a coherent result within a given time. A director is not free of responsibility—he is totally responsible—but he is not free of the process either, he is part of it. Every now and then an actor turns up who proclaims that directors are unnecessary: actors could do it by themselves. This may be true. But what actors? For actors to develop something alone, they would need to be creatures so highly developed that they would hardly need rehearsal either; they would read the script and in a wink the invisible substance of the play would appear fully articulated amongst them. This is unreal: a director is there to attack and yield, provoke and withdraw until the indefinable stuff begins to flow. The anti-director wants the director out of the way from the first rehearsal: any director disappears, a little later, on the first night. Sooner or later the actor must appear and the ensemble take command. The director must sense where the actor wants to go and what it is he avoids, what blocks he raises to his own intentions. No director injects a performance. At best a director enables an actor to reveal his own performance, that he might otherwise have clouded for himself.

Acting begins with a tiny inner movement so slight that it is almost completely invisible. We see this when we compare film and stage acting: a good stage actor can act in films, not necessarily vice versa. What happens? I make a proposition to an actor's imagination such as, "She is leaving you." At this moment deep in him a subtle movement occurs. Not only in actors— the movement occurs in anyone, but in most non-actors the movement is too slight to manifest itself in any way: the actor is a more sensitive instrument and in him the tremor is detected—in the cinema the great magnifier, the lens, describes this to the film that notes it down, so for the cinema the first flicker is all. In early theatre rehearsals, the impulse may get no further than a flicker—even if the actor wishes to amplify it, all sorts of extraneous psychic psychological tensions can intervene—then the current is short-circuited, earthed. For this flicker to pass into the whole organism, a total relaxation must be there, either God-given or brought about by work. This, in short, is what rehearsals are all about. In this way acting is mediumistic—the idea suddenly envelops the whole in an act of possession—in Grotowski's terminology the actors are "penetrated"—penetrated by themselves. In very young actors, the obstacles are sometimes very elastic, penetration can happen with surprising ease and they can give subtle and complex incarnations that are the despair of those who have evolved their skill over years. Yet later, with success and experience, the same young actors build up their barriers to themselves. Children can often act with extraordinary natural technique. People from real life are marvelous on screen. But with adult professionals there has to be a two-way process, and the stirring from within has to be aided by the stimulus from outside. Sometimes study and thought can help an actor to eliminate the preconceptions that blind him to deeper meanings, but sometimes it is the reverse. To reach an understanding of a difficult role, an actor must go to the limits of his personality and intelligence—but sometimes great actors go farther still if they rehearse the words and at the same time listen acutely to the echoes that arise in them.

. . .

In rehearsal, form and content have to be examined, sometimes together, sometimes separately. Sometimes an exploration of the form can suddenly open us up to the meaning that dictated the form—sometimes a close study of content gives us a fresh sound of rhythm. The director must look for where the actor is messing up his own right urges—and here he must help the actor to see and overcome his own obstacles. All this is a dialogue and a dance between director and player. A dance is an accurate metaphor, a waltz between director, player and text. Progression is circular, and deciding who's the leader depends on where you stand. The director will find that all the time new means are needed: he will discover that any rehearsal technique has its use, that no technique is all-embracing. He will follow the natural principle of rotation of crops: he will see that explanation, logic, improvisation, inspiration, are methods that rapidly run dry and he will move from one to the other. He will know that thought, emotion, and body can't be separated—but he will see that a pretended separation must often take place. Some actors do not respond to explanation, while others do. This differs in each situation, and one day it is unexpectedly the non-intellectual actor who responds to a word from the director, while the intellectual understands all from a gesture.

In early rehearsals, improvisation, exchange of associations and memories, reading of written material, reading of period documents, looking at films and at paintings can all serve to stimulate the material relevant to the theme of a play inside each individual. None of these methods means much in itself—each is a stimulus. In the *Marat/Sade*, as kinetic images of insanity rose up and possessed the actor and as he yielded to them in improvisation, the others observed and criticized. So a true form was gradually detached from the standardized clichés that are part of an actor's equipment for mad scenes. Then as he produced an imitation of madness that convinced his fellows by its seeming reality, he had to come up against a new problem. He may have used an image from observation, from life, but the play is about madness as it was in 1808—before drugs, before treatment, when a different social attitude to the insane made them behave differently, and so on. For this, the actor had no outside model—he looked at faces in Goya not as models to imitate but as prods to encourage his confidence in following the stronger and more worrying of his inner impulses. He had to allow himself to serve these voices completely; and in parting from outside models, he was taking greater risks. He had to cultivate an act of possession. As he did so, he faced a new difficulty, his responsibility to the play. All the shaking, shuddering and roaring, all the sincerity in the world can still get the play nowhere. He has lines to speak—if he invents a character incapable of speaking them he will be doing his job badly. So the actor has to face two opposite requirements. The temptation is to compromise—to tone down the impulses of the character to suit the stage needs. But his real task lies in the opposite direction: make the character vivid—and functional. How? It is just there that the need for intelligence arises.

There is a place for discussion, for research, for the study of history and documents as there is a place for roaring and howling and rolling on the floor. Also, there is a place for relaxation, informality, chumminess, but also there is a time for silence and discipline and intense concentration. Before his first rehearsal with our actors, Grotowski asked for the floor to be swept and for all clothes and personal belongings to be taken out of the room. Then he sat behind a desk, speaking to the actors from a distance, allowing neither smoking nor conversation. This tense climate made certain experiences possible. If one reads Stanislavsky's books, one sees that some of the things said are purely to evoke a seriousness from an actor at a time when the majority of theatres were slipshod. Yet at times, nothing is more liberating than informality and the chucking away of all holy, high-minded ways. Sometimes all the attention must be given to one actor; at other times the collective process demands a halt to the individual's work. Not every facet can be explored. To discuss every possible way with everyone can be just too slow and so it can be destructive to the whole. Here the director has to have a sense of time: it is for him to feel the rhythm of the process and observe its divisions. There is a time for discussing the broad lines of a play, there is a time for forgetting them, for discovering what can only be found through joy, extravagance, irresponsibility. There is a time when no one must worry himself about the results of his efforts. I hate letting people watch rehearsals because I believe that the work is privileged, thus private: there must be no concern about whether one is being foolish or making mistakes. Also a rehearsal may be incomprehensible—often excesses can be left or encouraged even to the amazement and dismay of the company until the moment is ripe to call a halt. But even in rehearsal there is a time when one needs outside people watching, when what always seem to be hostile faces can create a good new tension and the tension a new focus: the work must all the time set new demands. There is another point the director must sense. He must sense the time when a group of actors intoxicated by their own talent and the excitement of the work loses sight of the play. Suddenly one morning the work must change: the result must become all important. Jokes and embroideries are then ruthlessly pared away and all the attention put on to the function of the evening, on the narrating, the presenting, the technique, the audibility, the communicating to the audience. So it is foolish for a director to take a doctrinaire view: either talking technical language about pace, volume, etc., or avoiding one because it is inartistic. It is woefully easy for a director to get stuck in a method. There comes a moment when talk about speed, precision, diction is all that counts. "Speed up," "get on with it," " it's boring," "vary the pace," " for Christ's sake," is then the patter, yet a week before such old-timer talk could have stultified all creativity.

The closer the actor approaches the task of performing, the more requirements he is asked to separate, understand, and fulfill simultaneously. He must bring into being an unconscious state of which he is completely in charge. The result is a whole, indivisible—but emotion is continually illuminated by intuitive intelligence so that the spectator, though wooed, assaulted, alienated, and forced to reassess, ends by experiencing something equally indivisible. Catharsis can never have been simply an emotional purge: it must have been an appeal to the whole man.

Now the moment of performance, when it comes, is reached through two passageways—the foyer and the stage door. Are these, in symbolic terms, links or are they to be seen as symbols of separation? If the stage is related to life, if the auditorium is related to life, then the openings must be free and open passageways must allow an easy transition from outside life to meeting place. But if the theatre is essentially artificial, then the stagedoor reminds the actor that he is now entering a special place that demands costume, make up, disguise, change of identity—and the audience also dresses up, so as to come out of the everyday world along a red carpet into a place of privilege. Both of these are true and both must be carefully compared, because they carry quite different possibilities with them and relate to quite different social circumstances. The only thing that all forms of theatre have in common is the need for an audience. This is more than a truism: in the theatre the audience completes the steps of creation. In the other arts, it is possible for the artist to use as his principle the idea that he works for himself. However great his sense of social responsibility, he will say that his best guide is his own instinct—and if he is satisfied when standing alone with his completed work, the chances are that other people will be satisfied too. In the theatre this is modified by the fact that the last lonely look at the completed object is not possible—until an audience is present the object is not complete. No author, no director, even in a megalomaniac dream, would want a private performance, just for himself. No megalomaniac actor would want to play for himself, for his mirror. So for the author or the director to work for his own taste and his own judgment, he must work approximately for himself in rehearsal and only truly for himself when he is hemmed in by a dense bank of audience. I think any director will agree that his own view of his own work changes completely when he is sitting surrounded by people.

Seeing a first public performance of a play one has directed is a strange experience. Only a day before, one sat at a run-through and was completely convinced that a certain actor was playing well, that a certain scene was interesting, a movement graceful, a passage full of clear and necessary meaning. Now surrounded by audience, part of oneself is responding like this audience, so it is oneself who is saying "I'm bored," "he's said that already," "if she moves once more in that affected way I'll go mad," and even "I don't understand what they're trying to say." Apart from the over-sensibility brought about by nerves, what actually is happening to make such a startling change in the director's view of his own work? I think that it is above all a question of the order in which the events now occur. Let me explain this by a single example. In the first scene of a play a girl meets her lover. She has rehearsed with great tenderness and truth and invests a simple greeting with an intimacy that touches everyone—out of context. In front of an audience, it suddenly becomes clear that the preceding lines and actions have in no way prepared for this: in fact, the audience may be busy trying to pick up quite different trails relating to other characters and themes—then suddenly it is faced with a young actress murmuring half inaudibly to a young man. In a later scene, the sequence of events could have led to a hush in which this murmuring would be exactly right—here it seems halfhearted, the intention unclear and even incomprehensible.

The director tries to preserve a vision of the whole, but he rehearses in fragments and even when he sees a run-through it is unavoidably with foreknowledge of all the play's intentions. When an audience is present, compelling him to react as an audience, this foreknowledge is filtered away and for the first time he finds himself receiving the impressions given by the play in their proper time-sequence, one after another. Not surprisingly he finds that everything appears different.

"I can't go on, I'll go on"
Alan Schneider

Alan Schneider (1917–) joined the faculty at Catholic University in 1941 and began directing professionally in 1948. The director for all of Edward Albee's works, he has also introduced to America such playwrights as Samuel Beckett and Harold Pinter. Perhaps the American director most familiar with multiple theatre situations—New York, regional, and university—he here laments the conflicting roles enjoyed by the director in all of them.

Y ou must go on," writes Samuel Beckett, the man most responsible for my being able to do that. "I can't go on, I'll go on." Obviously he wasn't writing about the state of mind of American theatre directors circa 1971–1972, although he could well have been. For in a theatre environment in which everything worthwhile seems more impossible than ever (even though it occasionally somehow gets done), where nothing necessary is pleasurable, and where the procedures in between have become increasingly maddening and stupid, why do we go on? Because, again from the words of my favorite contemporary word-man, "There's nowhere else."

Of my fifty or so productions of all sorts directed in the New York theatre, on Broadway and off, "successful" or less than so except to my inner eye, in over fifteen years since I was foolish or foolhardy enough to stray northward from the pleasanter corners of the Arena Stage in Washington, only a bare handful—and I have to search for the fingers—have not turned out to be total agonies of one kind or another from beginning to end; the special agonies in each case always unexpected and surprisingly unique. Nor do I feel especially accursed in this regard. My best friends tell me the same story; Tommy Ewell once mentioned to me casually that the only show he'd ever not had his total agonies in had closed in Philadelphia. And recently, I noticed that Gerald Hiken, a fine young director-actor and ex-associate of mine, who has withdrawn himself completely from the "formula and noise" of New York for a kind of communal touring existence in California, confessed in the drama pages of the Sunday *New York Times* that in his nine years and twenty-two shows, he had hated rehearsing nineteen of them. To reverse one of Mr. Beckett's cheerier lines, it's an unreasonable percentage. But a normal one. That is to say, despair is normal in our work: it's the nature of the beastliness. Only, recently, despair like the smog has been reaching abnormal levels.

Before exploring some of the more specific and characteristic agonies of the directorial process, let me send up some smallish flares to illuminate the general landscape. For neither statistics nor the sordid details of individual miseries, neither journalism nor even sociology, is adequate. Only poetry will do. Pardon then, if you will, some preliminary images, some semi-hemi-demi-metaphors, some (I trust) somewhat poetic truths, or whatever, to set the mood of our Fun Citadel-on-Hudson:

There is a small square room, with peeling wallpaper and glaringly empty; suddenly, a few crusts of dry bread are thrown into it at random by some giant unseen hand or hands, to merge with the debris and slime of the rough, unfinished floor. At regular intervals, hordes of half-starved, struggling, naked human animals, all strangers and hostile to each other, and all previously goaded to desperation, are let loose to grope for the bread. Blindly, they join in the impossible struggle, most of them succumbing or giving up, a few surviving to grow less famished—and more frightened as they realize that next time they might not be among the lucky ones.

There is a container of irregular but definite shape, smallish but somewhat flexible, filled to the brink with water rushing out eternally from an inexhaustible spring deep under a mountain. The water continues to pour forth, steadily and strongly, timed somehow always to force the surplus liquid down through an invisible drainpipe below the surface of the ground somewhere—so that the container itself never overflows. Scientists have never been able to explain how nature is able to regulate the exact amount of water flowing in and out of the container; but it is very clear to them that the water in the container itself is never the same from one moment to the next.

An infinity of particles of live matter, infinitesimal but finite, revolve in endless orbit around a glowing, pulsating, mesmerizing nucleus of indistinguishable material, their path predictable and seemingly fixed. Suddenly, from time to time, random flashes of lightning dislodge one or more of the particles and blast it or them into a smaller constellation of other particles revolving in a different orbit, one higher and faster, around a brighter but equally indeterminate nucleus in a solar system of evidently higher magni-

tude. Once more the particles revolve endlessly, waiting for the next accidental lightning blast. The process is endless, the orbits arcing higher and more
unsteady, the successive nuclei always brighter and more intangible. The
particles retain one common quality: memory.

A crowd gathers in the marketplace at nightfall and listens, silently and
spellbound, to Brutus explain to them the horrendous crimes of Caesar.
They cheer Brutus long and loudly and curse Caesar. Immediately afterwards, the same crowd listens to Antony cautiously and then boldly praise
Caesar and muse on the awful crimes of Brutus. They cheer Antony even
more enthusiastically. The dead Caesar's body continues to lie in state, his
flesh slowly devoured by the worms. The crowd breaks up to have a cup of
coffee and a sandwich.

Some time ago, I was sent a script to read by a young playwright unknown
to me. Not having my home address, he sent it to me c/o Executive Office,
Sheridan Square Playhouse, where my off-Broadway *Godot* had been playing
for eight months—with four or five complete reversals of each of the roles,
constant administrative and artistic crises of every sort, even occasional difficulties with such psychological matters as the state of the plumbing and
the efficiency of the air conditioning (not to mention lesser matters, like the
roof leaking), and total suspension of royalties to playwright, director and
designer because of declining grosses (the theatre owners, the company manager and the press agent, of course, being more essential to the production,
continued to get paid); and most recently without a single understudy, because the management, even though it was making a fortune with another
production at the same time, refused to add to the weekly outlay. Can you
picture a stage manager going on to play the blind Pozzo—holding a book?
Ours did one evening.

The sender of that script, besides being a playwright of some promise,
was clearly a romantic idealist and therefore to be cherished. For the Sheridan Square Playhouse not only has no office space of any kind, executive or
otherwise, it has barely enough space to contain and costume the actors.
Dressing-rooms off-Broadway, and sometimes even on Broadway, are considered to be luxuries, not necessities; ask Kate Reid what would have happened in hers at the Longacre if she took a deep breath while a visitor was
present. Nor have I ever had any kind of office in a New York theatre (the
new regional playhouses sometimes offer some version of such an amenity,
in those cases where the Artistic Director has been able to sneak them into

the plans while the architect was dozing); although producers sometimes have offices of their own where, while the casting or the reading of scripts took place, I have occasionally been allowed a desk drawer (if not an entire desk) and a telephone (so long as I made no long-distance calls).

When I walk in to rehearse—assuming we happen to be rehearsing in a theatre rather than a small dance hall, a closet or a men's cloakroom some-where—dangling my inevitable briefcase, replete with baseball cap (not a fetish, as is commonly supposed, but actually a shield to keep the worklight from blinding me), my raincoat (for leaky roofs), and my daily paperbag ration of cheese sandwiches (to avoid luncheon at Sardi's) I may with good luck and a careful aim succeed in throwing all three neatly down on one of the first couple of rows of frayed and undusted seats, hoping that neither the silent doorman outside nor the talkative cleaning ladies in the balcony will mind—or throw away the sandwiches. (Maybe those ladies may even quiet down before we get to our big scenes onstage.) If my luck holds and rehears-als are proceeding well enough for some of the actors still to be talking to me, I can usually find one friendly enough to permit me to install my belong-ings in a corner of his dressing room from time to time. In a larger theatre, there's usually an abandoned dressing room up on the fifth or sixth floor, where the stage manager stores his stuff; he rarely minds if I huddle up in there—so long as I don't try to run up those four or five flights of stairs too often in order to fetch my sandwiches or my clipboard—the one without the light (or the battery or paper) in it.

None of which is critical, except that it dramatizes the persistent fact that the ordinary director, far from being the star of the American theatre, is, like the playwright, the actor, the assistant stage manager, and for that matter everyone else—except possibly the doorman—an outsider, picked for this one occasion and discarded afterwards. Although the director is, perhaps, more defenseless and vulnerable than the others. It is the director, first of all, who waits all alone somewhere to be asked by someone—with an office—to read a play. A playwright, after all, has a typewriter to keep him company. Nor can the director even audition to show how good he is, as can the actor—although I'm not sure actually which condition is to be the more avidly sought. Any-how, what's clear is that the director has to wait for an opportunity to direct which can come only after someone has seen him direct, a fairly vicious sort of circle. Also, he tends to get offered only the kind of play that he's just done. My first production in New York was an ordinary family comedy; all

I got offered after that was a series of ordinary family comedies. When I wanted to do *Anastasia*, the producer resisted because she thought all I could do was comedy. (I had rarely done comedy before coming to New York.) After *Anastasia*, I got only melodramas or plays with scenes for two women. And so on. Because I've done so many small cast elliptical plays lately (especially Beckett and Albee) most producers assume that I would be terror-stricken with more than four people in the cast. Actually, I would be delighted for a change.

In addition, very few persons with power in the theatre are qualified to differentiate between talent and success. So the director knows that he can only succeed by being successful, not just by doing good work. Therefore, he is doomed to be nervous about not being successful, a synonym for being unemployed. So he either repeats what he's been successful at for as long as possible, usually becoming less successful as he goes along. Or getting more successful, which may turn out to be even worse because he stops being good. Or he remains cautiously inactive for as long as he can survive, always recalling his last success as though it had been yesterday—or becomes dangerously over-active, the danger coming from the theatre's inevitable law of averages and its constant yen for new names and models. That's why our successful directors immediately turn to films.

If and when the director ever gets into rehearsal, he is always the convenient party to blame for whatever mysterious (or not so mysterious) plagues afflict the enterprise. Jehovah, as I recall, sent only ten plagues; but the theatrical gods, being much more imaginative, can afflict a production on its way to Broadway (or even to off-Broadway because plagues, being infectious, have now spread below Fourteenth Street) with hundreds: Nerves, Uncertainty, Tension, Intrigue, Emotions, Egos, Irrationality, Madness, Terror, Hysteria, among others. For instance, the leading lady, after two days rehearsal, calls her agent (who also happens to be the director's agent but the leading lady's salary is much higher so that the agent tends to side with her) to complain that the director has placed her co-star center stage eleven times in the first act and her stage center only seven times. If this artistic imbalance is not corrected immediately (regardless of what the text might suggest) she insists on getting another director with greater mathematical ability. Or, the leading man, whose personal draw while slightly above nil happens to be responsible for whatever theatre parties have been sold, even though he has no talent for doing anything but exploiting his personal idiosyncrasies, decides that the director's insistence on dealing with text or motivations is inhibiting his artistic flow—and refuses to go on rehearsing. Or a super-star, who has been eating out of the director's hand for three weeks and lavishing kisses and gold tieclasps on him as a token of her undying devotion, gets told by her fourth husband at the first run-through that the director is actually engaged in a diabolical plot to destroy her effectiveness and sex appeal; she immediately calls in her previous director to direct her scenes—and the two directors, hers and theirs, spend the next two weeks passing each other silently in the darkened auditorium.

The director who is in the meantime supposed to be concentrating on higher aesthetic goals related to the demands of the play, or setting a tone and style for the production, or advancing the art of the theatre, usually spends most of his waking (and sleeping) time during the three-and-a-half weeks of rehearsal (seven out of eight hours, though it usually turns out to be five or six because actors get tired in the afternoon) trying to keep that delicate balance among all the forces involved: to mediate between producer and playwright about the cuts, to spar for status with the stars, to soothe the ruffled egos of almost everyone, including the walk-ons, to be all things to all elements, in effect serving as an unlicensed but very much needed psychoanalyst without portfolio, and worrying a lot. I once directed a show in which the leading man kept wandering into my kitchen before dawn each day wearing various combinations of bedraggled pajamas and bathrobe, for a cup of coffee and a handhold all the weeks we were trying-out, out of town. I wanted to sleep so that I could face what he was doing at rehearsals; he wanted to talk so that we wouldn't be able to rehearse.

Then, finally and unavoidably, you open and those critics out of town tell you the show isn't ready—which is the only reason you went to Baltimore or Philadelphia in the first place. Or if you open in New York to previews and the word-of-mouth turns out to be awful, which is obviously what often happens, of course it's the director's fault. We should have gone to Baltimore but the director didn't want to leave his wife alone, for various reasons. The director hasn't been able to get the playwright to rework that second act scene, or he's gotten him to rework it and it was better before. The possibilities are infinite.

Or the word-of-mouth by some miracle is not bad or even good, which turns out to be equally if not so obviously a problem, because everyone tends to get overconfident, and the performances start to deteriorate. Or an agent or a brother-in-law comes in and tells one of the actors that he's going to be a big star on this one no matter what happens to the show—and then that particular actor becomes impossible to deal with. And so on. Everything that's possible suddenly becomes necessary.

The idea that rehearsals of all plays should have a fixed limit of what amounts in practice to be 20 to 24 days (that is allowing one day off each week for everyone to worry and shop for groceries), with a maximum of four weeks—five in cases of certain special magnitude—although it's Actors' Equity and not the director who defines that magnitude—is ridiculous enough; after all, some plays might need more and some might subsist or even be improved with less. (*Virginia Woolf*, incidentally, was rehearsed for only two weeks and two days, plus ten previews, because one of its performers was unavailable until a certain date, while our theatre had to be taken and paid for as of another date.) What is even more frustrating is the stupidity of not being able to rehearse with either the setting or the properties without incurring exorbitant stagehand expenses, which means that you don't get to use the props. This stupidity is compounded by the allowable presence of rehearsal props (like paper cups for real cups and wooden sticks for swords), some of which tend to be very similar to the real props, depending upon the cooperativeness and ingenuity—and convenience—of the prop man, who is usually a genial fellow, extremely anxious to please. So you wind up using a real telephone as the frying pan, and a real frying pan as the telephone. But woe betide you if you use the real phone as a real phone because then you'll have to put on a full crew. Or, if you are in Baltimore and trying to rehearse in the second setting of a three-set play, you will wind up rehearsing in the lobby while that second-act setting remains tantalizingly within reach but light years away from use.

Eventually, as it must to all directors, there comes a day at the end of all those weeks when "they" have to move the physical setting in. Furniture, chosen and viewed at various hurried times and in various under-lit places, doesn't always fit together (but then neither do the actors, who have had to be assembled and auditioned separately because of Equity regulations). Never mind, you are too busy reeling from the blows of the technical confusions to make any changes now. Later maybe, "we'll see." And without anyone but the director knowing it, you wind up getting used to what you started out with. Is there ever time to try something else, to sample other possibilities or hopes, even to change the wallpaper a bit because in spite of what the designer said, it does tend to stand out? You've read somewhere about how the Berliner Ensemble once discovered that its masks or costumes or something were all wrong on *Arturo Ui*, and started all over again; does that ever happen in our capitalist/materialist society? It doesn't to me, although I've heard tales whispered of sets entirely redone, costumes altered, even money spent. Oh, yes, I remember that on *Virginia Woolf* we actually got another sofa because the one we had was much too large. But the change brought on a major crisis and was only resolved, as I remember, by one of the producers buying the offending sofa for his own personal use at the price we had paid for it. Obviously, a very astute gentleman and a fine producer.

Nor is there ever enough time within those portions of the one or two days allotted to technical rehearsals in which to do more than make sure everything is nailed down and rendered roughly usable by the actors—and then to get on to the lighting. "We'll improve things later," although "later" rarely if ever comes. And the lighting is, of course, not finished in those two days, just sketched in—partly because the equipment, temporary and rented and hastily thrown together is left over from another century, and partly because lighting is always done while everyone wanders about the stage except the actors. Just as sound levels are always tested while someone is doing some hammering. The idea theoretically is that lights will continue to be refined all during the previews or out of town performances; although in practice, since lighting rehearsals require the presence and cost of complete crews, you rarely if ever get them again. So that whatever improvements or changes are to be made, have to be "winged," that is sneaked in ad lib, improvised, thrown in hurriedly at odd moments such as the period between "half hour" and curtain. As with every other part of the production process, ends become subverted by means, changed drastically in order to accommodate the means, and eventually entirely lost or forgotten—except later in retrospect.

And then, in spite of everything, the day comes, the play opens; and the Herculean labors of weeks or months or even years (the playwright's) rest on the throw of an unmarked but nevertheless loaded (in more ways than one) set of dice: the critics. You never know, not even five minutes beforehand, what they are going to say except that they'll tend to miss the most important things and concentrate on what is unimportant. You do know that if it's a serious play, which is what I tend to direct, all that has to happen is for whoever is reviewing for *The New York Times* that week to turn his critical thumb slightly downwards—or even not to be energetic enough in turning it upwards—and the closing notice will be visible by the end of the week, if not tomorrow. You also know, by experience, that a play at which preview audiences have roared for weeks doesn't get more than a few scattered chuckles opening night because the orchestra floor is jammed with working press all too busy judging and writing down things in the dark to laugh—and the following morning the director gets blamed for not having a sense of humor. Worse almost, you know that a play which has gotten a reasonably warm response though nothing special during previews will, once the rave notices saying "delicious hit comedy" are out, get gales of laughter and applause on every funny line, including one like "Good morning, so there you are." I once got reviewed on the sound of the radiator pipes clanging backstage; the pipes got better notices than the play, which happened to be Beckett's *Endgame.*

It's exciting all right, that opening night vigil, after the friendly congratulations have drifted off and the cast party is sagging a bit with tension and drink, to mill around, trying not to care, between the advertising agency's supply of liquor and its battery of special telephones; in the bunker waiting for the Russians. Or, better image, waiting for each district to come in with those election returns that are going to let you know whether you will be eating and breathing and living tomorrow morning—or for another season. I've been through it all too many times not to know that a little less of this kind of excitement wouldn't hurt anybody, much less the theatre. Especially since you also know that any resemblance between success in this system and quality is generally purely coincidental. My best work as a director has usually run a couple of weeks, see *Play* and *The Lover* and *Entertaining Mr. Sloane* and one or two others.

Other little quirks along the way, professional aberrations rarely written about in the Sunday drama sections:

The basic problem of filling the day while you're not working, or rather working harder looking for work. Working in an absolute vacuum. Waiting for that *Godot* of a play to come along. What do you do while you're waiting? How do you fill in the day, the month, the year?

The profusion of actors and the impossibility each time of getting the actors you need. If life is a brief flash between twin eternities of darkness, the

actor's life consists of a brief appearance between being unknown and becoming unavailable. (Cf. Dustin Hoffman, Stacy Keach, Paul Benedict, and
a host of others.)

Good unemployed actors turning down perfectly good but smallish roles
for reasons of career status—to make their living in television soap operas or
commercials. Then they complain that there is no work, or that the British
actors are taking all the parts. I recall Glenn Anders, one of the greatest of
them all, almost seventy at the time, taking a small part after some 50 or 60
actors had been offered it, and making it into the high spot of the production.

The arguments over billing: I've never alienated or lost an actor because
of salary disagreements but often over the location and size of his name—or
his dressing room or his place in the curtain call.

The pressure on everybody and everything to be "successful" at all costs,
always bigger and better than the last time. Always sensational, socko, ter-
rific. Why hasn't Edward Albee, for example, the right to come up with a
good play once in a while instead of a great one?

Those smelly dirty stage-door alleys, the dust and airlessness onstage under
the glare of that monster work-light. (Why do actors complain about everything else to their union but that!) The theatre, that "dwelling place of
wonder" is often not only a pigsty but an untended urinal.

The long dark tunnel you enter the moment you start on rehearsals; all
the director does is work with the actors eight hours a day, spend the rest of
the day rewriting, re-casting, re-arguing, begging, gulping down some food,
and sleeping once in a while. How much more productive if there were time
to think or walk or listen to music or visit an art gallery or read a book. Why
not a four-hour rehearsal day spread over a longer period of time?

Finally, a small matter but galling: we never take real production photographs of our plays, so that posterity—or our European friends—never get to
see a proper record of the performance the way our audiences saw it. In order
to meet various deadlines set by management or the publicity department,
we always have to take the photos before the sets and props and costumes
are ready; we improvise and shoot, and there it is forever. And we always
choose what we shoot and how we shoot it not because it looks interesting or
tells us something about the show but because it suits the topographical or
typographical requirements of the *New York Daily News*. I have marvelous

production photographs of every show I've ever done outside of New York—
and practically nothing from Broadway except a bunch of glossy closeups.

And so on.

The real evil in the way we work is ultimately psychological rather than
physical. Our lives in the theatre are, in Hobbes' words, "nasty, brutish,
short." But what we lack most is that which might be called a sense of being
involved within some purpose or process that extends beyond our own personal needs and ambitions, of being part of a larger theatre community. Not
just having lunch together at Sardi's to be noticed or envied. Not only having
greater opportunity to be involved with the same people, actors and staff,
over and over again in productions, as the British do; most directors, after all,
hate our system of one-shots enough constantly to seek out the people they
know; but the feeling that we are all part of one organism, whose health and
well-being depends on all of us. We know how to compete but not how to
cooperate.

Maybe it's just that the New York theatre, like the city itself, is just too
big and sprawling, too individualistic and selfish. Maybe it's just so hard for
each one of us that there is no time or space to consider somebody else.
There are dozens of first-rate theatre artists with whom I have never been
associated or even met; many of those I have met are interested in me only
when I am successful or in the public eye. Nor is it easy to meet other theatre
people if you are not at the moment involved with them professionally, nor
to hang on to their company after the show has closed. One is constantly
meeting new people and forgetting old ones with whom one has been working very closely. If I am sufficiently interested in a play or a production to see
it before its official opening, I have to hide in a corner because anyone who
sees me there automatically assumes I'm "taking over" the production. If I
come after a show has been running a while, the inevitable response is that
I'm probably there to steal an actor—or a piece of business. Motives are always distrusted. I know. Several times, well known directors of the motion
picture versions of plays I did on the stage came to see the stage performances
over and over again, and took notes. They never even bothered to write me
a note to thank me. As my union informs me sadly, stage business is not yet
copyrighted.

Were I to see a show and afterwards write a friendly but critical letter to
the director in order to help him, as say Arnold Wesker did once after he saw

Peter Brook's version of *US*, in preview—because he liked it but thought Brook had missed some essential elements—ulterior motives of some kind would immediately be ascribed. I've had directors even get nervous at Workshop sessions when they saw me going up to the playwright of the evening to congratulate him on his work. And so it goes. We're all in it only for ourselves. No one understands, as did that marvelous man, George Devine of the Royal Court, that after we do indeed get rid of our desire to exhibit ourselves, the creation of "conditions in theatre" is the only thing worth doing. But not enough people really believe that or care. In our theatres, as on the streets outside, we are all too busy fighting and hating, pushing and shoving, ever to look at each other and remember that we all live in the same place and are one.

And yet we go on.
Because we know no other way.

And because we are beginning to see that there is another way, to see the possibility of this old wornout pattern of selfishness and hostility vanishing from our lives. Mostly, it is the younger people who see this, but then there are many ways of being young. Some kind of Consciousness III is beginning to drift into our theatre as it is through the fabric of our political life. Both spontaneously and with great deliberation; from dissatisfaction as well as from positive faith that sees theatre as always greater than the sum of its individual sections or parts, a variety of new kinds of theatre is emerging. "Ensembles" of one kind or another, "free theatres," collectives, "street theatres," new theatre places and new theatre ideas. Some of them are already known: La Mama is ten years old, the Open Theatre, and the Public Theatre, and the Negro Ensemble Company only a few years younger. Others, some not so well known: the Chelsea Theatre Center in Brooklyn, the Company Theatre in Los Angeles, El Teatro Campesino, the New Lafayette. They are all striving through their own special techniques and feelings to find a better way of people coming together and creating the experience and excitement of theatre together. Some of them will fail and disappear, some of them are already succeeding and becoming subject to the very pressures and corruptions they have been struggling against. But their reasons for existing are very much there and steadily intensifying. Sooner or later they will reshape our theatre even if that shape may turn out not to be exactly what they wanted or dreamed.

What is clear is that we are all dissatisfied. Not only directors, but almost everyone in the theatre, with the possible exception of the hacks and the business men who happen to have a hit going for them at the moment. We have only two choices, that of leaving the theatre—which a great many of us are contemplating doing at the moment, either for the groves of Academe or the graves of Hollywood—or that of making the theatre over in some grander and less self-seeking image.

In the meantime, we go on. Into whatever comes.

Excerpts from
The director
Richard Schechner

Richard Schechner (1934–), long-time editor of *The Drama Review* and more recently founder of The Performance Group, has been widely influenced by cultural anthropology, sociology, and Jungian psychology as he has attempted almost single-handedly to define the limits of environmental theatre. In this selection he describes his own evolving directing process, one that involves considerable improvisation and far less directorial control than advocated by many others. The writing is based on his experiences with The Performance Group from 1967 to 1973.

At one level, especially during the first phases of training, the director acts as the neophyte performer's parent. Through the director's guidance, and by submitting to the exercises the director offers, the performer begins to find himself. The performer also finds an enemy: the director. And, ultimately, a crisis is faced for both director and performer. A small family is created by a workshop, and the struggles and rebellions characteristic of family life are not foreign to life in a group theatre. If the workshop is temporary—say a specialized course offered by a director to some fifteen actors over a period of two months—this crisis of children vs. parents may never come. The course will end amid thanks, even devotion; the process has no time to work itself out to a conclusion that liberates the actors from the director; or he/she from them. But in enterprises that achieve longer life this first, deep, definitive crisis is unavoidable.

If the parental crisis is faced and surpassed, the group enters a new phase. The parental function of the director is not discarded entirely; it is used selectively and with more and more consciousness. Each production, in fact, recapitulates the whole relationship; and there are cycles and phases within cycles and phases. The new phase, which succeeds the children vs. parent model, is that of All Are Brothers Together. This is a heady, delicious, brief moment in a group's life cycle. It is utopian in its ambitions, revolutionary in its spirit, celebratory in its mood, and comradely in its work. It assumes an equality among all members, divides work and responsibility and income

144

equally. It is the famous "leaderless group." In my experience this Group of Comrades is short-lived because the wish to do something does not equal the ability to do something. And in the contradictions between what a person wants to do and what a person does arises new bitterness and, ultimately, a new hierarchy.

What kind of hierarchy, is the decisive question. The group can become reactionary and restore the parent-children phase. Or it can move toward a version of communism: from each according to his abilities, to each according to his needs. However impossible this model may appear on the large stage of world political life, it is attainable within small groups. At least temporarily.

What happens now is extraordinary. Different people emerge into new roles. Different projects spring up, both within the group and outside it. Not only the director but others run exercises. The entire operation is heated up, without becoming hysterical. The group that had been self-isolating, focused almost entirely inward, built like a castle with walls and moat, all the energies directed toward the center, suddenly reverses its flow: The energy streams from the center into diverse places and projects; workshops and rehearsals that were "sacred" (closed) are now open, people just drop in to watch the work, sometimes to participate in it. Group members collaborate with outsiders on projects. The director's role is reduced, focused, and more flexible. He is no longer parent, enemy, outcast, savior, lover, friend, demigod. He is the one who is in charge of seeing that the story of the play gets played. And he doesn't do his job by himself.

For me personally the most important part of this development is that I am free of my own stereotypes. I no longer feel frozen in one mold or another. I play a number of roles consecutively and simultaneously, as do the others. The emergence is not into the clear light of rationality, but into a busy street of changing moods, roles, and activities. The focus is on work-being-done not on me-in-the-work.

I know that when I direct a play, I get totally absorbed in its web of themes, moods, actions, and people. And that writing about directing is the hardest thing for me to do because I know that everything I say is subjective. My theories bend like light around a strong gravitational source—the play I am currently directing. As I write, I am directing *The Tooth of Crime.* In my mind also are some projects for the future. Were this chapter to have been written while I was working on *Victims Of Duty, Dionysus in 69, Makbeth,* or *Commune,* my ideas would be different in tone, if not in substance. As a director I do not stand off from the play I am working on or from the performers. I do not measure my responses beforehand. I don't come into rehearsals with a prompt-book under my arm, literally or figuratively. I get inside the play I am directing at a level that determines the rest of my life. I don't do this willfully. It happens because I love every play I direct, grow to know it intimately, and experience its faults as well as its beauties and pleasures. And each time I direct a play, I proclaim a method only to find out when I am finished that what I've found is not something general but the particular ways of directing the play I've directed.

Looking back over five years of working in environmental theater, I don't despair acknowledging that my own way of directing remains a mystery to me. Self-awareness is the hardest thing to achieve, and I have not achieved it. What I can write about are some specific techniques.

EARLY WORK ON A PROJECT THAT MAYBE WON'T BE

The first thinking I do on a project is in pictures—drawings I make in my notebook—visual flashes of spaces-in-action. These *actograms* occur at the level where environment, physical action, knowledge of the performers, concept of the play, and my own drives are identical.

. . .

Early work is not making a prompt book. At the start of a project I think about my own life and of the people in the Group. To lay a foundation, one must dig deep, clear out spaces, rip up old things, turn over set ideas. At this level there is no separation between the personal, the given, and the found—between my fantasies, associations, experiences, workshops, texts, and the physical place I am in when this kind of thinking occurs. Everything that happens later is in some way a transformation of the early work.

SEVEN STEPS TO CREATING A MISE-EN-SCENE

A mise-en-scène is *everything that comprises what the audience experiences.* To create a mise is to create something whole. Developing the mise is the director's main job. The most pragmatic, and succinct, definition of a mise-en-scène is Brecht's: "What comes before the spectator is the most frequently repeated of what has not been rejected."[1]

Work on a mise takes a long time. But it isn't gradual, like the blending of colors in a rainbow. It develops in breakthroughs, periods of apparent stalemate shattered by a burst of discoveries. I've seen lasting changes come from a few hours' work; and weeks of work where seemingly nothing happens. The quiet periods prepare for the (excuse me) dramatic changes. A performance goes through many transformations on its way to completion. And when it's complete, it is no longer worth performing.

As a matter of convenience I divide the process of creating a mise into seven steps. This arbitrary division is useful mainly as a teaching device. I ignore it while working.

1 Free workshop: No attempt is made to work on a project. Exercises are reviewed and invented. Work on the self, and on the group. Free workshop is the original void/chaos out of which the definite order of a project may emerge. Free workshop continues through all phases of creating a mise-en-scène. Even in the last steps of rehearsal I recommend at least two hours of free workshop a day.

2 Introduction of an action or text: In *Dionysus in 69, Makbeth,* and *The Tooth of Crime* texts were used. *Commune* began with an awareness of certain themes, several scenes from Shakespeare and Marlowe, and exercises from free workshop, especially slow-motion running and the sound and movement exercise that became "Recapitulation." These first two steps are like a vortex, drawing into the center of the work everything that is around it. The determining factor is not thematic but temporal; associations occur not according to categories but according to coexistence in time. Later thematic links are forged. For example, while starting to define the themes that would ultimately condense into *Commune,* the Group was also working on three scenes from Shakespeare and one from Marlowe. I selected these as acting exercises, assigning roles according to particular needs of particular performers. I didn't have *Commune* in mind (consciously). I think that *any scenes* we happened to be working with at that time would have been attracted to the center of the *Commune* vortex.

1 Bertolt Brecht, *Brecht on Theatre,* tr. and ed. by John Willet (New York: Hill and Wang, 1964), p. 204.

Except for *America Courts the World*, where satire and parody were intended, the actions/texts of Shakespeare and Marlowe were amalgamated and transmuted at a level where (I hope) they are fundamental to *Commune* and not intrusive literary allusions/quotations. Material from earlier theater can be brought into a production in the same way as personal material is brought in. Just as the performer refines, distorts, condenses, and selects from his life experiences, so fragments from earlier dramas can be worked into the play at hand. Only since the intrusion of stupid laws and notions regarding originality has this rich vein of creativity been stopped. Shakespeare and Molière without their plagiarisms would be much poorer playwrights. An art that is in essence transformational and transmutational should not surrender any of its sources, its deep springs. The modern idea of originality is a lawyer-capitalist construction geared to protecting private property and promoting money-making. It is anti-creative, and inhibits the reworking of old themes in the light of new experience. It is the constant reworking and elaboration of old material—call it plagiarism if you like—that is the strongest sinew of tradition.

3 The project: The time comes when an agreement—not always spoken—gives definition to the work: a *project* is launched. Discussions flow about themes, actions, meanings, structures. A condensation of interest leads to a basis for bringing things in and keeping things out. Themes, movement, environment, music, and characterization converge. The end is in sight. Formulations reached at this step are the basis for all subsequent transformations. At this step *The Bacchae* became *Dionysus in 69* and *Makbeth* got its "k."

4 Performance space, roles: The environmentalist gets to work—maybe even building part of the environment. Roles are defined and permanently assigned. This is a time of crisis and uncertainty because everyone is aware of the horrible gap between what the project sounds like and what it is. There seems to be no way to bridge this gap.

5 Organization: A text takes shape, scenes make sense, a sequence of events—scenic and/or textual—is agreed on, the environment built. Even business affairs like publicity, price of admission, posters, and so on are worked on. The mise appears finished—if this were an orthodox production, step 5 would be equivalent to rehearsals and at the end of it the play would open.

Steps three, four, and five draw limits, close avenues—pull the project together, get it in shape. A very hard decision comes at the end of step 5: The play could go on, but it must be taken apart again, thrown into deeper doubt than ever, and reconstructed. *The Tooth of Crime* was worked on from May to September 1972 before our work got through step 5. Then came a series of open rehearsals and work-in-progress performances in Vancouver, upstate New York, and Paris. These seventeen performances were difficult because in the Group's mind the play wasn't finished; but the audience came to see finished work. Even when the play was interrupted, when a scene was repeated, and when we did not complete the play—never having rehearsed the last scene—spectators acted as though they had seen a finished production. The difficulty was compounded by the fact that many spectators liked the play very much. All the promptings were toward wrapping it up: rehearsing the last scene, polishing what we had, opening in New York. The Group did not want to do this, and we were helped by an accident. Spalding Gray, who plays Hoss in *Tooth*, developed a hernia and had to be operated on. He went into the hospital as soon as the Group returned from France. Physical work could not be resumed on *Tooth* until after a six-week pause. During that time we reread the play carefully—taking more than fifty hours of rehearsals to get through it. This work-around-a-table came after the play had been done seventeen times, and so our reference points were not academic or imaginary. The reworkings were very deep and rich.

6 Open rehearsals and reconstructions: Mise meetings, role exchanges, free workshops: working through the whole play again, from the start. The audience is invited into the work—to view it, talk about it, and criticize it. The play is examined in hard-nosed theatrical terms: Does a scene work, does it hold the audience, is it clear?

For me this step is the hardest. The presence of an audience makes everyone want to set the piece. Failures are humiliating. There is a credibility gap between what the Group knows and what the audience knows. Insist as we may, spectators come to the theater to see a "finished piece." Only recently have we found a way of allaying this expectation. For *The Tooth of Crime* the announcements of open rehearsals are made to individuals. These people are invited to the rehearsals knowing that things may come up that require the Group to work alone; then the audience will be asked to leave. Only a few people show up for each rehearsal, usually less than ten. The performance develops vis-à-vis an interested audience that has come to see rehearsals, not finished shows. This kind of open rehearsal later gives way to more formal, publicly announced rehearsals. This second kind of open rehearsal is more like a performance. It is during these public open rehearsals that I grow stubborn. I fight to keep what I have and resist criticism. My stubbornness has at times been cataclysmic. If the director can keep himself open—really be able to take the play apart in front of strangers—the work can progress. If not, mistakes freeze into the mise-en-scène. *Makbeth* never got beyond step 6, and mistakes were frozen in. *Commune* opened in December, 1970, in the midst of step 6, and it took many months of arduous work to liberate the work from its early clichés.

Taking the play apart and reconstructing it makes everyone grasp the work in concrete theatrical terms. Open rehearsals leave no room for anyone to hide in abstractions or proclamations. The audience is there; either they get it or they don't. In step 6 the production emerges as something outside the performers and the director. It achieves an objective reality.

7 Building scores: The need is to locate the exact physical actions, musical tones, and rhythms that embody the themes and moods of the production. Rehearsals are often technical. A through-line is developed for each role. And the entire production is *tuned* the way a sailboat is tuned for racing: taut, sparse, efficient, active.

I used to believe that the score was exactly like a musical score, set in every detail. I don't think so now. The performer's score gives him anchor points—moments of contact, an underlying rhythm, secure details: places to go from and get to. As Ryczard Cieslak told me:

The score is like a glass inside which a candle is burning. The glass is solid; it is there you can depend on it. It contains and guides the flame. But it is not the flame. The flame is my inner process each night. The flame is what illuminates the score, what the spectators see through the score. The flame is alive. Just as the flame in the glass moves, flutters, rises, falls, almost goes out, suddenly glows brightly, responds to each breath of wind—so my inner life varies from night to night, from moment to moment. The way I feel an association, the interior sense of my voice or a movement of my finger. I begin each night without anticipations. This is the hardest thing to learn. I do not prepare myself to feel anything. I do not say, "Last night, this

scene was extraordinary, I will try to do that again." I want only to
be receptive to what will happen.

    And I am ready to take what happens if I am secure in my score,
knowing that, even if I feel a minimum, the glass will not break, the
objective structure worked out over the months will help me through.
But when a night comes that I can glow, shine, live, reveal—I am
ready for it by not anticipating it. The score remains the same, but
everything is different because I am different[2]

Cieslak's metaphor of the glass and the flame is only an approximation;
it is misleading insofar as it supposes that the score and the performer's inner
life are separate: the container and the contained. The score is the most
visible part of the performer's life as lived during the performance. The score
is not hard like glass. It is a membrane, a skin of an extended life-system that
only an ensemble/group can create. The score is alive, sensitive, and responsive. What each individual's inner life is to him, the score is to the whole-
group-in-performance.

    For the director the score is somewhat different than for the performer.
The director is in the performance only by extension and identification. I go
to each performance of a play I am directing, not out of duty; and I am not
bored. I experience the changes in the score, the variations and modulations,
with an excitement. I reflect on the overall pattern of the performance: the
development of the story, the leitmotifs. I concern myself with the arrangements and relationships among all theatrical languages: verbal, body, contact,
and musical.

. . .

THE DIRECTOR

    The director is the performer's Tiresias, Horatio, Sganarelle, Pylades:
Friend, Servant, Sidekick, and Seer. This kind of character has dropped out
of drama as the director has come into full force. It is too fancy an idea to
connect their going out to his coming in? The director functions as leader
cum parent cum therapist cum colleague cum child: His roles during workshop and rehearsal are many, as long as he disappears during performance.
But some contemporary directors—Grotowski, Chaikin, Andre Gregory, and

2 Personal conversation, 1970.

I, for example—have a hard time becoming anonymous during performance. Grotowski is an *eminence grise*, Gregory laughs up a storm, Chaikin is shyly obvious, and I carry my big notebook. Up against the presence of the performers is the presence of the directors.

The performer is a doer, the director is a seer. The director is present, he sees, he says what he sees. But also he accomplishes many less mighty tasks, especially in a small group. These housekeeping duties are important because in doing them the director trains [himself] to respond in different ways to the myriad situations that come up in rehearsal and workshop. His responses are no more false than those of the performers. The director doesn't "play roles" in the orthodox sense.

> Each group requires more or less radical internal transformation of the persons who comprise it. Consider the metamorphoses that one man may go through in one day as he moves from one mode of sociality to another—family man, speck of crowd dust, functionary in the organization, friend. These are not simply different roles: each is a whole past and present and future, offering different options and constraints, different degrees of change or inertia, different kinds of closeness and distance, different sets of rights and obligations, different pledges and promises.[3]

The changes in the modes of sociality that most people experience among different groups, the director experiences in the *one* group. The performers are the masters of transformation, and the director learns to become a master adapter. The problem is to do this without, at the same time, becoming a schemer, an Odysseus, or a hypocrite.

I have been numb, unable to see. I have been distracted. I have seen things but lacked the courage to speak of them. I have manipulated people by not saying the kernel of what I've seen. I've been in terror of saying what I've felt. I have guarded my self-esteem and my public reputation, as well as my reputation within the Group. Worst of all I've lied to myself. There are ten reasons for not being present, one hundred reasons for not seeing, and one thousand reasons for not saying what one sees.

Lest the reader think that these things have little to do with directing, let me say that the fundamental life-feels of the director are what directing in a

3 R. D. Laing, *The Politics of Experience* (New York: Ballantine Books, 1967), p. 97.

group is all about. The director's life-feels are communicated in the way tasks are distributed, the way time is ordered in workshops and rehearsals, the way individual needs are balanced against group needs when the two conflict, the way in which the director's fantasies are brought into the work, or kept out of it.

The Cat only grinned when it saw Alice. It looked good-natured, she thought: still it had very long claws and a great many teeth, so she felt that it ought to be treated with respect.

"Cheshire-Puss," she began, rather timidly, as she did not at all know whether it would like the name: however, it only grinned a little wider. "Come, it's pleased so far," thought Alice, and she went on. "Would you tell me, please, which way I ought to go from here?"

"That depends a good deal on where you want to get to," said the Cat.

PART II
**CONTEMPORARY DIRECTING PRACTICE:
SOME POSSIBILITIES**

"I don't much care where—" said Alice.

"Then it doesn't matter which way you go," said the Cat.

"—so long as I get somewhere," Alice added as an explanation.

"Oh, you're sure to do that," said the Cat, "if you only walk long enough."

Lewis Carroll,
Alice's Adventures in Wonderland

Notes on the theatre of cruelty
Charles Marowitz

Charles Marowitz, an author and director most influential for his work with the Royal Shakespeare Company during the mid-1960's, founded his own theatre, the Open Space, in 1968. With Peter Brook he began an experimental studio group in association with the Royal Shakespeare Company in 1963. The account of that experiment presented here was compiled from notes he made during work and from reflections after the group had climaxed its activity with the production of *Marat/Sade*. Marowitz reveals many specific tools used by the group which now can serve a wider purpose.

THE AUDITIONS

Since we weren't casting any particular play and therefore weren't on the lookout for any *types*, and since our main concern was to find actors who were open, adaptable, and ready to rush in where rigid pros fear to tread, it was necessary to devise a completely new audition technique. I decided to do away with those murky soliloquies where a single actor, pulsating with suppressed but crippling hysteria, gets up and reels off the same speech he has been carting around since drama school. The auditions were collective—anywhere from eight to ten actors working together for at least an hour. The audition was broken up in the following ways:

DISRUPTED SET-PIECE

The actor is asked to perform his two-minute set-piece in his own way, without suggestions or interference. Once he has done this, he is given a new character and a new situation and asked to play these, still retaining the text of his original speech. (An actor who comes along with "To be or not to be . . ." is asked to play King Lear in the death scene or Romeo in the balcony scene *through* the Hamlet text.) The task is for the actor to throw himself into a completely different set of circumstances (to improvise) and yet to retain control over his original text (to operate formally). Once the actor has managed to create a smattering of the new character and the new situation, he is given yet another character and a different situation (a barrow-salesman on a market-day, a political candidate standing for re-election), until he has three balls to juggle at once: 1) his original choice; 2) the first variation; 3) the second variation. The actor is then given cue-words which refer to each of his characters, and he is asked to switch rapidly among the three different situations without breaking the flow of his original text.

TEXT AND SUB-TEXT

The actor is given a piece of nonsense text. There is no discernible character or situation. The actor makes of it whatever he can, but he is obliged to use the given words. (This enabled us to discover how the actor, on the most elementary level, coped with language—where his natural instincts led him. It is like a Rorschach test with words instead of ink-blots.)

OBJECT ASSOCIATIONS

An object is thrown out onto the stage—a toy shovel, for instance. The actor proceeds to build up a scene (in mime only) using the shovel. When something has begun to develop, when the actor feels he is finally *on* to something, another object, entirely unrelated (a briefcase, a shoehorn, a telephone directory, a plant) is thrown out and the actor is obliged either to create a completely new scene or develop a bridge between the unrelated objects.

DISCONTINUOUS IMPROVISATION

An actor performing a simple, recognizable action (digging, golfing, wallpapering, exercising) enters. The others choose actions which relate to that actor's choice and a scene (with words) develops. A enters digging with a shovel; B mimes a pneumatic drill; C grabs a wheelbarrow; D becomes a works-supervisor checking his stopwatch. Then a new actor enters performing a completely unrelated action (making lyrical kneebends), the other actors adapt to the new action as quickly as possible. (One begins to *plier*, another, Martha Graham-like, rolls his body into a ball; a third begins marking time with a stick.) As each new situation is perceived and developed, another one, as far removed as possible, is begun. Eventually, three separate teams are chosen—each with its own built-in changes—and these three groups, working simultaneously, weave among as many as twelve different situations. The cleanliness of the changes is what counts, also the rapidity with which actors cotton on to the changed situation. The scenes themselves are, of necessity, superficial, but the object is not to create substantial, well-sinewed improvisations, but merely to follow up dramatic leads as quickly as they present themselves.

THE FIRST COMPANY

Out of about fifty actors, a dozen were selected, and then presented to Brook for approval. (Ironically, there was a slight hassle only in the case of Glenda Jackson, over whom Brook took some convincing. She turned out to be—along with Alexis Kanner—one of the two most resourceful members of the group.)

The average age of the group was twenty-four. Only one member was over thirty, and most were just over twenty. The backgrounds were television, drama school, a minimal amount of repertory, no West End experience to speak of. The general formation was naturalistic—a grounding in Stanislavski techniques as attenuated and distorted by English drama schools. I felt the need to start from scratch, to plunge the whole company into elementary Method exercises before totally demolishing the Stanislavski ethic. Brook disagreed. He felt the level of proficiency was high enough to tackle the new work directly. I thought this a mistake because Stanislavski was the grammar out of which we were going to build a completely different syntax and I wanted the basis to be sound before shifting it. It is difficult to say, in retrospect, whether we were right or wrong in plunging a group of twelve young actors and actresses into the swirling waters of Artaudian theory, but, of course, there was the time factor. We had only twelve weeks for training and a preliminary workshop performance. We worked in a small church hall behind the Royal Court Theatre in Sloane Square; a bare, wooden room littered with Brownie posters and the relics of ancient whist-drives. It was a long day, beginning at 10 a.m. and ending at 6 p.m. Each night Brook and I consulted by phone about the objectives of the next day's work. My notes of these sessions are not chronological, and so what follows is in no particular order.

INTRODUCTION TO SOUNDS

On the very first day of work, before the actors had properly met each other and without Brook or me delivering any orientation lectures, the actors were handed objects: boxes, bangers, scrapers, vessels, sticks, etc. Each actor had something or other to bang with, and something or other to bang on. They were then asked to explore the range of their instrument (the sound the thin end of a ladle made on a tin can; the sound the tin can made against the floor, muted with one palm, held suspended, in two hands, tucked inside a sweater, rapped with the knuckle instead of the ladle, with the forehead instead of the knuckle, the elbow instead of the forehead . . .). Once the range of the instrument had been explored, a series of rhythms were rapped out. Some of these were then varied while others remained the same; some were accelerated while others were slowed down; there were combinations of twos and threes; dialogues between broomhandles and empty crates; scenes from *Romeo and Juliet* played out between metallic tinkles and bass percussions; mob violence with soapcrates and pitched battles with tennis rackets.

Eventually *rhythm*, a generalized and over-used word in the theatre, got redefined in exact, physical terms. Not only did actors experience the basic changes of rhythm—slow, fast, moderate—but the endless combination and counterpoints that rhythms were capable of. Shortly, the same attitude the actors had taken to their objects was applied to their voices and bodies. This was a tortuous adjustment, and one was always fighting the primordial instinct in English actors that believes the voice is the medium for *good speech*, *projection*, and *resonance*, the carrier of the theatrical "message," and the body a useful but secondary adjunct. Little by little, we insinuated the idea that the voice could produce sounnds other than grammatical combinations of the alphabet, and that the body, set free, could begin to enunciate a language which went beyond text, beyond sub-text, beyond psychological implication and beyond monkey-see-monkey-do facsimiles of social behaviorism. And most important of all, that these sounds and moves could communicate feelings and ideas.

SOUND AND MOVEMENT SIMILES

Exercise: You come back to your apartment after a hard day's work. Enter, take off your coat, hang it up, pour yourself a drink and sit down at the table. On the table is a letter which you suddenly notice. You put down the drink, open the letter and begin to read. The contents of the letter are entirely up to you; the only condition is that it contains news which put you into a highly emotional state of one sort or another. Express this state using only a sound and a movement.

The movements in the exercise leading up to the final beat are entirely naturalistic, but the final beat is an externalized expression of the character's inner state and totally non-naturalistic. At first, all the choices were commonplace. People jumped for joy, fell into weeping, bolted upwards with surprise, stamped with rage. When none of these simple expressions was acceptable, the actors began to realize the nature of the exercise. With all their naturalistic choices dismissed out of hand, they had to go in search of a more stylized means of communication. Eventually, the choices became more imaginative. Sounds were created which had the resonance of wounded animals; of prehistoric creatures being slain by atomic weapons. Movements became stark and unpredictable. Actors began to use the chairs and tables as sculptural objects instead of functional furniture. Facial expressions, under the pressure of extended sounds, began to resemble Javanese masks and Zen sculpture. But once the actors realized what we were after, some of them began to select an arbitrary sound or movement, effective in itself but unrelated to the emotional state growing out of the exercise. Very quickly, frighteningly quickly, actors became as glib with non-naturalistic sounds and movements as they were with stock, dramatic cliches. One wondered if Artaud's idealized theatre ever were established whether, in five or ten years, it too would not become as practiced and cliché-ridden as the present-day Comedie Francaise, or the West End.

DISCONTINUITY

One of the main objects behind the work was to create a discontinuous style of acting; that is, a style which corresponded to the broken and fragmentary way in which most people experience contemporary reality. Life today (I am not philosophizing, merely trying to illustrate) is very much like the front page of a daily newspaper. The eye jumps from one story to another; from one geographical location to another; from one mood to another. A fire in Hoboken; an election in Paris; a coronation in Sweden; a rape in London; comedy, passion, ceremony, trivia—all flooding one's consciousness almost simultaneously. The actor, however, through years of training and centuries of tradition, moves stolidly from point A to point B to point C. His character is *established*, his relationships *develop*; his plot thickens and his conflicts resolve. In short, he plods on in his Aristotelian way, perpetuating the stock jargon of drama and the arbitrary time system of the conventional theatre.

To break the progressive-logical-beginning-middle-and-end syndrome, one uses improvisation (personal and organic material rather than theatrical données) and uses it simply as rhythmic matter.

Exercise: The life of a character is briefly built up. X is an out-of-work writer:

Scene 1: His landlady asks him for rent which is months in arrears.

Scene 2: His girlfriend wants to know when they're going to get married.

Scene 3: His father urges him to give up writing and take a job with the firm.

Scene 4: His pub-crony exhorts him to come out, have a drink, and forget his troubles.

Scene 5: His schoolfriend drops in and wants to re-live old times.

Scene 6: An insurance salesman persistently tries to push an unwanted policy on him.

Each scene is built up independently for five or ten minutes; just long enough for it to have a little meat, but not long enough to develop any real sinew. Then X is placed in the center of the room and each character—on cue—resumes his scene with him. The scenes, all unrelated except that they all center around the same main character, follow hard upon each other. With the addition of each new scene, X quickly adapts to the changed situation, the different relationship. Eventually, three and four scenes are being played at once. Soon all are being played simultaneously. At one point, the exercise becomes unbearable and impossible, but before that point, X and his fellow actors have experienced a frantic sense of discontinuity that just begins to convey the complexities to which any, even the simplest, sensibility is prone.

A COLLAGE HAMLET

A couple of years before the Royal Shakespeare Experimental Group, I had invited Brook along to a play I was doing at the In-Stage studio theatre at Fitzroy Square. It was a short play by Lionel Abel called *A Little Something for the Maid*. Originally intended for radio, it consisted of a series of short, discontinuous scenes in which the female character became, by turns, everybody in the male character's life: wife, sweetheart, charlady, male employer, secretary, mother, etc. Discussing it afterwards, Brook had said it would be facinating to see *Hamlet* played that way, re-shuffled like a deck of familiar cards. A year and a half later, Brook's idea still knocking around in my head, I sat down to restructure Shakespeare's play.

The idea of the LAMDA [London Academy of Musical and Dramatic Arts] *Hamlet* was to condense the play into about twenty minutes, without relying on narrative. This was on the assumption that everyone knew *Hamlet*, even those people who hadn't read or seen it; that there was a smear of *Hamlet* in everyone's collective unconscious and that it was possible to predicate a performance on that mythic smear.

The play was spliced up into a collage with lines juxtaposed, sequences rearranged, characters dropped or blended, and the entire thing played out in fragments which appeared like subliminal flashes out of Hamlet's life. In every case I used Shakespeare's words, although radically rearranged.

Of all the discontinuity exercises, this had the firmest foundation, as all the actors knew the original play and therefore had an emotional and narrative frame of reference. The first version was essentially a clever exercise in Burroughs-like cut-ups. In the later, expanded, 85-minute version which played in Germany, Italy, and later London, the style was better assimilated, the play had more intellectual content and was at the service of clear-cut interpretation.

CONTACT

The building of company-sense demands the construction of those delicate vertebrae and interconnecting tissues that transform an aggregation of actors into an ensemble. A protracted period of togetherness (at a rep, for instance) creates an accidental union between people, but this isn't the same thing as actors coiled and sprung in relation to one another—poised in such a way that a move from one creates a tremor from another; an impulse from a third, an immediate chain reaction. Contact doesn't mean staring in the eyes of your fellow actor for all you're worth. It means being so well tuned-in that you can see him without looking. It means, in rare cases being linked by a group rhythm which is regulated almost physiologically—by blood circulation or heart palpitation. It is the sort of thing that exists between certain kith and kin; certain husbands and wives; certain kinds of lovers or bitter enemies.

GROUP INTERVIEW

Exercise: A is a social outcast, who has spent some time in jail. He has now been released and is being interviewed for a routine job by an interviewer for a large firm who knows his background but is prepared to consider him for employment. A needs the job, hates the idea of being patronized, and is torn between ingratiating himself and venting his hostilities. The rest of the group (sixteen actors) are personality adjuncts of A. One represents his social hostility; Two, his economic need; Three, his attempt to conform; Four, his rebellious nature; Five, his innate cowardice; Six, his suppressed social ambition; Seven, his fantasy-image of himself as a Great Man, and so on. None of A's personality extensions initiates any material in the scene. They speak only as and when A replies to the Interviewer's questions, and their response is determined entirely by what A actually says and what they glean from the way he says it. Depending on those replies one or another of A's personality adjuncts take prominence. But with every response, all sixteen actors pick up, echo, modify, or extend A's replies in the scene.

Interviewer: Do you think you would be happy in this job?
A: Oh yes . . . I think I'd like it very much.
B: *viciously.* Who wants to know.
C: *pleadingly.* Just try me out for a week, you'll see.
D: *imperiously.* I'll be sitting behind that desk, in a month's time.
E: *tentatively.* Could I wear a suit like that, I wonder?
F: *fretfully.* I wonder whether I'm going to be kicked out of this office.
G: *aggressively.* I'd love to put my fist in your eye.

The exercise musters an agonizing degree of attention and, as each actor must speak simultaneously with A, compels actors to grasp implications and innuendoes instead of responding mechanically to word cues. In other words, it forces actors to cope with sub-text, and to recognize top-text only as a kind of tackle that leads down to the underwater world where all the essential action lies.

IMPROVS AND ESSENTIALS

There was a good deal of conventional improvisation (built up on actions and reducible to beats), but the more useful came from variations and extensions of the stock Method approach. For instance: after a scene was played, the actor was asked to divide the improv into three units, and to give a line-title to each unit. Once this was accomplished and it was generally agreed that the line-titles were appropriate to the situation just played, the scene was replayed in its entirety with the actors using only their three line-titles as dialogue. Then the actor was asked to choose only one word from each of the three line-titles, and the scene was played a third time with the sound components of those words serving exclusively as the dialogue. Then (and only then) the actor could choose a sound which accurately reflected the main quality of his scene and play the scene for a final time, using variations of that sound. The playing in sound invariably prompted a non-naturalistic use of movement, and it was fascinating to see how, once the situation had been ground down to basic impulses, the movement graphically expressed the true intentions behind the scene.

Example: Scene—A wants to break off long-standing affair with his girl-friend, B. He now realizes he does not love her, and it would be lunacy to marry. B, however, has become helplessly attached to A and cannot bear the idea of parting. She tries desperately to maintain the relationship.

Scene Breakdown in Terms of Line-Titles: *1st Replay.*

Boy	1	I want to break off this affair.
	2	I want to be as kind as possible.
	3	I won't be persuaded to change my mind.
Girl	1	I want to keep my hold on A.
	2	I want to reason with him so as to change his mind.
	3	I refuse to be hurt.

Second Replay: Essential words.

Boy	Break
	Kind
	Won't
Girl	Keep
	Reason
	Refuse

Third Replay: Sounds

Boy   Ey-ayeOoghn

Girl   Eey-zoohz

(The sounds are fluid and free, merely based on the vowels and consonants of the essential words.)

STANISLAVSKI AND ARTAUD

Having been brought up on Stanislavski and the idea of inner truth, it was a major adjustment for me to discover there was also *surface truth,* and that in certain contexts, the latter was more persuasive than the former. An even more difficult adjustment was to realize that artifice and downright artistic fraud could create a plenitude of truth for an audience and was therefore, according to the pragmatic laws that govern acting, legitimate. The Method argument for inner truth holds water only if its main contention is true: that is, that the spectator experiences feeling to the same degree the actor does. But we all know this is not always the case; that there are hundreds of instances of turned-on actors, splitting themselves with inner intensity, communicating nothing to an audience but effort and tension. It is equally true that an actor who is almost totally turned-off but going through the right motions in the right context can powerfully affect an audience—almost involuntarily.

The Method actor's test for truthfulness is the intensity and authenticity of his personal feeling. The Artaudian actor knows that unless that feeling has been shaped into a communicative image, it is a passionate letter without postage. Whereas pure feeling can be mawkish or leaden, a pertinent stage image—a gesture, a movement, a sequence of actions—is a statement in itself which doesn't require the motor-power of feeling in order to register, but when emotionally charged is many times more potent.

There is no fundamental disagreement between the Method actor and the Artaudian actor. Both rely on consciousness to release the unconscious, but whereas the Method actor is chained to rational motivation, the Artaudian actor realizes the highest artistic truth is unprovable. Like certain rare natural phenomena that defy scientific analysis, they *can* exist—and the actor's task is to conjure them into being.

The Artaudian actor needs Stanislavski in order to verify the nature of the feelings he is releasing—otherwise he becomes merely a victim of feeling. Even Artaud's celebrated actor-in-trance is responsible to the spirit that is speaking through him. A seance where nothing is communicated but atmosphere is not half as rewarding as one in which messages are received loud and clear. The very state of trance itself is arrived at methodically. The medium's secret is knowing when to let go of the mechanisms that have produced it, in order to transcend them; the same is true for the actor—any actor—who uses either intellect or instinct to bring him to an important jumping-off point.

CHANGING GEARS

Three actors, A, B, and C, are given cue sounds (a bell for one, a buzzer for the second, a gong for the third). When A hears his cue, he initiates a scene, and B & C, adapting themselves to A's choice, enter into the situation as quickly as possible. After two or three minutes, when the scene is either approaching a highpoint or running down because of lack of invention, B is given his cue. B suddenly leaps into a completely new situation, entirely unrelated to the one preceding: A & C adapt themselves immediately. Short development, then C is cued, another unrelated scene, the others adapt again, etc.

As important as the actual material thrown up by the scene is the moment chosen for breaking it and beginning another. There is a moment in almost every improvisation where things reach a head and are moving quickly towards a resolution. If one can trigger off the new scene just at that moment, the actor's emergency equipment is instinctively brought into play. Improvisations like these feed on (and sometimes are destroyed by) their sense of danger. There is an inescapable imperative forced on the actors. They must think and act with lightning speed. They know that within a seven or ten minute period, they have to devise as many as five or six different situations, and they soon discover they cannot cheat by planning ahead, because a prearranged choice is immediately apparent—as is the instinctively appropriate choice which could not have come from anywhere else but the given circumstances. It brings into play a quality that actors tend to think they do not possess: the ability to associate freely and without regard to fixed character or logical consistency. For me, the great eye-opener in this exercise was how, under the pressure of changing gears, actors who had never heard of surrealism, were able to make the most stunning surrealist choices; and actors who claimed to have no sense of humor suddenly found themselves dipping into deep wells of fantasy and absurdity that lay on the threshold of their consciousness. Choices which, if actors had time to deliberate over them, would never be made, or would be doctored or modified, leaped out with astonishing clarity and boldness.

ACTORS AND ACTORS

The hallmark of a good actor is his attitude towards change. Most actors make their decisions in the first stages of rehearsal, chart the shortest distance between two points and then proceed in a straight line. For these, the rehearsal period is a tunnel with light on one end and light on the other, and a great stretch of darkness in the middle. Another sort of actor retains the ability to re-think and reorganize his role throughout. He follows every lead and yields to every permutation, and isn't put off by detours and secondary routes. He may take longer to arrive but when he does, he brings a better-rounded result.

This attitude towards change almost distinguishes two separate breeds of actor, and in England today these breeds intermingle in almost every company. It is too sweeping to designate one *traditional*, and the other *modern*, but there is a grain of truth in that distinction—those actors who have passed through the Royal Court, Theatre Workshop, and ferment of the past ten years tend to have a more open attitude than can be found among the academy-bred, rep-orientated actors of an older formation. Each of these types almost has a vernacular of its own.

Trads	*Mods*
Let's get it blocked	Let's get it analyzed
Fix inflections and "readings"	Play for sense and let inflections take care of themselves.
Block as soon as possible	Move freely for as long as possible
Play for laughs	Play for contact
Final decisions as soon as possible	Final decisions as late as possible and always open to reversal

It was a bad house	It was a bad performance
I take orders	I give suggestions
Am I being masked?	Am I important at this moment in the play?
Can I be heard?	Are my intentions clear?
I'm getting nothing from my partner	I'm not getting what I expected, so I shall adjust
Just as we rehearsed it	As the immediacy of the performance dictates
Let's get on with it and stop intellectualizing	Let's apply what reason we have to the problems at hand
More feeling	More clarity of intention so as to produce more feeling
Hold that pause	Fill that pause
Everything's in the lines	Everything's in the sub-text
I'll play this role symbolically	I can't play concepts; only actions
I am the villain	I refuse to pass moral judgments on my character
My many years of professional experience convince me that	Nothing is ever the same

SPEAK WITH PAINTS

Exercise: You have just come out of your flat, locked the door, and put the key in your pocket. You walk over to the elevator and ring. Casually you look through your newspaper as you wait for the elevator to arrive. On a sound cue, the elevator arrives, the doors slide open and in the elevator you discover a completely unexpected person towards whom you have a strong, specific attitude of one sort or another. (The actor decides background beforehand.) At that instant, you rush to the easel and immediately express that attitude in paints.

As in the similar exercise with the letter, the most delicate moment in the exercise is the one in which the actor confronts his stranger and moves to express his attitude. If he can organically link one with the other, the result is clear and communicative. If there is even a second's hesitation, the result is self-conscious, unnatural, and merely illustrated. A later version of this exercise, which proved more successful, was for the actor to play out an improvisation with the stranger in which the chosen attitude was actually manifest, then to have an interim scene inside the flat, followed by the exercise situation. Otherwise, the actor is working too exclusively from a mental frame of reference.

At first, the paintings were sloppy and crude. On the third and fourth repeat, they were almost artistic, in that they were meaningful, impressionistic blotches which did suggest an internal state, interpretable by the other group members. The paint exercise was used directly in Artaud's *The Spurt of Blood,* by author's direction in *The Screens,* and in a more sophisticated version in the *Marat/Sade.* (The red, blue, and white paint sequences in *Marat/Sade* stem from a similar effect in Brook's production of *Titus Andronicus* where Vivien Leigh used an unfurled red ribbon to symbolize the flow of blood.)

Reforms: One must assume that Artaud's "fragile, fluctuating center that forms never reach" refers to states beyond the reach of *linguistic* forms, but accessible by other means. Otherwise it is soapy mysticism. The potential superiority of an Artaudian theatre—compared even to an overhauled and much-improved realistic theatre—lies in the fact that its language is not yet discovered, therefore not yet tarnished and empty. The danger is that a backlog of five centuries filled with verbal debris may never enable us to hit bedrock. Or to put it even more pessimistically: the actor's social and psychological conditioning is both the main obstacle to be removed, and the one factor which is immovable.

THEATRE OF CRUELTY

The first showing of the group's work unfortunately was titled *Theatre of Cruelty* and ran a scheduled five weeks at the LAMDA Theatre Club in London. It was never intended as a *show,* but merely a demonstration of work in progress, of interest, we assumed, to the profession. The press was not invited in the usual way, but letters were sent explaining that if they felt like coming along, they were welcome, but that we were not particularly desirous of reviews, as this wasn't strictly speaking a show. All of which was a kind of self-delusion that both Brook and I swallowed whole. Only after the event did the obvious truth of the situation strike us. Any presentation, call it what you will, that is done before an audience, invited or otherwise, becomes a show, and is judged according to traditional criteria. This is not a harangue against the critics. On the whole, we got interesting, up-beat notices, but the point was that we weren't really intending a theatrical performance, and the overriding point was that it seemed impossible, in London, to present anything short of one.

The program consisted of two short nonsense sketches by Paul Ableman, similar to our sound exercises; a production of Artaud's three-minute *Spurt of Blood* (played through first in sounds, then as Artaud wrote it); a dramatization, in movement only, of a short story by Alain Robbe-Grillet; two collages by Brook, one (*The Public Bath*) a splicing-together of newspaper accounts of the Kennedy funeral and the Christine Keeler testimony; the other (*The Guillotine*) made up from original sources; three scenes from Genet's *The Screens*; an anti-Marceauvian mime-sketch called *The Analysis*; a short play by John Arden, *Ars Longa, Vita Brevis*, and the collage *Hamlet*.

There were two sections in the evening which were deliberately marked out as "free." One, the improvisations, the forms of which changed every evening with the actors never being forewarned; and two, a section towards the close of the second half, into which we inserted whatever "specials" occurred to us. On the first night, Brook used this section to rehearse a scene from *Richard the Third*. Another night, the section was used for a spontaneous exchange between Brook and myself in which we questioned the audience's motives in coming to the theatre, and the whole point of what we were doing there. Early in the run, on the night John Arden was in the audience, without warning we asked him to come forward to justify his short play, and for the occasion we set against him one of the actors from *Ars Longa, Vita Brevis* who hated the play and what it was saying. For the improvs, which I supervised from the stage, I tried to invent new and different challenges every night. On one occasion, we played the Changing Gears exercise entirely in sound; on another, entirely in musical phrases; on another, using only animal noises. The audience was incorporated every evening and, very much like *The Premise*, actors worked from suggestions thrown out to them on the floor. The random factors maintained a degree of freshness almost to the end of the run, but their main point was not simply to keep actors on their toes, but to break the hypnotic effect of continuous performance, and to un-settle the myth that grows up once a performance has begun a run. No two audiences saw the same show, and so no two people from different audiences could recount exactly the same memories. Towards this end, roles were swapped (frequently at the last moment); bits altered or dropped, and one piece (written by Paul Abelman) completely unstaged and unrehearsed, played out each evening as the spirit happened to move the actors. Some nights, this was disastrous; others, after it seemed that every possible interpretation had been tried, startlingly new moods would appear. The playing of this particular dialogue was greatly enhanced by the fact that the two players, who were sometimes required to play quite lyrically with one another, hated each other's guts. The tensions that charged, disfigured, and enlivened the piece prevented it from ever becoming dead material. It is to the everlasting credit of Peter Hall and the Royal Shakespeare Company that it was understood from the start that this work required total subsidy. There was no question of making money or breaking even, for that matter, and it went without saying this was unrecoverable money (therefore, seats were deliberately cheap—five shillings each). There was no balking after the event, when accountants would solemnly point out £5000 had gone down the drain in a matter of twelve weeks. The drain, in this case, led to a very interesting cellar where certain rare wines were being cooled, and even if it should turn out they had all gone sour and had to be dumped, no one was going to burst a blood vessel or demand an official investigation.

PHASE TWO

After the Theatre of Cruelty showing, the plan was to begin work on Genet's *The Screens*. The group was enlarged to seventeen and training was re-started. The newcomers, who had seen the LAMDA program and heard fanciful tales about the work, were wary and suspicious. The mother company was either distrustful or openly antagonistic towards the "mutation at Earl's Court," as one senior member described it. The original group of ten, although still committed to the work, was beginning to eye the mother company covetously. They wondered what was going on at the Aldwych and where they would fit in. An inevitable concern and natural in the circumstances: twelve young actors working for peanuts with the prospect of graduation into a major London company. (An in-group definition of Theatre of

Cruelty was twelve actors working for twelve pounds a week.) I mention this now, not to descend into theatre gossip, but to point out how even the best intentions can be subverted by an over-powering commercial atmosphere. Ostensibly, we had an experimental group concerning itself with craft-problems and difficult stylistic pursuits, but in fact, we had a group of talented, underpaid actors who were wondering how long they would have to work for subsistence wages. I don't want to exaggerate this undercurrent. It wasn't crippling or disastrous, but it did generate preoccupations that affected the work. Training and rehearsals became, in some instances, miniature auditions for the better-paid work, and because, the group, or some of them, were going to be assimilated into the larger company, it became impossible to build a healthily incestuous group-feeling; the kind of group-feeling that companies like Grotowski's in Poland, or the Becks' Living Theatre, build automatically because a shared attitude and mutual allegiance bind the company together. Good work can be done without such an adhesive; but not exceptional work; not enduring, unselfconsciously creative work.

THE SCREENS

The work on *The Screens* could be an essay in itself. The early exercises continued, and were gradually adapted to the specific needs of the play. The crucial production problem, apart from perfecting a style that would cope with such a monumental structure, was to communicate both the poetic and political tremors in the play without veering too far in one direction or the other. The Artaudian exercises had prepared us for Genet's metaphysic, and we now began to apply a Brechtian approach to get at the play's political bedrock, and also to define for ourselves precisely what each of those extravagant little scenes was about.

The early rehearsals were spent in reading, discussion, and translation amendments. After rehearsing each scene, key characters were asked to tell the story of what had just happened: (1) as a factual news report; (2) as a policeman summing up before a magistrate; (3) as a fairy tale ("once upon a time . . ."); (4) as a horror story; (5) from the Marxist point of view; (6) from a Freudian standpoint; (7) as it might be described by a highly poetic sensibility, etc.

Brechtian titles were employed as epigraphs for each scene:

Said Reluctantly Goes to Meet His New Wife
The Colonists Discuss Their Possessions
Said's Mother Insists upon Being Included at a Funeral

Sometimes the work sessions threw up more material than we knew what to do with, and eventually the problem became one of discarding highly interesting but irrelevant insights. More and more, we concentrated on the text: its coloration, its timbre, its weight and feel. As with Shakespeare, one began to test the truthfulness of every moment in terms of the ring of the words in their context. We found that every moment of naturalism, even the most obvious and unquestionable, benefited by being knocked off balance; by being winged by a metaphor, or studded with a stylization. *Ritualistic* may be a critic's cliche when writing about Genet, but it becomes a directorial Rosetta Stone in rehearsal. Even the crudest situation, three soldiers farting a farewell to their dead Lieutenant (Scene 15), becomes both more comic and more understandable by being acted ceremoniously, instead of in a loose, naturalistic manner.

Like *The Blacks* or *The Balcony*, *The Screens* appears to be about some great social topic (the Algerian War) but is essentially a private fantasy couched in convenient social imagery. Said's salvation through progressive degradation is portrayed with all the relentlessness of a thesis-playwright laboriously proving his point. As a play, it proliferates incidents without opening up new ground, and keeps winding back on itself like a badly-wrapped package which becomes fussy without becoming any firmer. Which is not to belittle the genius of certain individual scenes; nor breadth of the conception; nor the grandiose lunacy in the character of Said's mother; nor the hypnotic other-worldliness of the scene where Madani is transmuted into the Mouth of the murdered rebel-leader Si Slimane; nor the easy, unpretentious shuttling between the worlds of the rebellious living and the settled dead; nor the black, urinal comedy between the Arab hooligans and the Algerian Cadi; nor the stunning scene where Arab rebels paint their atrocities onto a series of ever-multiplying screens. But on studying the entire play Brook felt, and I concurred, that the first twelve scenes contained all the gnarled genius of the work, and the remaining two and a half hours held only endless out-riding variations.

One last observation on *The Screens:* in the work of no other writer is the external life of the play quite so essential. In the last weeks of rehearsal,

The Screens looked murky and gauze-covered in spite of many weeks of trying to cut sense and meaning into the scenes. Then, using Genet's own color suggestions, Sally Jacobs' stark-designs, and Brook's faultless eye for surface-effect, a great wave of color was spread over the entire play. In the space of four hours (the hours during which costumes and design were added), the play was transformed into something bold, brazen, aptly rhetorical and hieratic, as if the arrival of objects and color seemed to coincide with the arrival of Jean Genet. One part of me rebelled at what I took to be the spreading of dazzling camouflage, but another was entirely swept up by the camouflage itself. I am not simply describing the extra-dimensionalism dress rehearsals bring to a production. No amount of fancy surface can obliterate a faulty foundation, but in the case of *The Screens*, the costume and decor produced—in one day—two-thirds of the truth, only one-third of which had been evoked in six weeks of rehearsal.

Still, for me, *The Screens* was never an organic production, but a sub-structure and an overlay with a vital middle layer missing. The production made a kind of stark, physical sense in spite of, not because of, our work, and the intellectual uncertainty of cast and producers, the unresolved ambiguities in the text, left an inner fuzziness which a longer run would undoubtedly have revealed.

BROOK IN PERSPECTIVE: A DIGRESSION

Extended exposure to Brook enables one to balance him up. His greatest asset is that, because of personal charm and acknowledged past achievement, he inspires contributions from actors. They want to please him, and this desire makes them exert themselves more than is usual for actors. Brook is cunning in his use of praise or admonishment, cold-bloodedly applying one or the other depending on what effects he thinks he may achieve. He has a strong visual sense and an uncanny instinct for the structural needs of a production, but his approach to actors is too restrictedly intellectual and not always very practical. He knows how to describe the result he wants, but isn't always capable of producing it methodically. If an actor can transform Brook's verbal descriptions into acting-results, then the actor works well with him. If the actor either cannot understand what is being asked or cannot find the route to the result, Brook often cannot provide specific-enough guidance. His approach to improvisation is external, seeing it mainly as acted-out stories that supplement a text rather than carefully-devised provocations designed to induce missing qualities. Perhaps he distrusts the methodology of Method work because he has never grasped the technique of building beats and organizing systems to produce internal results, but because of this he is too often hoodwinked by flashy external choices.

Brook tends to work "off" rather than with people, and the preliminary spadework of aides and consultants helps him to eliminate possibilities in his own mind. In the midst of a stew of contradictory suggestions and ideas, he is able to bring to the boil a clearly defined line of his own, but he seems first to need the stew. He works best with outsize personalities like Scofield and Olivier because there it is simply a matter of adapting himself to highly creative instincts which already have a direction of their own, and Brook fully appreciates the value of letting talented actors have their own way. He could never build a characterization as Kazan does, nor could he ever exert that much personal influence on a role, but he is brilliant at using actors as objects. Although he has a firm intellectual grasp of a play's ideas, his natural instinct for violence and stark effects seduces him into irrelevant sensationalism, and often, as in his Paris production of *Serjeant Musgrave's Dance*, he is incapable of interpreting a play except of his own personal obsessions.

His great attribute is a deep-seated distrust for any—even the best—of his rehearsal achievements. Being dogged by other and better ways to do a thing, he postpones final decisions until he is sure he has explored every possibility. His great liability is that he hasn't the knack of exploring acting possibilities, and too frequently, he settles for a *coup-de-theatre* or a disarming stroke of cleverness. Although the *enfant-prodige* of the 1940's is now a well-tucked-away image and the serious *metteur-en-scène* is more prominent, an impish cleverness remains Brook's constant enemy.

MARAT/SADE AND COMPLETION

When Peter Weiss's play *Marat/Sade* came along, it was the natural conclusion of the Group's work; a play which could not have been contemplated before the Group's existence and which now, after the work on Artaud and Genet, could not be ignored. The play even contained certain features from our first Theatre of Cruelty program: Marat's bath tub was mystically related to Christine Keeler's in *The Public Bath*, the guillotine imagery to Brook's collage-play. Weiss acknowledged Artaud as his mentor, Artaud had played Marat in a film for Abel Gance, sounds and "happenings" were embedded in the play in a way that had been integral to the group's thinking from the start.

Although I cannot be absolutely objective about the *Marat/Sade,* I can be somewhat detached as I wasn't directly involved in its production. That it is a spectacular and breathtaking production—perhaps the boldest we are to see this half-century—seems to me unquestionable. It restores something riotous and vital to the theatre, a kind of stylized mania which is closer to the personality of Antonin Artaud than any other single thing. But just as the Group's work itself had been diluted by being a demonstration of techniques, so the production of the *Marat/Sade* appeared the ultimate application of a theory which had been hatched before the egg of the play ever arrived. It seemed to say: this kind of theatrical expression is soul-stirring and mind-widening—if only there was a play to accommodate it. Weiss's play, at base, is a rather old-fashioned and long-winded polemical tract. In the original Swinarski production which I saw at the Schiller-Theatre before the London production, it was an indictment of revolutionary fascism that set out to make a Marxist point. One either took the play or left it alone, but it was what it was, and there was no question about its point of view. In the London production, its ambiance was neither political (despite polemical longeurs) nor philosophical, but exclusively theatrical. All the time it was saying: an Artaudian inspired theatre, strong on imagery, disrespectful of plot and suspicious of these, can resuscitate something in our jaded senses and overhaul our aesthetic appreciation. That I happen to agree with that implication does not blind me to the fact that this is not what the play is about. One tends to appreciate the work in somewhat the same way one admires the resilience of a diving-board that allows a world champion to perform a breathtaking triple somersault. Once the swimmer is in the water, that diving board looks mighty bare.

Marat/Sade marked the dissolution of the Group, or rather its assimilation into the larger company; the end for which it was intended. One of Peter Hall's aims had been to use the work of the Group as a kind of healthy antitoxin which, after being injected into the bloodstream of the mother-company, would produce a greater robustness. Actually, the arithmetic was all against that, as there were seventeen in the Group and over a hundred in the Company. I expected the LAMDA work would simply disappear. As it turned out, it was the pivotal factor in the *Marat/Sade* rehearsals, and the

key by which the over-all company developed the style of the new production. It was unfortunate that the LAMDA program was called Theatre of
Cruelty and that serious work should have spawned yet another label for
journalists to bandy about. Where, in all reflection, I have asked myself,
where, in all of this, was Artaud? It was never our intention to create an
Artaudian theatre—to do what, in fact, Artaud himself never did. But there
were too many provocative insights and tantalizing challenges in *The Theatre and Its Double* not to take him up. What was Artaudian in our work was
the search for means, other than naturalistic-linguistic means, of communicating experience and insights. Also, our attitude to the classics—not as
peerless masterworks, but simply as *material* that could be reworked and
rethought in very much the same way Shakespeare reworked and rethought
Kyd, Holinshed, Boccacio, and Marlowe. And what was characteristically
Artaudian was the shared distaste and impatience the group's directors felt
towards prevailing theatre trends; the well-upholstered, self-esteeming *cul-
de-sac* in which the contemporary theatre found itself.

The quest for Artaud, if it's lucky, will not simply discover sounds, cries,
groans, and gestures, but new areas that never even occurred to Artaud. His
value is that of the devasting skeptic whose very posture and tone of voice
questions the validity of highly coveted achievements. How important is the
accurate reproduction of the trivia in our lives, asks Artaud? How significant
is the arbitrary social thesis that elaborates a partial insight so that we are
persuaded this is the whole story? How valuable, asks Artaud, is a theatre
that elegantly, excitingly, and wittily reiterates the clichès of our lives—compared to a theatre that suddenly opens up, like a mountain crevice, and sends
down a lava that scours the lies, half-truths, and embedded deceptions of our
civilization? "Metaphysical" has become a pretentious word with high-
falutin' connotations, but if one defines it as a form of imagery through
which we can rediscover the essential links between sky, rock, land, sea, gods,
and men—that is a lesson worth learning, and one the theatre is not yet able
to teach. The cruelty that Artaud referred to (this is a truism worth repeating) did not refer exclusively to torture, blood, violence, and plague—but to
the cruelest of all practices: the exposure of mind, heart, and nerve ends to
the grueling truths behind a social reality that deals in psychological crises
when it wants to be *honest,* and political evils when it wants to be *responsible,* but rarely if ever confronts the existential horror behind all social and
psychological facades. This is where Artaud becomes practical and level-

headed, because he declares: if we want to have a theatre that isn't trivial or escapist, we have to find a new way of operating such a theatre: a new way of generating the actor into action, the playwright into meaning, and the public into consciousness. An exhortation couched in rhetoric isn't the same as a body of work and achievement, but at certain junctures in history—and I believe we're at one at this moment—it is the healthiest noise we can hear.

The making of make-believe
Paul Sills, Larry Arrick,
Mildred Dunnock, and Alvin Epstein

Paul Sills founded the first American improvisational theatre company in 1956. Called the Compass, it gave way two years later to the now famous Second City. He developed the technique now known as story theatre, and directed the production by that name which opened in New York in 1970. The following article is a collection of views by Paul Sills, Larry Arrick, who is also a director, and Mildred Dunnock and Alvin Epstein, who are actors.

"The Making of Make-Believe," by Paul Sills and others. First published in *yale/theatre,* Volume 3, number 2. Copyright © by *yale/theatre,* 1971. Reprinted by permission of the publisher.

aul Sills Story Theatre was very frightening for me to do, very difficult to get to, to face the fact that I was a grown man putting my adult theatre career through the eye of this fairy story needle, but I felt it was something I and the theatre had to do.

In the oral tradition of Homer, the theatre is concerned with the spoken as opposed to the written word. Theatre has to remain with the spoken word. That's why I'm very interested in stories and not just any stories, but *the* stories, *true* stories. The point is to connect the audience today with what has lasted by word of mouth—with *what has been passed down.* In Story Theatre what wants to come through is the story. It must be done under compulsion. As a gimmick it's nothing.

I'm not trying to reach anything but the stories. The stories themselves are the teaching. We're passing on the teaching. It's so simple, all intuitive. I don't know what they mean exactly, but I do know they touch people.

These are parables. A story like "Simpleton" with the usual moral "share your bread and cake and you get the golden goose" is a true story in my understanding. All these stories have a great deal to say about what is in some sense salvation, not merely a life lived in struggling with the truth as comprehended by the people. What Story Theatre is after is the poetry. A story is a peculiar kind of a journey. There is nothing extraneous. You can perform the whole thing.

Mildred Dunnock Children do things so freshly, without any premeditaton, without any acquired veneer, and that is what I found in working with Paul Sills—that sort of spontaneous approach to theatre—in trusting the material, trusting him, not demanding too much from ourselves. Paul didn't lead me on. He didn't say, "Go as far as you like," but he did reinforce me. His one statement was "Let the material do it for you." My coming to the Grimm's material was so simple compared to the way one works on a play, because it is so simple. We all knew the plot. The plot didn't get in our way. And nothing came between us and the plot.

Sills We tell the story, then we eliminate by ear what isn't necessary because it's complemented by the action, although in some cases you do both. You say it and do it. That's a very interesting moment in the theatre, and it takes you into a very different space. . . .

The whole trick is to create the story with the actors. The music aims at the same thing, especially Dylan and the Beatles. You can harken 'way back to the bard, to the poet who sang, and Dylan is our man, no question about that. The two of them make me feel the same way. Dylan's music and the stories have much in common.

The key word is *share* with the audience. What actually happens in that moment is happening to the actor as opposed to having it all figured out and laying it on the audience. The actor transforms into the character. But he's not going to become the character for more than a very brief moment, so the third person narration is a way of helping him make that jump.

Larry Arrick In Western theatre everything always happens in the present tense and has a linearity . . . which stems from an Aristotelian view of the drama as the imitation of an action. It immediately suggests a straight line. The whole training of American theatre is related to the teachings of Stanislavsky, in which the play is constructed as a series of actions leading toward an objective. In literature, however, other things happen . . . there is an interesting tension set up. For instance, in a simple declarative sentence, *"I want you," he said,* the *"I want you"* is absolutely in the present tense. That line can be taken directly and put on the stage; the actor can say it. But what happens in a book is that there is a comma, and then there are the words *he said,* which means that now it is in the past tense so that the sentence exists simultaneously in the present and the past. Besides existing simultaneously it also suggests that someone is overhearing that line, not just the reader but the writer; the writer's sensibility is there. Now he can characterize. He does not simply have to say *"I want you."* He can write,

"I want you," he said, lying in his teeth. The reader receives this as one lump. We know that the character's need is to convince the person he's talking to, and that the author is telling us he's lying.

One of the interesting things about this technique of using literature or the means of literature more directly on the stage is that we can manipulate time, and we can attempt to manipulate sensibilities so that we have more than one voice speaking. We have the character's voice and the author's voice speaking simultaneously. We have the present and the past existing simultaneously. That sets up an extraordinary tension that I am just at the beginning of exploring.

Also one is liberated [from the idea] that a scene is not a scene unless it pushes the action forward, linearly. Well, it's extraordinary to be able to push the action backward, not as flashback which usually functions to push the story forward anyway, but so that in dealing with something going in a linear fashion—that is, horizontally—you have a chance to go vertically.

Alvin Epstein   You're never unconscious of the audience, and even when you're talking to them, all you're doing is making another character out of them as if you were talking to somebody else on the stage. Whatever you might be doing to another character when you're talking and relating to him, you're doing that to the audience. That has to do with some kind of basic acting which I think is unchanging, and which is practiced in different ways by different people. The Stanislavsky thing was really to create some kind of relationship among the actors on the stage, but a lot of acting before that was very frontal. It was done to and for the audience. In countries where the Stanislavsky system has had a profound effect there is a tendency to ignore the audience.

Sills   There are three traps for the actor: the traps of character, story, and emotion. The only way you can escape the trap of character is to become the character. It actually occurs in the on-going moment. That's a becoming. That's a transformation. The only way to get that is to be out of the character; otherwise you certainly cannot get into him. Most actors aim at mock-up characters. They put on characteristics from sociology or psychology until they look almost like life. But they're not alive. The theatre's concerned with reality. When it works it *is* reality.

Dunnock   Story Theatre is just what it says. It's theatre with a story, and a story is a plot. It's not a characterization. It's not a deep involvement between the subconscious of two people. I don't believe you could act that in the Story Theatre form . . . I think I felt freer [in this type of theatre] because the demands of the material were not so specific.

Epstein   Paul didn't want characterization. He didn't want conventional character acting in the stories. He wanted the story elements, the story-telling elements, to be prevalent so that you wouldn't drop in and out of character, you wouldn't stay in character, you were never really portraying a character. You were somehow indicating a character, telling about a character and you never lost the narrative approach to the character. For instance, in one of the *Grimm's Fairy Tales* I had to play an old man, an old king, and then I would have to do the lines of the old king. In rehearsal he told me, "Don't characterize, don't act an old king. You say he's an old king, that's enough. Do something other, less, something less." His whole approach to the stories at the time was to get into the space. He wanted you to act out things with your body and to be in the space. It was the space which somehow had to become expressive. It was just "get into the story, just tell the story, don't drop out of it into character." Larry is just the opposite. Larry wants you to play the character. It's more traditional in terms of acting. In terms of Story Theatre, I can't see that one is more traditional than the other since there is no Story Theatre tradition.

Arrick   In Story Theatre the means should become metaphorical instead of just the results being metaphorical. A photographer uses his camera to capture a moment of reality and yet if the photograph is more than a snapshot, it becomes a metaphor for an experience. But the means are natural, whereas in painting the means are not. Story Theatre is closer to the means of a painter who uses metaphorical means to fulfill the larger metaphor.

Of course there is always the danger that you will find not a metaphor but a decoration. The danger of a Story Theatre production is that it can look like an illustrated Children's Book since elements of Children's Theatre are still left. What we're doing is coloring in to illuminate an experience which comes through the text.

To put it systematically, it is the difference between simile and metaphor. A simile is a one-to-one relationship. "She looked like a lion." The test of the simile is its one-to-one validity. Did she look like a lion? If so, what have you really proven? Whereas, if you find a metaphor for the experience of that girl at that moment, then you've done more than simply describe what she looked like, you have illuminated an experience. Therefore, in the work in which we do a lot of transformations I try to keep the actors from imitating anything. The animals are never on all fours; flowers move. They are rooted in their own humanity and truth, but as in all heightened experience we transform it into something else.

Picasso has a series of lithographs about the sex act where what he's involved with is metaphor. His males are half-bulls, half-fawns, satyrs, centaurs. What he's really searching for is some way of illuminating the variety of sexual experience. Paul feels that the simpler the presentation the more complex it would be in the viewing. We are using more complex means for simpler ends. We should move toward excess, deliberately, just to find some limits, to find out where we're over-extending beyond our real imaginations and have moved only toward cleverness and toward decoration.

Epstein   An actor's whole attraction to acting I guess is transformational, to pretend a life that is not his own, to pretend a kind of existence, a form even, a shape, a sound that is other than his own. Story Theatre is a place where you have to do a lot of that, so maybe its attraction to an actor is from that point of view. It gives him scope for the thing which makes him want to act in the first place, more obviously than other plays would. It occurs more often and it never has to be very complete. It's always a sketch, and it's more varied.

An interview with myself about story theatre

A. J. Antoon

A. J. Antoon has directed in such places as the New York Shakespeare Festival Public Theatre and in San Francisco. At the time this article was written he had just completed a story theatre experiment at Yale University.

INTERVIEWER   Can you define Story Theatre in a few words?

ANTOON   No.

INTERVIEWER   In as many words as you want, then.

ANTOON   Well, the way I see it, Story Theatre is a narrative form of drama in which actors tell a simple story as simply as possible.

INTERVIEWER   Maybe a few more words.

ANTOON   When in the old days people wanted to know why, say, there was evil in the world, the wise men told a story about a man, a woman, a tree, and a snake—a very simple story. The people listened and the story struck home, it touched something "inside" them. Story Theatre tries to recapture that simplicity of storytelling. It takes away everything; there is no scenery, no props, nothing except some actors telling a story, and the imagination of the audience. The old man on the back porch telling tales about the haunted house makes his listeners imagine all he wants them to see, hear, feel, etc.—the rest he acts out for them. He assumes the characters' voices and their faces, if he is a good storyteller.

INTERVIEWER   That's the job of the actor then in Story Theatre.

ANTOON   I guess so.

INTERVIEWER   Simple.

ANTOON   Yes, it should be, and magical.

INTERVIEWER   Magic?

ANTOON   Sure. Trees appear, doors open, apples are eaten—but there is nothing there. Something out of nothing is either creation or magic. Paul Sills' mother, Viola Spolin, has some games for improvisation based on the Who, the Where, and the What: a character in an environment doing something. To tell that clearly without props and things is magic.

INTERVIEWER Do you use a lot of improvisation and games to do Story Theatre?

ANTOON No, I'm not very good at that kind of thing, I'm afraid . . . Where were we . . . Oh yes, Simple, Magical, and Lyrical. I think the form is rather folksy when it's at its best. It has a purity about it like a good poem or a real folk song.

INTERVIEWER Is music absolutely essential to . . .

ANTOON Yes. (pause)

INTERVIEWER What about the narrative?

ANTOON Wait a minute. Can I say some more about music? So far I have not used songs with lyrics for the actors. Allan Jaffe, who wrote all the music for my Chekhov/Tolstoy stories, and I tried never to make the music stand out. I think his music is extraordinary. It is lyrical, haunting, funky, sad or whatever when it needs to be. He'd always stop me from overdoing it. Larry Arrick wants songs: a more "musical" or "cabaret" (his word) kind of Story Theatre. That's cool. Paul has used familiar pop sounds to give added relevance or resonance to the Grimms. That's cool too. But that's not where I'm at now. I just use the music in the background, hoping it helps open up the audience's souls—if that's not too corny. No matter what you say about underscoring in movies, if it's done right, you cry. OK. The narrative.

INTERVIEWER What? Oh yes. Does the narrative break the action?

ANTOON Never. I don't want to keep the audience at a distance, not for a moment, not at any cost. No Brechtian alienation here. The third person doesn't have to objectify. The Yale Story Theatre productions I've seen use this objectivity. I want to keep bringing the audience in. "Once upon a time . . . come closer and hear . . . and what do you think the Government Clerk did . . . Huh. . . ." Keep them at the storyteller's feet. That's what the narrative can do. "Bring them in closer and closer"— that's the way I explain it to the actors. Paul used to use the word "share" a lot. I've learned a lot from Paul.

INTERVIEWER Does Story Theatre work with longer pieces?

ANTOON I don't know. The longest ones I've ever done are the Tolstoy *Master and Man,* and the *Story of Buddha,* both about twenty minutes. Much longer, I have a feeling, wouldn't work. I'm not sure.

INTERVIEWER Is there a formula? What makes a story right for Story Theatre?

ANTOON No formula, no. I've tried stories, then rejected them as not Story
Theatre. I'm fascinated now with the idea of journey and a sort of magical repetition. It comes from the folk tales. A circular movement. Most of
my stories have a journey in them and some task tried more than once.
Cain and Abel go to the mountains, Cain tries three times to light the
fire; Tobias escapes to the land beyond the river, tries to kill the fish three
times; Buddha wanders the world, tries three ways of life before he becomes the Buddha; Chekhov's Government Clerk goes back and forth to
the General three times; Master and Man get lost in their journey in the
snow three times. And come full circle.

INTERVIEWER Stories are more for children than adults. Don't you think
adults are too complex to really believe in Story Theatre?

ANTOON Well, there's a secret kid in all of us, of course. But I believe acting is simply a children's game played by adults anyway. Pretend, or
better, make believe. When children make believe they act. The emphasis is on believe, though. I've seen a five-year-old boy pretending to be an
old man—all the adults concurred, he was over fifty. No gimmicks, no
method, no fake walk, just pretending with belief. This is the kind of
acting that is especially right for Story Theatre. We've got to believe
again. We're so stuffed with irony and cynicism—I don't know. It's too
easy to be ironic; too easy to be cynical. That's for insecure high school
teachers. I feel directors of Story Theatre don't trust the form, so they
allow actors to camp it up, to do their thing, make fun of the very stories
they're telling—that's a joke, not a story. A storyteller who doesn't believe his own story soon starts talking to himself; nobody wants to listen.
I think we want simplicity very badly. We want to have a story read to us
at bedtime—any good story after the horrible eleven o'clock news. We
want above all to be told, at least by the purity and honesty of the art
form itself, that there is something pure, something honest left in the
world. Story Theatre.

INTERVIEWER Thank you.

ANTOON Yeah, thank you.

Guerrilla theatre
Dwight Steward

Dwight Steward is a playwright and director who has written and staged plays for the alternative theatre of the 1960's such as *The Dance* and *Third World*. He is also the author of *Stage Left: New Scripts for the Radical Theatre,* from which this article and the other writings by him in Part Two are drawn.

The New York Guerrilla Theater gave several performances at the Mobe demonstration in Washington on May 19, 1970. Wearing ragged clothing and smeared with blood, the performers ritualistically carried the innards of animals in their hands. Rarely has costuming been so effective. Jackson State, Kent State, and Cambodia were fresh in the audience's mind, so the performers used grim reminders to show that what they were protesting was real indeed: real blood, real life, real death.

Unquestionably the New York Guerrilla Theater is one of the most competent radical theater groups in the country. But are all their performances really guerrilla theater? By my definition, no. What distinguishes guerrilla theater is its purpose.

Guerrilla theater—like guerrilla warfare—has as its main end the disruption of an enemy's activities. The styles of guerrilla theater are many, but its function is always the same: disrupt the proceedings, whatever they may be, possibly with an eye toward taking them over.

What proceedings? Any proceedings. College commencements and classes. Conventions. Trials. Political rallies. Meetings. The proceedings can be taking place indoors or outdoors, but the desired result remains constant: the event must stop. It must stop suddenly and dramatically. Especially dramatically.

Guerrilla theater differs from strong-arm, takeover tactics in that it is entertaining—or at least it should be. The audience being deprived of the scheduled meeting gets something in its place. Ideas are important, not random violence, and guerrilla theater is designed not to alienate, but to instruct. Also, guerrilla theater makes good copy for radio, TV, and the press.

The use of force is often too commonplace to mention, but certainly disruption via theater is not. In addition, strong-arm takeovers elicit individual responses, whether those responses are passive acceptance, bored yawns, swinging fists and clubs, or retreat. By its very nature guerrilla theater elicits a collective response to specific issues, especially if they have been dramatically presented.

Obviously, practitioners of guerrilla theater are usually the most militant members of today's radical theater. This causes special hazards, and the "rules of the game" listed later should be carefully considered.

Many people ask if "dramatized disruption" is really a part of theater. The answer is, yes. Consider a typical disruption staged by a Maoist group in West Berlin called the Red Panthers: group movements are disciplined and stylized, almost choreographed; there is strong rhythmic clapping, accompanying responses and chants, occasional skits and blackouts; all led by a man with a bullhorn! This may sound like football cheerleaders in action, but the way the Red Panthers do it is enormously effective, besides having many points in common with the Greek dythrambic chorus, from which all Western theater evolved.

RULES OF THE GAME

Move in and begin quickly. Even the most hostile audience will take time to react and will show some interest and curiosity.

Plan your production to arouse maximum interest, curiosity, and suspense. These elements go a long way toward winning at least the grudging acceptance of your actions.

If possible, capture the sympathy of some of the audience. Although not always possible, it *can* be done.

If possible, plant some members of your group to applaud, cheer, to touch-off and continue any audience reaction favorable to your skit.

Always have the skit or play bear *directly* upon the subject of the meeting you are interrupting.

Use humor and satire to "put down" your chosen opponent.

Know your audience and the precise *response* you wish them to make, as well as the impact you wish to have on them.

All forms of noise makers and musical instruments should be used. It is more entertaining and it saves wear and tear on the vocal cords.

Costumes and props are a must, since they will increase visual interest and curiosity.

If you are aiming at a large audience, then multiple or simultaneous productions can be a great help.

Have the skits well rehearsed, as interruptions are very likely.

It is assumed your presentation has some merit, so insure its completion by protecting the actors with body guards if necessary.

Have exits planned in advance.

A short statement on street theatre
Ed Bullins

Ed Bullins, a leading figure in the growth and development of Black theatre in America, and long a playwright-in-residence for the New Lafayette Theatre in New York, has written such plays as *The Electronic Nigger, Clara's Old Man, Goin' a Buffalo, In the Wine Time,* and *The Duplex.* This short piece on street theatre concentrates on agitprop purposes, but Bullins's insights have equal validity also for non-radical, informal theatre of all kinds.

Street theatre is the name given to the play or dramatic piece (i.e., skit, morality or political farce, or black "commercial" that subliminally broadcasts blackness) written expressly to be presented upon the urban streets or adapted to that purpose.

When one envisions contemporary America, one is compelled to think of faces moving, faces facing upwards, faces in crowds, faces in dynamic mobs—expanses of faces in the streets.

Faces in the streets and in the cities: Broadway, Main Street, Market Street, Broad Street, Grand Avenue, the thoroughfares of New York, Detroit, Providence, Chicago, San Francisco, Philadelphia, Atlanta, L.A.—BLACK FACES.

STREET PLAYS (BLACK REVOLUTIONARY AGIT-PROP)

1 Purpose: communicating to masses of Black people. Contact with Black crowds. Communication with diverse classes of people, the Black working class, or with special groups (e.g., winos, pool hall brothers, prostitutes, pimps, hypes, etc.) who would not ordinarily come or be drawn into the theatre.

2 Method: first, draw a crowd. This can be done by use of drums, musicians, recording equipment, girls dancing, or by use of a barker or rallying cry which is familiar and revolutionary and nationalistic in connection (Burn Baby Burn). Or the crowd can be gotten spontaneously where masses of people are already assembled—the play done within the mob (Mob Action—Mob Act): immediacy—or done with a minimum of fanfare, in the street, upon a platform or a flatbed truck. The truck can carry the equipment and

191

be used as an object of interest if decorated attractively. Also, girls can ride atop the truck and aid in crowd-gathering (fishin'). Monitors can circulate throughout the crowd, distributing printed information, doing person-to-person verbal communicating, and acting as guards for the performers and crew (The Black Guard).

3 Types of plays: short, sharp, incisive plays are best. Contemporary themes, satirical pieces on current counter-revolutionary figures or enemies of the people, humorous themes, also children's plays with revolutionary lessons are good street play material. Also, startling, unique material, something that gives the masses identifying images, symbols, and challenging situations. Each individual in the crowd should have his sense of reality confronted, his consciousness assaulted.

Street theatre
Dwight Steward

In the lexicon of today's radicals, not all theater presented in the streets can be considered street theater. An example is the New York Free Theater with a company of thirty including student apprentices, supported by grants and donations of nearly $40,000 for 1970 alone. Last summer the Free Theatre presented "an original music drama" on the streets of Manhattan and Brooklyn. In addition to its entertainment value—which no one would dispute—the aim of the play was to help people better understand the problems of urban life (for which read how to be happy though you reside in New York and are (a) living in a slum, (b) poor and (c) black or Puerto Rican). Performances were scheduled on various city streets throughout the summer, and citizens were urged to call the department of recreation to learn when and where they could receive their allotment of official summer entertainment.

Any program that brings theater to people should be encouraged. However, the methods and aims of radical street theater are in sharp contrast to those of the New York Free Theater. Street theater doesn't call an audience together, it goes out and finds an audience on the street. Indeed, it is street people that you want, people who know the street and have spent much of their lives there. The audience you are looking for is not generally the one that will telephone a city's recreation department.

The action of the play should represent something familiar and natural, something that is realistic, that people on the street and in houses overlooking it can relate to. But care must be exercised. Don't be overly realistic. One actor playing the part of a cop was so realistic that he was nearly mobbed by the crowd who had stopped to watch. It is necessary to inject some stylization to give the audience a degree of aesthetic distance. Music and masks will help.

Whatever your subject for street theater, it should be handled directly, simply, perhaps harshly, and with "street knowledge." The subject or story should deal with an easily identified, well-known problem, yet it must furnish the audience with a new perspective. The language (vocabulary, syntax, images) must be immediately entertaining. Minutes passing with no *yea's*, *no's*, or groans spell no entertainment. Most important, the message should linger. It should be talked about and thought about long after you have left.

RULES OF THE GAME

Keep your play brief. You will probably be blocking a sidewalk, or street, so you can expect to have your performance stopped at any time.

Know the audience you are playing to and the precise impact you hope to create upon them.

Practice. Each performer must know his role well enough so that audience interruptions and comments won't throw him off stride.

Keep in character. A performer's effectiveness depends on this. Remember that you are not making a speech, but presenting something unusual on the audience's home ground.

Have an elastic beginning for your script, allowing time for a crowd to gather. Once the audience has assembled, begin and work without stopping.

Have a definite, clearly unmistakable end to your play.

Make full use of sight and sound, especially those usually found on city streets—auto horns, sirens, posters, shouting, firecrackers, street music.

Experiment. Borrow a page from W. B. Yeats's theater, and have two or three sides of your "stage" enclosed by banners held by company members.

Use the bizarre or grotesque. Masks. Unusual clothing. Strange hats. But use it sparingly. Too much and your message gets lost in the spectacle.

Have your entrances and exits well planned. If you are moving to another location, the "parade route" should be established ahead of time. If you are finished, and exit by automobile is best, leaving nothing behind but curiosity and the memory of your performance.

Info and tips on street theatre
Patricia J. MacKay

Patricia J. MacKay wrote this article as the editor of *Theatre Crafts Magazine*. It was included in the special 1972 *Theatre Crafts* issue devoted entirely to street theatre. More than other writing about street theatre presented here, it suggests specific possibilities for the non-political, non-radical uses of theatre for an informal audience in the streets, and the author includes information on subjects from sound systems to crowd control.

What equipment to take to the street? How to run it? How to adapt indoor equipment for outdoor use? How to get it there? These are concerns that all street theatre groups have in common. Here are some of their technical tips:

Sets, props, and costumes should be considered after the other technical problems have been solved. Unless carefully thought out, sets can be too cumbersome and heavy for street performances. Simplified props are easier to use. Costumes are light and easily used in the streets and can create the right mood for the performance.

Transportation for actors and equipment should be efficient. If you are not using a self-contained mobile unit, try to borrow or rent a station wagon, school bus, or truck of the appropriate size. Avis and Hertz always have a selection.

Security for truck and equipment is important before, during, and after a performance. Assign people to watch lights, speakers, and generators. Numbers of staff should include enough people to operate equipment, insure its security, and make possible a fast set-up or tear-down. It helps if actors double as technicians. Plan on getting help from the community, especially from the children, but they must be well supervised. Few public garages will take trucks larger than a standard van. If you cannot or don't want to unload equipment, try to arrange some safe parking place—perhaps with a local industry, the department of schools, parks, or sanitation. Don't forget to provide return transport for the driver of the unit or truck.

Stages, even if they are a minimal height, help a group to be seen. Milk crates, the steps of a building, a soap box or parallel platforms ($\frac{3}{4}$ inch ply-

wood topping, fold-up legs) are easy do-it-yourself solutions. More complicated flatbed truck units, or stages that fold out of a closed truck, can be
designed and built. A street theatre group should aim for something that
sets up and tears down relatively quickly. Try consulting a local parade float
builder or display house.

Setting up the stage or parking a mobile unit should be done off the street
center to permit fire truck and ambulance traffic, and should be done near a
street light, which will provide enough light to tear down.

Electricity can be tapped from several sources, depending on the wattage
the equipment demands. With small electrical requirements, an extension
cord can bring current from a nearby house or store. In New York, arrangements can be made through Broadway Maintenance to plug equipment into
a lamp post where 30-60 amps of power is usually available—all for free. If
all other methods fail, you have to supply your own generator. They come in
all sizes and wattages. The amount of gratuitous noise they generate is usually in inverse proportion to the amount you paid for purchase or rental.
Most groups have found them cumbersome and too much trouble. Noisy
ones have to be parked around the corner. When the lights go out—try car
headlights, flashlights, candles, or a recently developed substitute, Coolite.

Traditional stage lights may be heavy and expensive, but if they are available use them. Many street theatre groups who go indoors in the winter
make do with that equipment during the summer. For a lot of light, Tom
Munn suggests scoops or 500- to 1000-watt fresnels. The City Street Theatre
found that fresnels gave a soft light that is more desirable than that of a
leko. The New Heritage Repertory has found that their four follow spots
work well outdoors, but require extra men to operate. News Voice International uses follow spots with a horizontal frame for some of their clients.
Another group warns against using quartz lamps in the street because they
retain heat and can be dangerous if knocked over.

Inexpensive alternatives to traditional theatre lighting can be rigged:
using PARs or 150-watt reflector floods with barndoors attached. Also check
into sealed beam lights.

Telescoping stands for lights are recommended to make adustments and
storage easier. Lights can also be attached with gator clamps to microphone
and speaker stands.

Standard theatrical gels can be taped over the lights or attached with
clothes pins to the barndoors.

Dimmers which are small and portable are available from most manufac-turers. Many groups recommend making your own inexpensive dimmer by wiring together four or five standard household dimmers, which usually cost $5.95 to $6.95. Each dimmer has a 500-watt capacity and can handle three 150-watt reflector floods.

Sound equipment is usually the biggest area of the "unknown" for most groups; consequently there is very little consensus about what is the best mike or speaker to use and why. Tape recorders for music and sound effects or live music from an amplified combo have become standard, yet many groups bemoan the lack of impartial information about how to compile compatible components. Local audio suppliers can help get something up to meet requirements and budgets. Ed Bagwell of News Voice International, who has spent the last 13 years setting up sound for groups working in the streets, makes the following comments on equipment: Sound column speakers are precise but without much bass; trumpet or horn speakers have a lot of treble, but hardly any bass. Tubs have a warmer, richer sound. Bagwell uses the standard theatrical A7 speaker by Altec Lansing or combinations of others, depending on a group's budget. Shotgun microphones don't work outdoors. An omni-directional mike will give too much feedback unless the actors are performing in a circle around it. Cardioid mikes, which have a heart-shaped pick-up pattern can work. Bagwell prefers using directional mikes but notes that means "the actor has to be within the mike's range to be picked up and not many directors think about microphone pick up when they rehearse."

Waterproofing provisions should be made. Tarpaulins, umbrellas, and raincoats will cover equipment and actors. Wrap microphones in foam rub-ber or toss a Baggie over them. Rain will not stop a good performance.

Simulated environments
Alvin Toffler

Alvin Toffler, formerly an Associate Editor of *Fortune Magazine*, has written *Future Shock*, as well as *The Culture Consumers, The Schoolhouse in the City, The Futurists*, and *Learning for Tomorrow*. This particular piece of his writing discusses one possibility for current and future theatre practice: the creation of a total environment in which the audience becomes a participant in a scheduled activity which is central to the environment itself.

One important class of experiential products will be based on simulated environments that offer the customer a taste of adventure, danger, sexual titillation, or other pleasure without risk to his real life or reputation. Thus computer experts, roboteers, designers, historians, and museum specialists will join to create experiential enclaves that reproduce, as skillfully as sophisticated technology will permit, the splendor of ancient Rome, the pomp of Queen Elizabeth's court, the "sexoticism" of an eighteenth-century Japanese geisha house, and the like. Customers entering these pleasure domes will leave their everyday clothes (and cares) behind, don costumes, and run through a planned sequence of activities intended to provide them with a firsthand taste of what the original—i.e., unsimulated—reality must have felt like. They will be invited, in effect, to live in the past or perhaps even in the future.

Production of such experiences is closer than one might think. It is clearly foreshadowed in the participatory techniques now being pioneered in the arts. Thus "happenings" in which the members of the audience take part may be regarded as a first stumbling step toward these simulations of the future. The same is true of more formal works as well. When *Dionysus in 69* was performed in New York, a critic summed up the theories of its playwright, Richard Schechner, in the following words. "Theater has traditionally said to an audience, 'Sit down and I'll tell you a story.' Why can't it also say, 'Stand up and we'll play a game?'" Schechner's work, based loosely on Euripides, says precisely this, and the audience is literally invited to join in dancing to celebrate the rites of Dionysus.

Artists also have begun to create whole "environments"—works of art into which the audience may actually walk, and inside which things happen. In Sweden the Moderna Museet has exhibited an immense papier-maché lady called "Hon" ("She"), into whose innards the audience entered via a vaginal portal. Once inside, there were ramps, stairways, flashing lights, odd sounds, and something called a "bottle smashing machine." Dozens of museums and galleries around the United States and Europe now display such "environments." *Time* magazine's art critic suggests that their intention is to bombard the spectator with "wacky sights, weirdo sounds and other-worldly sensations, ranging from the feeling of weightlessness to hopped-up, psychedelic hallucinations." The artists who produce these are really "experiential engineers."

In a deceptively shabby storefront on a Lower Manhattan street lined with factories and warehouses, I visited Cerebrum, an "electronic studio of participation" where, for an hourly fee, guests are admitted into a startling white, high-ceilinged room. There they strip off their clothing, don semitransparent robes, and sprawl comfortably on richly padded white platforms. Attractive male and female "guides," similarly nude under their veils, offer each guest a stereophonic headset, a see-through mask, and, from time to time, balloons, kaleidoscopes, tambourines, plastic pillows, mirrors, pieces of crystal, marshmallows, slides and slide projectors. Folk and rock music, interspersed with snatches of television commercials, street noises and a lecture by or about Marshall McLuhan fill the ears. As the music grows more excited, guests and guides begin to dance on the platforms and the carpeted white walkways that connect them. Bubbles drift down from machines in the ceiling. Hostesses float through, spraying a variety of fragrances into the air. Lights change color and random images wrap themselves around the walls, guest and guides. The mood shifts from cool at first to warm, friendly, and mildly erotic.

Still primitive both artistically and technologically, Cerebrum is a pale forerunner of the "$25,000,000 'super' Environmental Entertainment Complex" its builders enthusiastically talk of creating some day. Whatever their artistic merit, experiments such as these point to far more sophisticated enclave-building in the future. Today's young artists and environmental entrepreneurs are performing research and development for the psych-corps of tomorrow.

Happenings
Dwight Steward

Frequently labelled "painter's theater," happenings are often dismissed as just another afternoon's entertainment for simple-minded aesthetes with no potential whatsoever for political adaptation. This is nonsense.

It is true, however, that the early happenings were staged by painters, not in a theater but in lofts or galleries. In fact, the first happening this author witnessed was in the back room of an art gallery. Seated in darkness, the small audience faced an end of the room where colored lights flickered. Large silver balloons were suspended from the ceiling in a net. Suddenly the net was released and the balloons floated slowly down, casting odd shadows, reflecting strange tones. At last they settled in a jumble on the floor. *Finis.*

But happenings have matured and grown away from their original conception as kinetic painting. The changes occurred because their potential for human involvement was recognized. Live actors began performing for larger and larger audiences. Soon the audiences themselves began to participate: a happening was announced, tickets distributed, a city block was roped off; then the audience arrived, stood around, talked, sat, looked in the store windows, milled about generally for two hours and left. The audience itself was the happening. Finally, more recent happenings, such as Allan Kaprow's *Birds*, have had distinct social and political overtones.

Happenings thrive for two reasons. The first is *variety*. There is the variety of things that can be used, of sounds, of actions. There is the variety of locations (almost anywhere), of subject, treatment, and style. In addition, the various talents that make up a happening (actors, sculptors, painters, musicians) ensure that practically everyone will have something to do.

The second reason happenings thrive is *suspense*. Not only are the actions/nonactions of happenings unknown but, since happenings have developed a sense of "staged violence" toward the objects used and the people employed, the suspense is tinged by danger. Further, the very randomness of action/nonaction selection heightens suspense. It should be kept in mind, however, that the creator of the happening sets the rules and limits the possibilities.

Because of its variety and suspense, because of its complete freedom from formal requirements and the effective use of mixed media, the happening, probably more than any other form of theater, can be used to make polemical points—make them directly, almost wordlessly, and perhaps even humorously.

RULES OF THE GAME

Know the audience you are playing to and precisely what impact you hope to have upon them.

Determine, at the outset, whether you want the audience to be spectators or participants. And stick to that decision.

Keep your political message constantly in view through the settings and objects of your happenings. Keep the message simple, easy to understand.

Make all actions bigger than life, or smaller. Avoid the natural or familiar. The success of political happenings depends upon extremes.

Productions must be in the extreme also. Give full rein to your imagination. To startle the audience, you might use a bizarre combination of colors and sounds, or a total production utilizing just one color for costumes, set, props, and perhaps even makeup—all accompanied by one musical instrument playing just one note.

Maintain a brisk pace. If nothing is happening, have it happen quickly and in a stylized way. Happenings should assault the audience's senses.

Preserve the quality of randomness, of chance, of suspense.

Rehearse. Then rehearse some more. The effect you wish to create is apparent randomness in a sequence of events, not actual chaos.

Building a play from improvisation
John Hodgson
and
Ernest Richards

John Hodgson and Ernest Richards, both teachers and directors of creative drama, included this article in their book titled *Improvisation*. Here they consider getting ideas for improvised performance and the various emphases possible for improvised drama. They include not only a discussion of useful techniques but also specific illustrations of how the techniques can be utilized.

E very improvisation is to some extent a play. Different approaches will yield different kinds of plays. At some stage it will probably be felt desirable to set out to build a definite play from the creative efforts of the group. This means that the play performed will be shaped by those taking part from their particular gifts and talents, as far as these have been developed. Usually the leader will act as the director or coordinator, but he will constantly find himself, in discussion with the group, devising new ways of stimulating their imaginations, encouraging them in their responses and, with the group, sifting and selecting what to work on further and what to reject. There is a sense in which the play will never be completed, because it will never be static, but the aim will be to devise a fairly satisfactory form within which variations and discoveries can continue.

When a satisfactory shape has been achieved tremendous sensitivity is required by all taking part in order to retain the freshness and vitality without losing the shape and satisfaction in what has been created. One of the hazards of dealing with living things is that the creature grows out of control or to a point at which it no longer fits its clothing. At this point it is as well to recognize the fact, and instead of trying desperately to recapture something which has already been lived through, we need to turn to a new creation. Anyone who saw the film *The Picasso Mystery*, in which the camera watched Picasso painting, will remember how in some creations he went on altering and modifying his work beyond the point of satisfaction, either to viewers or himself. At this point, he shrugged his shoulders and turned to a fresh set of material.

There are all kinds of ways in which ideas may be started: established stories from literature; incidents from history; ideas from newspaper accounts;

word association in a stream-of-consciousness response; visiting a police court; characters met in pubs, cafes, trains; local incidents, such as mine disasters, fires, floods; listening to music which might suggest stories or characters or moods; listening to sounds which could begin a story or set off an association of ideas.

Then once some ideas have been discussed, the group can consider how the material can be treated.

There must be as many ways of group play-building as there are groups likely to attempt it, and, of course, the method of approach will be conditioned by the kind of play we decide to build. Alternatively, the kind of play which we find ourselves with at the end will be the result of the methods we have employed in group creation.

The following main approaches are considered here: (1) Where plot is predominant. (2) Where character is our prime concern. (3) Where dialogue shapes the play. (4) Where a theme is the starting point. (5) Starting from an incomplete script.

1 WHERE PLOT IS PREDOMINANT

Possibly the easiest way of play-creating in the early stages is to take an established plot which we find in either verse or prose, or in history, mythology, or literature and explore ways of treatment. It is necessary to decide whether it is going to be most effective to take the plot and deal with it chronologically or whether we want to focus our attention on one aspect and let other elements be revealed.

Straight narrative   For instance, if we took the Norse legend of the Aesir and the Vanir and decided to bring out the clear struggle between the forces of creation (the Vanir) and the forces of destruction (the Aesir) we could look at the legend from its possibilities of interpretation in movement and action.

One day the Vanir sent to the Aesir—on a mission which is not explained—a goddess by the name of Gullveig. This goddess was highly skilled in all the practices of sorcery and by her art had acquired much gold. When, alone, she reached the Aesir they were, it is supposed, tempted by her riches. They seized her and submitted her to savage torture. The Vanir demanded satisfaction. They insisted that either a large sum in money should be paid in reparation, or else that their rank should be recognized as equal to that of the Aesir so that they hence forward would receive an equal right to the sacrifices made by the faithful. After taking counsel the Aesir decided to settle the question by fighting. But in the long and cruel war which followed they were very often defeated by their adversaries. They therefore came to an understanding and resigned themselves to treating the Vanir as their equals. On both sides hostages were exchanged. The Aesir turned over the robust Hoenir and the wise Mimir. The Vanir sent their former enemies the mighty Njord and his son Frey, who, from then on, lived in Asgard and were often confused with the Aesir.

In the first instance we might discuss in the group the main elements of the story and bring out:

I A scene in which Gullveig is sent by the Vanir with gold to go to Aesir. The group might invent some reason—to entreat for peace. It might be as well in the first stage to enact the scene without words and later dialogue could be introduced.

II Gullveig's arrival at the Aesir. They are tempted by her riches, seize her and ill-treat her.

III They dispatch a messenger to the Vanir with their demand for ransom and equal rights.

IV A battle follows which could be either symbolically carried out, or with a certain amount of realism, in which first one side and then the other gains the advantage.

V A withdrawal in which the Aesir allow the Vanir to be regarded as their equals.

VI Hostages are exchanged, the Vanir sending Njord and Frey to Asgard.

Such a play could be carried out to a background of appropriate music or sound effects, and dance, song, and dialogue might be developed. The first rough run-through would reveal where more imagination was most required and it would be useful to have several groups working on versions of the different parts of the story. Discussion and selection can follow at each phase and some of the better moments might be written down.

In the middle of things   From this kind of improvised development of a play we can turn to a less chronological shaping of the plot. If we decided to take the Oedipus story, we could present it in scenes like this:

I Laius, warned by the oracle, takes his son, whose feet are bound and pierced, to leave him on the mountainside.

II A shepherd brings the child he has found to King Polybus, who names him Oedipus.

III Oedipus as a young man hears of the oracle's prediction and exiles himself from Polybus and his wife, believing them his true parents.

IV On the road to Boeotia he meets and kills the unknown man, who is, in fact, Laius, his father.

V Oedipus arrives at Thebes and learns that the Sphinx is devouring all who cannot solve her riddles. He hears also of the promise of Creon that he who delivers the city from the scourge shall marry Jocasta.

VI Oedipus meets the Sphinx, solves the riddle, and is united with Jocasta.

VII The scourge of an epidemic over Thebes and the oracle's pronouncement that this is due to Laius's murderer being in the city. Oedipus decides to find him himself.

VIII The terrible discovery that the man he is looking for is himself.

However, another way of treating the same story might be to begin as Sophocles did with the incidents in scene VII, and let the incidents in numbers I–VI be revealed as reported action during Oedipus's quest, or, as Cocteau did in *The Infernal Machine*, we may begin round about number V and imagine Thebes in a state of unrest, followed by the visit of Oedipus to the Sphinx and so on.

Focus and insight   Or we might take a different approach altogether, making Jocasta the central figure and following her thoughts and feelings, beginning, say, with her first meeting with Oedipus. Clearly, this kind of approach throws much more emphasis on dialogue and imagination, and in creating plays from improvisation some kind of progression like this will help a natural development from the play of action and incident to the play demanding insight and imagination into human conflict.

Ballads are a useful source of material with children, and folk tales are capable of different kinds of treatment according to the age group. There is a wealth of English narrative verse from Beowulf to Auden.

Almost daily, the newspapers contain paragraphs and reporting which are capable of dramatization. For example, here are two paragraphs from the *Daily Express*:

A rector, who was asked by a Tyneside chain store if a new employee was honest, told her bosses in confidence that she had been convicted of theft ten years ago. The woman was told about the rector's note and was sacked.

Said the rector yesterday: "This is a complete breach of confidence and I intend to do something about it. This person made a slip, but that is no reason why she should be hounded for the rest of her life."

In the first instance, we can give a copy of this to various small groups and get them to discuss ways in which the story might be treated. Some might place the emphasis on the rector, and some might tell the story placing the woman in the center of the picture, while a third group might try to keep the balance between the two. It might be treated as a scandal that the woman's theft has been disclosed, or it may be presented as a moral dilemma from the rector's point of view. Scenes might be imagined in which the woman asks for a reference, in which the rector learns of the effect his action has had on the woman. We can imagine that the woman, about whom the paper tells us little, has a family dependent on her, or that she has during the past ten years been a particularly loyal servant to the rector's church.

Such an incident presented like this to groups will call for the exercise of the imaginative powers they have been developing throughout their improvisation work. When many of the possibilities have been explored and groups have looked at each other's versions, we can experiment by combining scenes which seem the most promising, and then begin to shape these. Notes can be kept by a group leader and gradually the material sifted until a satisfactory development begins to emerge. Then we need to follow this by work in detail on each of the aspects of the play which we have worked through in previous improvisation sesssions. The beginning and ending of the play will probably call for special attention. The characters, the relationships, and the mood can be refined until at last we have a play which we would like to rehearse and perform to an audience.

Other starting points for plays based on plot might be simply the giving of a word or a phrase, such as "independence," "lost," "no luck," "reproach," "tradition," "tis not so sweet now . . . ," "let us grasp this nettle, danger," "the hungry lion roars," "O! brave new world."

We could begin simply by giving the word or phrase to the group and asking them to jot down or say anything which comes to mind as a result of this stimulus. Then some of these can be followed up. Two or more ideas can be combined until a story line is emerging. This can then be developed, along the lines of previous examples, to the polished play.

As has been seen already, one very useful source of material is to be found in literature and especially dramatic literature. Playwrights have always found it useful to take the plots of other playwrights and give them a new twist or a new setting. Jerome Robbins took *Romeo and Juliet* and placed the conflict in the West Side of New York. For Montagues and Capulets he read Puerto Ricans and white Americans. For Friar Lawrence and his retreat he gave us Doc and his drug store. For Juliet's ball we had a dance in a gym, and so on. Such a story of antagonism and frustration is capable of all kinds of settings—we might think of a dockside story where the conflicts are religious or labor, or the story might be set in the context of political battle, where the parents are on the one hand Conservative and on the other the son is a young Communist. Other plays are capable of similarly being set in a modern situation. Othello's color insecurity might well be placed in a Southern U.S.A. setting, or we could visualize a middle class King Lear unfolding the present-day problem of age and parent-child relationships. But it is not only the plays of Shakespeare which can be given contemporary settings. Tyrone Guthrie has shown that *The Alchemist* has considerable humor and impact played in modern equivalents, and other Elizabethan and Restoration dramatists, as well as, of course, the Greeks, lend themselves to presentation in terms of the present-day world.

2 WHERE CHARACTER IS THE PRIME CONCERN

In the chapter on characterization we saw ways of approaching character building, and in this approach to improvised play making, we begin with the creation of the character. The aim now is to develop the conflict, especially within the person, and between him and other characters on whom we are working. It would be possible, for instance, to take a study of an historical character and develop this in the light of our understanding of present day psychology.

From history This is the sort of thing that Osborne did with Luther, and Bolt with Sir Thomas More in *A Man for all Seasons;* and studies are fairly readily available on people like St. Francis, who could then be seen not simply as a romantic animal and bird lover, but a complex character struggling against his own maladjustments in a medieval world. Groups could be given early incidents in the life of St. Francis and asked to discuss them and develop them, bringing out the psychological makeup of the person, then later incidents could be explored in a similar manner, until there was sufficient material to allow for the arrangement and general treatment to be seen.

All kinds of historical personalities will readily spring to mind, such as Plato, Socrates, Nero, Bruno, Boadicea, Augustine, Cromwell, Fox, Wordsworth, Wellington, Pitt, Peel, Mrs. Pankhurst, Dick Turpin, Fanny Burney, Samuel Pepys, Samuel Johnson.

Then, as we worked with the creation of a play beginning primarily from plot, so here we decide upon the starting point and develop the play from that stage, watching the character unfold. This is again more complicated, and at this level it would be necessary to make notes in considerable detail. We could either arrange for each group to have its own scribe or for one writer to be engaged in making notes from the work produced by each of the groups at the different stages of exploration. At some point it will very likely be essential to have one person who is entrusted with the task of final selection and shaping, but if he is sensitive and observant he will all the time be open to the development which the groups reveal. At some point a fairly detailed script may result, but it would always be useful to allow a certain amount of flexibility, so that new insight could be discovered.

From literature   Similarly, literature abounds with characters who could be used as a basis for play building, and it would be especially rewarding if we can apply our understanding to them so that we realize more and more the complexity of the motivation of human action. Personalities like the following would make stimulating studies: Huckleberry Finn, Merlin, Rip Van Winkle, John Gilpin, Pandarus, the Wife of Bath, Moby Dick, Roderick Random, Becky Sharp, Moll Flanders, Pamela, Nicholas Nickleby, Silas Marner, Wordsworth's Michael, Dan McGrew, Frankie and Johnnie, Mr. Polly.

Everyday observation would also supply ideas; the obituary column of *The Times* and other newspapers can be read with insight and penetration into the person behind these notices, and especially significant turning points could be explored through improvisation.

3   WHERE DIALOGUE SHAPES THE PLAY

More than ever today we are discovering the dramatic significance of dialogue, and starting from a conversation overheard in the supermarket, at the bus stop, outside the theatre, or any other place where people meet and talk, we can develop the play based upon the rhythm of interchange and silence.

In the first instance, groups might be given a few lines and asked to develop the language from there. For example:

(1) —He's not a bad player.
  —He's what?
  —He's not a bad player.
  —He played a bad game last week.
  —Yes, but he's usually not bad.
  —Yes, but he's not good, is he?
  —What?
  —He's not good, is he?
  —No. I didn't say he was. But he's not bad.

(2) Radio is on full volume.
  ALICE Just listen to that.
  DORIS That's the new singer.
  ALICE Isn't it terrible?
  DORIS Just listen to her voice.
  ALICE The way it goes on.
  DORIS It beats me how anybody can listen to it.
  Radio blares on.

(3) He married the girl down the road, the one that lives next to Mr. Black—you know, him that married twice and his wife came back to dig the garden—his first wife, that is—'course, she's having a baby—the girl, that is—she's going into the Salvation Army home—that's the one where they take the unmarried mothers in—'course, she's married, but it doesn't make any difference—they still take you in.

(4) HIM I see they're out again.
  HER Do you want one or two?
  HIM You'll never satisfy them.
  HER Fried or boiled?
  HIM Take 'em out and shoot 'em—that's what I'd do.
  HER Well, you can have yours boiled, and I'll have mine fried.
  HIM They'll be importing them from Germany, if they're not careful.
  HER I'll have them both ready before the news.
  HIM Then we'll have to get the union in again.
  HER You'd like that, wouldn't you?

It might be useful in such exercises to use a tape recorder and be prepared to discard a good deal, but from the outset it would be interesting to observe those pauses and moments of silence which spring out of genuine appreciation of personality and situation. Or (as in No. 3 above) sometimes the conversation can be built around a particularly garrulous character—the landlady who talks incessantly, constantly jumping from subject to subject, sometimes interposing one line of thought in complete opposition to another, or, having introduced a topic, the mention of a name reminds her of all sorts of other irrelevancies. Or a character might repeatedly drop names casually in order to build up his own prowess and make his listener feel more and more out of it.

Once the dialogue begins to flow, the place and the stiuation will most probably present themselves, and although the situation itself may have little development, the conflict will spark off the dialogue development.

In presenting plays of dialogue, groups can experiment with the overlapping of circles of conversation. Begin, say, with two characters apparently talking to each other, but in effect each remaining in his or her own world, such as in the Pinter sketch *The Black and White*. Each of these characters might develop his or her own world and dialogue separately at first, and then come together to interweave their words. Or they may prefer to tune in to each others' wavelengths first, before developing their separate trends of conversation.

From here we can go on to cyclic conversations in pairs, where one couple hold a conversation and another couple have a separate discussion, but the two overlap or interweave and then move on to larger groups. This will call for heightened group awareness and sensitivity, as well as a considerable sense of timing. Observation in bars, and coffee houses, where groups sit around separate tables holding their own conversations can be heard simultaneously, will allow the imaginative person to observe the possibilities of developing this on an artistic plane. An example of this in a written play will be found in the first act of Ionesco's *Rhinoceros*.

These ideas can be developed in situations such as the following: a conversation in a room and another overheard from outside; one side of a telephone conversation and a conversation in a room; parents talking, preoccupied, and children playing; a city or village square, in which we become observers of two or three families at the same time (as in *Sparrers Can't Sing* by Stephen Lewis).

It will soon be seen that we are now becoming very concerned with the rhythm both of individual and community life, and in shaping the play the group editor will be much more concerned with sensing the rise and fall of words and emotions than with a more conventional approach to plot and character.

4 WHERE THEME IS THE MAIN CONCERN

Group entertainment can effectively be constructed around a theme. If people are thinking especially of a more conventional play, they will be likely to find their theme and then discuss a plot and character which will highlight or illustrate this.

If, for example, they have decided upon prison reform as their theme, they may look for a specific example from the newspapers, or they may prefer to build a more fictional situation. In either case, they will explore several ways of bringing out their ideas before finally deciding upon a line of approach. Then the shaping and development of the play proceeds very much as already outlined.

There is, however, a place for treatment using the theme as the unifying factor. In this case, we may, in fact, have several smaller plots or situations in which a variety of characters might appear, or the end-product might be a combination of some dialogue scenes, some character scenes, some movement scenes, and some songs, all illustrating different aspects of the topic chosen. For example, if a group decided on violence as its topic, we might begin by a general discussion or some research. The group could work in the first instance on looking through newspapers and periodicals of that week for references to violence. They might keep a lookout on television and radio for examples of scenes of violence in fiction or the news and could check their own reading and film-going for other illustrations.

Then comes the time to act out some of these, and almost certainly, even at this stage, different styles will appear. Some might burlesque, some might take a naturalistic approach. Others might present the scene in a different dimension, such as playing it in a music-hall convention, or a circus ring, or as a play within a play as in *Oh, What A Lovely War* and *Hang Down Your Head and Die*. At some stage, it would be necessary to decide upon the method to be adopted to shape the piece, and probably out of improvisations an idea would arise. It might simply be a narrator who would link the sequences, or it might be that one aspect of society or life is seen in terms of another—for instance, business seen in terms of a supermarket, politics in terms of a holiday camp, or life seen in terms of any kind of game. In this case each separate item would require to make its own impact and improvisation would be arranged so that the best effect was obtained. Then again, through trying the various sections in different orders, the most effective overall shape might be obtained.

5   STARTING FROM AN INCOMPLETE SCRIPT

Sometimes a group has a member who is keen on writing or perhaps someone outside the group may submit part of a text to the group. By taking this script as a starting point, the writer can be stimulated into developing his ideas and the group can explore possibilities in and around the script.

We might, first, ask the group to play the script as they found it, each giving their own interpretations of the ideas obtained. Then if, after having read the script through several times and talked about it, they put it by, and, working from their understanding of it, improvise, many spontaneous developments will result. Depending on how much script is at first presented, the groups can take specific sections of the script and improvise on these.

Should it, say, begin by a small family moving into a new . . . house, they might take the characters as they know them and play around with moving in and the various things which might happen. At this stage it would be as well to let them act first and discuss later, and if the author can observe all along, he can draw from the imaginations of each member of the group, and very often some of the things they do will suggest even further possibilities to him. So each sequence can be explored, developed, altered, in the light of these improvisations, and other ideas can be passed back to the groups by the author or leader. Completely new scenes may well emerge which will have been seen to be necessary or effective as a result of this improvised work around the text. At times the group may focus their attention solely on occupational improvisations concerned with the situation; at other times they will explore the characterization. Similarly, mood and climax can be worked on in improvised form, until the author or leader sees the most satisfactory solution. Finally, the author may write his completed script in the light of all this experience. He may decide that at certain moments he wishes to leave the situation flexible, so that improvisation may take place during performance, to ensure that words and situation can build to the most effective climax at the moment of playing.

Improvisation
Dwight Steward

The latest edition of the weighty *Oxford Companion to the Theatre* has no entry for "improvisation." Strange, since the art of improvising around set situations and speeches formed the backbone of the Italian Commedia dell'Arte, to say nothing of the many pieces of "improvised" theatre that have been performed at Oxford itself. The omission is even stranger when you consider that Joan Littlewood's original production of *Oh What a Lovely War* grew out of her company's improvised reactions to certain historical facts of war. In much the same way, the script for Megan Terry's highly successful *Viet Rock* was molded into its final form by the performers themselves, as were Brendan Behan's first two plays. Today dozens of drama coaches—as well as many psychologists—use improvisation as a technique for understanding a character (or oneself), and for building a part within a play.

The simplest description of improvisation as a dramatic form is found in the title of a set of improvisations published several years ago by Kenneth Koch. He called his scripts "Blueprints," and in improvised theater the blueprint or outline of a skit or play is given by the playwright. After that it is the job of the director and actors to flesh out—from the hints provided—the deeper meaning and substance of the work.

Obviously, in order to suit local circumstances, improvised plays must allow for a great deal of adaptability and change. To achieve maximum political impact, this immediacy should be exploited to the fullest. Like most of today's radical theater, improvisations will be presented, not before a nationwide audience, but before a local group with a particular identity and bias. Productions should be tailored accordingly.

Such adaptation should not prove difficult. Improvisations depend more on the wit and skill of the actors than on props, sets, or costumes, and they can be performed practically anywhere. In addition, adapting improvisations to particular situations (or writing them for specific occasions) permits a group to make optimum use of any particular skill, appearance, voice quality, etc., which its members may possess.

Members of the audience can be brought into an improvised skit—and should be whenever possible. For example, if you are staging a protest for improved housing conditions in a slum and have assembled a number of tenants, you might first dramatize their plight with a skit built around slum-lord exploitation, then do the skit again, the second time with a member of the audience playing one of the parts. Most likely you will be surprised by the wit and insight brought to the role. Also, such spontaneity and immediacy breaks down the barrier between *you* as performer and *them* as audience, and provides a much greater sense of participation. You might also learn something that can be incorporated into the skit the next time you perform it. Audiences are great teachers.

Improvisations can be either tightly structured or loose and open. Examples of both types follow.

RULES OF THE GAME

Know the audience you are playing to and *precisely* what impact you hope to have.

Be sure you understand the main points—both political and dramatic—of the script you are working around. Use your best pieces of improvised business to reinforce these points.

Have various members of the group improvise different parts of the script. Talent turns up in unexpected places and should be used.

Employ music whenever possible.

Keep a close record of what works during rehearsals, and use those bits whenever possible. The same for performances. Also, remember that successful bits can be used in many different improvised scripts.

Be humorous and satiric whenever possible. Humor is an excellent audience relaxer and a corrective for overdoses of tired rhetoric.

Performers should "play-off" among one another to develop the habit of falling into a situation or character quickly and grasping its possibilities.

Rehearse. You may be on the right side of history, but that doesn't mean theatrical competence can be taken for granted.

Casting the non-play
Michael E. Rutenberg

Michael E. Rutenberg, teacher and director, was on the faculty at the City University of New York when he wrote this article. In it he discusses various audition techniques for nonverbal, kinesthetic theatre, with emphasis on ensemble preparation for performance. His ideas focus on the role of improvisation. Rutenberg is also the author of *Edward Albee: Playwright in Protest*.

"Casting the Non-Play," by Michael E. Rutenberg, from *PLAYERS: The Magazine of American Theatre,* Vol. 44, No. 4, ed. by Byron Schaffer, Jr., April/May, 1969. Reprinted with the permission of *PLAYERS*.

Gordon Rogoff has said of the current theatrical trend that "today's inclination is not as much toward the perfect text, something finished, unbending, or marbleized, as it is toward the collaboratively suggestive, improvisational architecture of a fluid, open text." Directors influenced by such new theatre ensembles as Cafe La Mama, The Open Theatre, Theatre of the Ridiculous, The Living Theatre, and the plethora of recent off-off-Broadway experimenters, have begun to think in terms of presenting an evening of theatre consisting of short, nonnarrative works: songs, dances, burlesques, improvisations, acrobatics, magic, clownery, film clips, and psychedelic, mixed-media bombardment of the senses. They are forming ensembles dedicated to the nonplay. Building such an ensemble requires tryout procedures quite different from those usually employed in auditioning actors. What follows is a description of methods of auditioning used by one director. These procedures are offered not as the final answer, but as a springboard from which each director might move as he devises his own method of selecting actors for the New Theatre.

Traditionally, actors are selected for a company on the basis of closeness to the physical and vocal type of the *dramatis personae* of the plays scheduled for the season. Type casting prevails, and those actors who seem "right" for the parts available are given a series of readings, the best readers usually winning out. This practice is not feasible for the director of the non-play since he is often forming an ensemble without having decided on the evening's program. (He could still advertise an evening of "provoking improvisations and theatre pieces" in advance publicity releases, which is vague enough to allow the creation of the program during rehearsals.

The first step in casting an ensemble for the non-play is to devote a good portion of the initial interview to putting the auditioning actor at ease. The director engages him in a cordial chat about his background, interest, and aspirations, thus building his confidence and trust. Most actors, like most people, carry with them unresolved feelings of fear and distrust. It is up to the director to allay these negative feelings by letting the actor know through the tone of the interview that the director fully accepts him, and hopes to use him in the ensemble. Once the actor begins to relax, much can be learned about him from questions that show an interest in his education, present job, travel plans, etc. The astute director can get a sense of the actor through the visual and emotional cues he registers as he sits or moves about during the interview. He can also check the degree of proficiency the actor has attained in his articulation and pronunciation.

When the director feels the actor is comfortable enough to start the second phase of the audition, he may put the actor to work on a simple improvisation. The improvisation, the director can explain, is nonverbal and built upon the imaginative use of small objects. Two or three related objects (such as soap, towel, or a shirt) are given to the actor, and he is encouraged to create an event in pantomime using the objects as an integral part of his story. When the actor is in the midst of his pantomime he is given a third and fourth unrelated object (perhaps a plant or monkey wrench) and asked to incorporate them. Using the new objects tests his willingness to alter the story spontaneously. The exercise also indicates something of his intelligence, because he must find a logical thread that ties unrelated objects together. His imagination is obviously called into play since we can assume that the more imaginative the actor, the more imaginative the story.

After the improvisation is over, and if the director is pleased with the results, the actor is asked to read a sheet of nondescript sentences aloud. It is the actor's task to find or give meaning to this text. The exercise is much like the Thematic Apperception Test psychologists use in having patients project their feelings onto the nonevent picture. The nondescript text utilizes the same principle of projection, and helps reveal to the director where the actor's natural instincts lead him. If the results of the nondescript exercise are favorable, the director may ask the actor to go on to the next phase of the audition.

A simple one-action improvisation is given to the actor. The exercise requires two actors, each presumably having reached the same plateau in separate auditions. (The traditional use of the stage manager as one of the auditioning partners is an intolerable burden on the actor and should be discontinued.) The two actors are told where the improvised situation is to take place—perhaps a bench in the local park on a hot summer's day. The actors are then told their objectives. If one or both are inexperienced, the director should not use the word "objective" as it will confuse an untrained actor. Simply give suggestions naturally such as: "In this improvised scene you will make up your own words based on the premise that you'd rather be alone than talk. But if someone does strike up a conversation with you, answer him as best you can without offending him. Remember you are the kind of person who takes other people's feelings into consideration." In this way the director has given the actor an objective to play, and also begun to hint at such other acting elements as justification of the objective and the awareness that attitude must be taken into account in any dialogue. The other actor is also given an objective to play which will produce conflict in the improvisation. The director suggests that "you are lonely and feel the need to talk to someone—even a stranger. If you meet someone in the park, try to get to know him." Both actors are also given activities. One is asked to "feed the pigeons, or read a book, or sketch a picture," while the other actor is told "to eat a hot dog or munch on popcorn."

During the improvisation the director watches to see how well the actors carry out his suggestions. Are they playing their objectives? Is the activity continued, and is it truthful and fully developed in terms of sense memory techniques? Is a distinct relationship evolving out of the encounter? Do they listen to each other? Have they let the environment and the weather affect their behavior? The actors' level of suggestibility can be determined by the depth of their involvement in the situation. When the improvisation is over, or stopped by the director, he should ask them to repeat it again—this time offering an *adjustment* which will alter the circumstances. He may propose that one character now introduce a *physical state* as his adjustment. The physical state may be a headache, or stomach cramps which he is hiding out of embarrassment. Perhaps he is suddenly overtired, but must continue to talk. The addition of a physical state should produce a corresponding change in the character's behavior. The director is free to make other adjustments. He might change the objectives, but leave the scene in the park. He might keep the same objectives, but place the meeting at a railroad station, or at a dance, or in a hospital. Then the director observes how well the actors have made the adjustments.

In order that both display their own personalities, the actors should be discouraged from playing "characters." The director should instruct them to use their own names in the improvisation. This approach to an improvisation helps the director learn how willing the actors are to expose themselves. If one of the actors shies away from direct personal involvement and seems reluctant to use his own name, he is not ready to assume the actor's responsibility which is *to be private in public*. The improvisation also tests the actor's willingness to depend on his partner. Since there is no script he must listen to the other actor in order to know what comes next. Learning to play for one's partner is essential in the training of actors for participation in the non-play ensemble. If the actors seem to handle their adjustment well, work uninhibitedly and in communion with each other, then they should be invited back to a second audition.

At the second audition two different returning actors are brought together with the director who again talks with them about family, mutual friends, favorite artists, or anything else that seemed of interest to the actors at their last interviews. When the actors seem sufficiently relaxed, they are given a short scene to read. It may be published or original material, but short enough to be read twice through in a few minutes. When they have finished reading the script they are told to approach it in the same manner they did the earlier improvisation. They are asked to play an objective, an activity (at least attempt to indicate an activity with the book in hand), a relationship, and a physical state. The director tells them where the scene takes place. An example (taken from the new theatre plays) might be a living room in which the main character talks to his television set or his pet alligator. The actor's objective is "to make love to his television set," or "to comfort his alligator." The activity might be "preparing supper for the beast" or "primping himself for a night of love." The relationship is one of sexual attraction and the physical state is hunger. The other actor (the one playing the television set or the alligator) is given another group of tasks to produce conflict in the scene. The director then watches his actors to see how well they can handle his instructions.

When the scene is finished, the actors are asked to make specific adjustments. Now the actor hates his television set or his alligator, but must continue to flirt, charm, and woo it. The other actor playing the television set or the alligator (both of whom were content in this home) now is told that his character can no longer be tied down and wishes to leave. Directorial adjustments can take other forms. The director might ask the actor to play the scene as if he were in a huge balloon, or taking a warm bath, or walking about in a pool of molasses. If the actors successfully fulfill their new adjustments, they should be called to a third and final audition and told to bring a record of their favorite vocalist. The actors are also asked to bring leotards or other appropriate gymnastic attire.

The third audition is the most difficult because it asks the actor to be his most uninhibited. The audition is concerned with accomplishing a series of physical and animal exercises. The purpose of this final set of exercises is to find out what kind of physical condition the actor is in, as well as to discover some of his acting inhibitions. When the actor arrives, a few minutes are devoted to relaxation exercises. For example, the actor is asked to lie down on the floor. Then he is instructed to tense his toes for fifteen seconds and then relax them. Each major muscle group is then tensed and relaxed until the actor feels comfortable. If there is still tension in a certain area he is instructed to tense and relax that area again. Next, he is told to think of whatever it is that relaxes him when he experiences it. Perhaps it is basking in the sun or taking a warm bath. Finally, he is instructed to think of the floor as water that he is floating upon. After the relaxation exercises music is begun, and the actor is asked to dance to it. The music (acid rock is recommended) should stimulate the actor to let loose and dance as wildly as possible. It should be stressed that this portion of the audition process is paramount, because so much of the new ensemble work is physical. The director should check the actor's styling, his grace and coordination as he dances to the music. After the dance the actor's record choice is played on a machine equipped with earphones and a long extension cord. The actor is told to wear the earphones and sing and dance along with the record. The exercise allows the director to hear how the actor would sound with the ensemble. It also gives the actor courage to sing out loud so that the director can test his stamina and breath control as well as his singing voice.

When the song and dance exercise is finished the actor is given the opportunity to try certain physical stunts. He is asked to try a headstand, a cart wheel, somersault, and certain simple movements such as a duck walk with hands on ankles, back bend, yoga lotus position, deep knee bend using one leg, or any other basic tests of strength, balance, and coordination. If he is unwilling or can't do the physical exercise, it is highly likely that he will hold back and not extend himself to the limits of the various roles he will have to play during one evening of non-play theatre. Ability to react fully to an emotional experience or state requires that the actor be in excellent physical and emotional condition. During these exercises the director should determine how many "blocks" the actor has that stymie free and uninhibited expression. Out-of-condition actors force the director to settle for less in the rehearsal situation. Having satisfactorily come through this stage of the audition, the actor is now ready for the last phase of his screening.

The director now suggests certain animal improvisations that will help further reveal the actor's inhibitions and vocal range. This improvisation can take the form of a group exercise with a few of the finalists participating. The director may either assign each actor an animal or (preferably) allow him to portray his own favorite. Much can be learned about an actor's personality from the animal with which he identifies. Similar to the earlier improvisation, the group is given an environment, perhaps the zoo at feeding time, or a water hole in the jungle. Next, each actor plays an objective (for example, to protect his drinking area), an activity (drinking, or washing, or playing), develops a relationship to the other animals, and concentrates on a physical state. (Possible physical states could be that he is hurt, tired, thirsty, or hungry.) The improvisation then proceeds and the actor is asked to use his voice to make the guttural sounds of the animal he is portraying. If the actor is truly involved with the animal life of his character, he will forget about "correct" vocal production, keep his throat open, and display an unobstructed series of sounds that tell the director his vocal strength and range. The exercise also shows the degree to which the actor is able to observe and imitate life around him. When the exercise is over, or stopped by the director, the actors are instructed to retain the animal characteristics as they re-read the scene used at their second audition.

If the director still needs a further test of the actor's talent, he has the opportunity to put each finalist through an *affective* or *emotion memory* exercise. This exercise should be done privately with all other finalists waiting in an adjoining area. Since most emotion memory exercises have been used to relive episodes of psychological trauma, the exercise has been severely limited in its use as an acting tool. It is not at all necessary for the auditioning actor to have to attempt recreating a moment of terror or hysteria through affective memory. Since the actor going through an emotion memory is required only to recreate a particular event in his life, the experience can certainly be a pleasant one. (It isn't necessary to mention that the director plans to take him through an affective memory.) Just ask him to talk about when he last had an uproarious time, or relate that moment when something truly inspiring happened to him. The director could, if he wishes, ask the actor to talk about a rather sad experience without suggesting that he search his memory for moments of utter desolation. If the actor becomes animated, is caught up in an eager and uncensored telling of his story, if he easily relives the experience, it shows the director that his actor is highly receptive and responsive to suggestion. The director then asks him to incorporate the feelings of the affective memory into the reading of the script used earlier. The actor who is able to color the reading with the feelings aroused by the emotion memory is one the director wants, because the art of acting is the art of calling upon past experiences which have been revitalized by spontaneous and open response to present stimuli.

The specific auditioning procedures described here are by no means the last word in developing the non-play ensemble. Each director will develop his own wrinkles. However, to have a successful ensemble for the theatre, the director must find a way of determining what these procedures are designed to search out—first, the ability of the actor to build imaginatively from a few key stimuli; second, the actor's willingness to become interested in the pursuit of situational objectives; third, the actor's freedom and willingness to be private in public; fourth, the actor's responsiveness to outside direction; fifth, the actor's stamina, physical control, and vocal range; sixth, the actor's fluency in emotional recall and projection.

Open rehearsals
Richard Schechner

Richard Schechner discusses here both the goals and techniques for holding working rehearsals open to the public, using the audience as a tool for production improvement. This selection is from his book *Environmental Theatre.*

Open rehearsals don't mean running a play in previews in order to make money before the critics murder the production. A genuine open rehearsal is showing the play, or parts of it, in an unfinished state. The audience is present so that the production can be revised in reference to how the audience reacts. Open rehearsals are a way of following through on Meyerhold's declaration of 1929. "We produce every play on the assumption that it will be still unfinished when it appears on the stage. We do this consciously because we realize that the crucial revision of a production is that which is made by the spectator.[1]

I want open rehearsals to accomplish the following:

1 Work on parts of the play that involve the audience such as the Tag Chorus of *Dionysus in 69,* the March to Death Valley of *Commune,* the soliloquies of *The Tooth of Crime.*

2 Locate difficult passages in the sense that a ship makes a difficult passage through shoal water. These passages may be problems for either the performers or the audience or both. For example, the first banquet scene of *Makbeth,* where the performers bite into each other, worked out okay in closed rehearsal but fell apart in front of an audience. The performers were rigid, inhibited, and terrified. The open rehearsals pointed to the kind of help needed in closed rehearsals.

3 Test the environment. No matter how carefully the construction is planned, many problems come to view once an audience uses the space.

1 Vsevelod Meyerhold, *Meyerhold on Theater,* 1969 (1929). Tr. by Edward Braun, p. 256.

Only spectators can make these discoveries because over a period of a few days hundreds of different personalities explore thousands of possibilities.

4 Repeat scenes in different variations, different stagings. Not only can audience reactions be tested, but so can performer reactions. Many scenes in The Performance Group productions have developed this way. Sometimes there are discussions with spectators about variations. Always people stay after the rehearsals to talk to the director and individual performers. Playing variations has several advantages. First, one can experience the immediate changes in reaction; secondly, spectators learn the process from which plays are made—the cold task of selecting from alternatives.

5 Eliminate illusion-breeding "magic." By letting audiences participate in unfinished work—by insisting that the work be shown "in progress"—in the midst of the struggle to advance it—by washing dirty linen in public—a barrier is clearly confronted, and maybe lowered. The important thing is to distinguish between the dirty linen that is purely personal and must be dealt with behind closed doors (or trust is lost) and those problems that center on the production. Audiences have a great deal invested in the illusion that performers are special people (as distinct from people with special skills) who live magic lives vicariously for the audience. Performers are both terrified and immensely pleased by the roles projected onto them by the audience. The director too. Nothing shames a performer or director more than making a mistake and knowing that everyone knows that he has made a mistake. Open rehearsals help reduce the pressure for instant success; or for success that comes from living life vicariously. Often performers can feel the genuine warmth spectators have for them, and vice versa. New, more relaxed and genuine audience-performer relationships can begin.

6 Spread word concerning a production. I don't believe in theatrical surprise. The only worthwhile surprise is watching an artist surpass himself/ herself while doing the work. From this viewpoint, each performance can be astonishing. Also, the monopoly reviewers have over the "reception" of new work must be broken—and the only weapon against the Reviewers' Trust is word-of-mouth. Open rehearsals give audiences a chance to make up their own minds, to tell their friends, to watch a play develop over a long period of time.

7 Abolish, or at least reduce, the distinction between rehearsal and performance. This is tied to the anti-illusionism of open rehearsals. I want people to become more aware of the crafts of theatre-making and to confront

the themes and rhythms of the work rather than either the personalities of the performers as such, or a "character" into which the performer has vanished. I believe in a highly conscious, critical, ironic middle ground. Too sharp a distinction between rehearsal and performance makes for evermore "safe" productions or more flashy techniques. Too much rides on the outcome of a single, opening night performance toward which all energies are directed. Performances are stuck in preparatory phases or frozen at a "successful" moment, losing vitality through routine repetition.

A few more words on points five and seven: The formidable task is to raise the consciousness of both audience and performers regarding not only each other but themselves. People become performers sometimes in order to live fantasy lives, magic lives. A performer with such illusions resists rehearsing in front of the people he wants to fool. Such a performer *performs rehearsing*. I have often found myself *performing directing* at open rehearsals. Becoming conscious of the game is the first step to ending it or changing it into something more wholesome. What is needed is a demystification of the entire process so that theatre workers can work on making theatre just as construction workers work on a building while the sidewalk superintendents watch. With one great difference: The watchers at an open rehearsal may effect changes in the play.

Open rehearsals go along well until there is a stop. Up to the stop the rehearsal is like a performance. The stop introduces a strong tension. If the director speaks privately to the performers, the audience gets uneasy: They're being cheated from witnessing precisely what they came to witness. If the director speaks out loud to the performers, they get uneasy: They are being treated like children by a parental figure in front of guests. Only if the performers themselves stop the rehearsal and ask to repeat a scene or discuss something, is the situation relatively easy. The contradiction is, simply stated, difficult to deal with: Performers don't want the parental aspects of the director-performer relationship exposed in public; the public wants either to see a finished performance or to be privy to intimacies concerning the rehearsal.

The director breaking in exposes the apparent diadic relationship between performers and spectators as an illusion. The actual relationship is triadic— with the director standing back because of convention. (In a symphony orchestra the director/conductor is present even though his role during an actual performance may be perfunctory. In music the illusion is the opposite to that of theater: the conductor appears to be more necessary during the performance than he actually is.) Not only is the apparent diad of theater an illusion, but the hidden third figure, the director, emerges in some kind of control. He interrupts, makes suggestions, requests different solutions to the problems at hand. Granted that the director's power is on loan from the performers—still, when the director interrupts, it is hard to not appear to be the *deus ex machina*, the Big Daddy.

These problems of director-performer communication in front of an audience must be worked on more deeply. I know that my own personality contributes to some of the difficulties TPG has had in open rehearsals. I tend to be more authoritarian in open rehearsals than I am in closed rehearsals. My Daddy role is puffed up, and I feel on the line. But I think the problems run deeper than my own inabilities. The performer's training is designed to support and enhance the diadic relationship. The director is supposed to prepare the performer for the diadic relationship. His work is out of sight by the time the performance is ready. At the moment the public is let into the theater the director is by convention supposed to retire. For, in fact, the director's chief role in orthodox theater is to serve as a surrogate public. If the director remains visible and active, then there are two publics, and perhaps a conflict between them. Which is the performer to pay attention to? During open rehearsal the performer plays with the spectators and then, suddenly, the director steps in—asserts himself as the important public—and demands/suggests changes in accord with his own tastes. The performer may feel betrayed at this moment of intrusion. And the director may feel too powerful, having usurped the rights of the audience.

It is easier to be positive regarding point seven. Theatre does not approach the finished state of a sonnet, a film, or even a well-turned letter. Each of these may be revised until the author is satisfied or feels he can't do better. Then he abandons his project—which means he publishes it, screens it, sends it, files it, or destroys it. Once abandoned, the project exists independent of its creator. Not so with theatre. Theatre is a group project, and part of the group is the audience. Theatre incorporates into its structure the dynamics of change. Its authors include the audience, the writer, the performers, the director, the environmentalist. The authors of theatre are always in the process of authoring it. Theatre is the interaction between its "finished" components (text, mise-en-scène, score) and its "unfinished" components (audience, performers, director).

Textual montage
Jerzy Grotowski

Jerzy Grotowski has become well known for his treatment of texts—rearranging, realigning, and reordering them into a nonlinear collage that maintains the integrity of the author's intention while altering completely his prescribed sequence of action. This selection is part of an interview which first appeared in *The Drama Review*.

"Textual Montage," by Jerzy Grotowski, from "An Interview with Grotowski" by Richard Schechner. First published in *The Drama Review*, Vol. 13, No. 1 (T41). Copyright © 1968 by *The Drama Review*. Reprinted by permission. All Rights Reserved.

The initial montage is done before rehearsals begin. But during rehearsals we do additional montage all the time. The principle is the following—it is very clear if you understand the creative situation of the actor—one asks the actors who play *Hamlet* to recreate their own *Hamlet*. That is, do the same thing that Shakespeare did with the traditional *Hamlet*.

Take the principal elements of the text as context for the creativity of the actor. The text forms a unity and a contradiction. For the speaker it reveals a character, Hamlet, with certain human and mysterious sides which are very tangible and comprehensible. But in art it is not life itself that makes the contact—it is the objects of art. That means, to do a great work one must not observe life. That effort is artificial. We observe life as we live it. To say that in order to create I must observe society is wrong. Society is always there in our experiences.

Every great creator builds bridges between the past and himself, between his roots and his being. That is the only sense in which the artist is a priest: *pontifex* in Latin, he who builds bridges. It is no accident that Joyce wrote *Ulysses* or that Thomas Mann wrote *Dr. Faustus*. It is rather easy to take a myth and to form one's work around it. If that is all you do, it is either an illustration or a travesty. What I prefer are new works which are eternal—I may not even know what objects are being referred to—perhaps Joyce wanted to write his own *Odyssey*—but clearly many things in *Ulysses* are important to him. These are invisible and so *Ulysses* is not an illustration or travesty. I am conscious of Joyce in his work, and the result is that his work is part of our world. At the same time something archaic exists in the book and in that sense it is eternal.

It's the same with the creativity of the actor. He must not illustrate Hamlet, he must meet Hamlet. The actor must give his cue within the context of his own experience. And the same for the director. I didn't do Wyspianski's *Akropolis*, I met it. I didn't think or analyze Auschwitz from the outside; it's this thing in me which is something I didn't know directly, but indirectly I knew very well.

One structures the montage so that this confrontation can take place. We eliminate those parts of the text which have no importance for us, those parts with which we can neither agree or disagree. Within the montage one finds certain words that function vis-a-vis one's own experiences. The result is that we cannot say whether it is Wyspianski's *Akropolis*. Yes, it is. But at the same time it is our *Akropolis*. One cannot say that this is Marlowe's *Faustus* or Calderon's *Constant Prince*. It is our *Faustus*, our *Constant Prince*. All the fragments of the text which were unnecessary were eliminated, but we interpolated little. We did not want to write a new play, we wished to confront ourselves.

It's a meeting, a confrontation. That's why there must be little interpolation. But there is rearrangement of words, scenes. We organize the event according to the logic of our cues. But the essential parts of the text—those which carry the sense of the literary work—remain intact and are treated with great respect. Otherwise there could be no meeting.

Extract from
Of time and design
Peter Wexler

Peter Wexler is a scene designer with interest in the evolving roles of various theatre artists. He argues here only for the simple, but often ignored, necessary interrelationships between different aspects of performance in a production-oriented theatre, where responsibility for performance rests with more than one artist.

"Of Time and Design," by Peter Wexler, from *PLAYERS: The Magazine of American Theatre*, Vol. 44, No. 4, ed. by Byron Schaffer, Jr., April/May, 1969. Reprinted with the permission of *PLAYERS*.

There is a great deal of talk today about the current theatre being a "director's theatre"; actors, especially, are very tender regarding this concept. What people really mean when they say it's a "director's theatre" is that it's a production-oriented theatre, which I happen to think is very good. That is, the idea of the production is the most important thing. We at the production end, the designer, the director, the composer and so forth, are very used to being subservient to that total idea. Actors, however, have a more difficult time because they, physically, are on the line every night whereas we are not. Either our collective work succeeds or it does not, and we tend to be pretty happy with our work when the whole idea succeeds. It's very rare that a designer feels he's done a good job on a bad production. We ask of the actors today that they try to see the production in that light. I know we are a little intolerant of the fact that it's not quite as easy for them. When an actor gets out there and the audience is not responding, the actor feels they're not reacting to him *personally*. It would be very good if we begin to think of the actors sooner or worked with the actors longer. Certainly it would be better to bring the actors in early, not to rehearse but to have time to talk and discuss and feel the thing out sooner. That will supply a bit more insight and information earlier, and it's important to all of us to get as much information as soon as possible.

I don't want to suggest that everybody who reads this article should irresponsibly go out and begin a production in which all the actors, directors, and so forth will have two months together before first rehearsals. I'm suggesting that intelligent, good-minded people make an attempt to keep involving themselves in everybody else's objectives. After all, it is a community work. Every show is different; each one has to be packaged differently; each one needs the ability of the designer, director, author, and actor to investigate their objectives and solidify their goals.

This is not to imply, however, that we all work in unison all the time. We are not like brick layers; we don't have to appear on the job every day and lay the bricks together. That's why there is more than one of us. Most designers visualize physical, graphic things better than most directors. Most directors deal with words and people better than designers do. Most authors deal with words better than most directors do. When they meet, they each give a piece of the crutch that the other needs, then they can take their pieces and go home and make them stronger. No one limits himself, necessarily, to just his special area. When the Cabinet of the President of the United States meets concerning Vietnam, the Postmaster General does not suggest that they ought to issue a commemorative postage stamp. He is committed to a certain area of the government, but he contributes to all. That's the whole thing about having the ability to meet together; you learn something from each other and each contributes something.

It used to be that the designer painted pretty pictures; "designer" is no longer that highly defined, nor is "director," or "author," or "actor." There are functions which must be met for every production. A decision as to who performs a specific function is, in the end, unimportant; the only thing that is important is that theatre production involves a group of people. Early-on time is essential if those people are going to communicate effectively and use one another's talents to best advantage.

Directing for the open stage
Irvin J. Atkins

Irwin J. Atkins is an actor and director who, at the time of writing this article, was on the faculty at the University of Minnesota. His description of techniques for the open stage are based on actual practice at the Stratford Festival Theatre in Ontario.

"Directing for the Open Stage," by Irvin J. Atkins, from Hub Electric Company reference manual #109, *The Open Stage,* from their publication of the designs of James Hull Miller. Reprinted by permission of Hub Electric Company, Inc.

The proscenium stage presents a play to the audience from behind the frame of a picture. On this stage, pictures of each moment are designed by the director to transmit some sort of information to the audience.

The setting and properties convey the environment. Picturization, composition, and movement concentrate on clarifying the drama. Transmission of direct information of this sort is made possible by the fact that all of the audience are disposed before the proscenium opening. The maximum angle allows each spectator to view the same basic relationship between objects in space.

OPEN STAGE DYNAMICS

Where the open stage takes the form of an end stage there is little difficulty. The pictorial principles and dynamics of proscenium hold. The caliper stage is closely related to the medieval multiple stage form and can be said to be a series of end stages.

Problems start to arise, however, with the forethrust or peninsular form. With this type of open stage we begin the process of ranging the audience about the action and pictorial principles break down, for here we find for the first time the challenge of multiple perspective.

Not all non-proscenium stages are multi-perspective stages. For example, anyone who has toured with a show which was blocked for the proscenium stage knows that, regardless of the architectural shape of the room he finds on arrival at an unknown destination, he must play his show at one end, or side, with the audience before him.

This is the arrangement which best suits his presentation, and best solves his technical problems. The most important component of the proscenium is impressed upon the available space—the audience seating directly in front of the stage area.

As long as this matrix is maintained, an actual proscenium arch is not a necessary feature; nor, for that matter, is a raised platform, though it may help sight lines. Our perceptual patterns have organized the space into a virtual proscenium.

THE MULTI-PERSPECTIVE STAGE

A multi-perspective stage organizes the audience about the playing area, not before it. The actual arc subtended is relatively unimportant.

What is important is that the audience see different relationships between the actors on stage and so interpret differently. The inability to perceive an intended relationship is the chief difficulty the director must overcome on the multi-perspective stage.

SPATIAL RELATIONSHIPS

The main problem on the multi-perspective stage is the problem of spatial relationships. The auditory, cognitive, psychological, and interpretative problems of the play can be solved adequately with the tools available through training for the proscenium stage. It is exclusively in the sculptural, pictorial, and kinetic aspects that difficulties are encountered.

In this area, the stage director must take his cue from the modern sculptor rather than from the pictorial artist.

SCENE PLACEMENT

Generally speaking, with the audience disposed in a semicircle, the area upstage has been regarded as a virtual proscenium stage and has been used for scenes of static dialogue, tableaux, pageantry, and strictly pictorial scenes.

The area below has been used for scenes of action, dynamics, soliloquy, conflict, and other spatial scenes. Not all open stages today have such area divisions, and a system of scene placement must be evolved in terms of a truly peninsular stage.

POSITION

Stage geography on the fore-thrust stage becomes a rather confusing jumble of terminology unless a new system is devised. Upstage and downstage refer in the proscenium situation to an imaginary axis at right angles to the proscenium arch. So long as the audience is deployed before the actor, the terminology is excellent; once the audience begins to surround the actor, it breaks down.

It becomes much more expedient for the director to give directions in the system utilized by directors in the round, where directions are given according to aisle number.

To utilize the system to greater advantage, the director can set points arbitrarily about a sort of compass rosette. . . . Crosses are then described to the actor by referring to the number assigned to the point toward which he is to move. Thus the actor on the stage can be asked to cross toward "8," "4," "12," or where you will without confusion.

AREA STRENGTH

The relative strength of "areas" on the proscenium has been the subject of discussion by authors of directing texts for some time. On the open stage, the subject again takes on a new configuration.

While center still holds the key spot in regard to relative strength for the single actor, the upstage to downstage axis is no longer axiomatic. Once the actor moves downstage, he becomes relatively weaker. This phenomenon is due to another cause which we might call "frontality," i.e., the greater the portion of the audience able to see the full front of an actor, the stronger he appears.

SOLUTION: FOCUS OF ATTENTION

The focus of audience attention on the proscenium stage is usually controlled through movement, composition, and picturization. As used on the proscenium stage these terms refer to pictorial qualities.

The front-of-the-stage director blocks his show looking straight onto the stage from center, then adjusting slightly for extreme sightlines. In transferring to the peninsular or round, he finds himself frequently doing the same thing from habit. He will build a scene from one part of the house, then another and still another, each time creating a straight-on scene which has little validity for other locations in the audience. True, at some time, every part of the audience will have a scene of its own, but the result is a choppy and unsatisfactory performance of the play.

A better result can be obtained through a shift of directorial perspective from the objective onlooker to the subjective center of the particular grouping. The ability to see the action from the center of focus rather than from an audience viewpoint is an invaluable asset to the multi-perspective director.

PRINCIPLE IN ACTION

The solution, then, is either to put *them into motion about the focal center,* or to remove them to a place outside the sightlines along the circumference they now occupy. The choice will depend upon the qualities of the particular scene in question: if the scene is fluid, the first suggestion may be acted upon; if static, the second.

The principle to be grasped here is simply that *the center of focus on this stage becomes the nucleus about which everything moves.* Thus the figure at center is more static than the figures about him, who are viewed as "ground."

Focus can then be shifted quite easily by selecting the figure about whom the ground will move. It will soon become apparent that the motion need not be circular, as the single illustration might imply, or even symmetrical, to achieve its effect, but that even the slightest shift in the pattern of motion will reinforce focus, shift focus, or even unfocus.

Scorn not the proscenium, critic
Robert Brustein

Robert Brustein is now Dean of the School of Drama at Yale University. An active critic and author, he has also acted and directed in various theatres since 1950. This particular article, presenting arguments for proscenium staging, has as much validity now as when it was written in 1960 for *Theatre Arts*.

Like the sonnet in the nineteenth century, the proscenium stage in our own time has been frowned upon, scorned, vilified and condemned by the country's most influential critics; lacking a Wordsworth to take up cudgels in its defense, it is now in process of being battered and broken by the abuse. "How did the hoax begin?" queried Brooks Atkinson at the beginning of a recent article in which he agreed with William Poel and Tyrone Guthrie that the proscenium stage is "the principal cause of staleness in the modern theatre." For Walter Kerr, who is generally quite sanguine about Broadway products and productions, the proscenium is that "jam-packed peephole stage that was wished upon us by the nineteenth century realists," and leads inexorably to bad imitations of unpopular "minority" playwrights like Ibsen and Chekhov. As for Thornton Wilder, he has often concluded that the proscenium—and especially the box set (the proscenium's most frequent tenant)—is the main enemy of theatrical truth, since it "stifles the life of the drama" and "militates against belief." It is true that these critics rarely agree on precisely what kind of "staleness" the proscenium is responsible for—for Atkinson, picture-frame plays are "violent and sensational"; for Wilder, they are "soothing," "evasive," and distrustful of the passions—but they all shake hands in blaming it for practically every shortcoming of American drama and dramatic production.

Now, it is easy enough to agree with one of these critical assumptions— that contemporary American theatre certainly has its failings. Weary, stale, flat (though not always unprofitable), flabby, dishonest, dull, slushy, sentimental, and soporofic, while belching with occasional bursts of energy, it alternates between somnolence and hysteria, like a beatnik hopped up on Benzedrine. Since most of our plays sound as if they were written by the same dramatist, staged by the same director, and performed by the same actors, let us also agree that the American theatre is in real danger of drying up in its own juiceless and dreary conformity. But now let our pleasant harmony with the critics come to an end. For though Atkinson, Kerr and Wilder all show a real awareness of the need for some radical change in the theatre, they have not convinced me that they have any effective idea of the direction the change should take.

Which is not to say that, on a purely formalistic level, their anti-proscenium arguments are unsound or unperceptive. I am easily persuaded that the picture frame stage is partially responsible for many dramatic excesses of a purely technical nature: that it "boxes a performance in" (Atkinson), that it tends to force the playwright into "contriving, curtailing, and distorting" (Kerr), and that it sometimes "fixes and narrows the action to one moment in time and space" (Wilder). I have also heard, and do in part believe, actors who swear that the proscenium arch cuts off their communication with the audience, leaving them with the sensation of dropping their emotion into a great dark mouth that swallows it up without sending anything back. And from my own observation, I am becoming convinced that the proscenium permits the secondary talents of the theatre—the scenic artists, costumers, and lighting designers—to usurp the stage from the playwright by introducing opulent and irrelevant "effects" that often distract attention from the main dramatic action. Although none of these seems to me a problem that smaller theatres, firmer playwriting, or more modest designers could not solve, I will certainly not deny that the open stage would solve them more effectually. So let us grant that the open stage is a more flexible instrument than the proscenium and that it helps establish a more intimate relationship between the actor and his audience.

Now, if our critics had had nothing more extravagant than that in mind, there would have been little need to quarrel with them. But their animadversions upon the proscenium extend a good deal further. And what begins as a perceptive technical argument almost invariably leads to an aesthetic conclusion of the most extreme and illogical kind: that if the theatre would only dispense with the proscenium stage, jettison the box set, and get rid of the curtain, the general spinelessness of American drama would somehow magically disappear.

What is more, this idea (if one can call it that) is now hardening into dogma even in the most sophisticated theatre circles. The Ford Foundation is currently awarding large sums of money to stage and theatre designers (all of them charter members of the Broadway Establishment) in the expectation that architectural innovations will have some effect on the quality of American drama; with the same hope, other philanthropists are underwriting the openstage Lincoln Square theatre, even though the whole project is already controlled by the same people who now bring such dubious distinction to the commercial stage. We have precedents enough to doubt the efficacy of such backdoor approaches to excellence. After a disastrous opening season, attributed by most of the reviewers to the theatre's conventional proscenium stage and settings, the American Shakespeare Company in Stratford, Connecticut, completely redesigned their house so that it featured a wider apron, downstage exit areas, and scenery that moved in and out on mechanical dollies. Result? Overwhelming physical productions but no appreciable improvement in the interpretation of Shakespeare's plays. The Phoenix Theatre, whose offerings have been plagued by unevenness and failure primarily because the company has never developed a firm and courageous artistic policy, now produces all its plays on a raked apron stage, using open curtains and unlocalized scenery. Result? No appreciable improvement in the quality of their productions. And, as for Broadway itself, the huge apron stages that designers like Jo Mielziner and Will Steven Armstrong have introduced to mollify the critics have had absolutely no effect on the quality of the plays or production techniques, except to call unnecessary attention to the sets.

I do not mean to imply that there is any harm in all this enthusiasm for architectural reform; *externally*, it may do a lot of good. What *is* harmful is the assumption that such a reform will solve any internal problems. The danger is one of false emphasis, for by blaming the proscenium for all the evils of American theatre, the real source of those evils remains unexplored. Let us examine some of the critical objections to the picture-frame stage to see if there is any justification for all the abuse.

1 The picture-frame stage "confines the theatre as an art to variations on a standard mode of performance." Wrong. What makes Broadway performances so standardized, unimaginative, incoherent, and inaudible is simply that no other kind of performance is taught or tolerated—and experiment is probably impossible anyway, given the inadequate rehearsal time and the

pickup quality of the cast. Our dominant schools of acting, led by the Actors Studio (whose members hold classes as well), have chosen to confine their instruction to the most narrowly realistic techniques, and—dedicated to internal "truth" even when faced with non-illusionistic plays—have reduced acting to mere imitation, turning out actors who all look and behave alike. Anyone who saw the Piccolo Teatro Milano during its recent visit to the City Center (a great barn of a theatre with a huge picture-frame stage) could observe for himself that authentic histrionic imagination survives very well within proscenium walls when the actors are audacious and well trained, the director conversant with other than Method techniques, and the company as a whole equipped to break out of the conventional molds. (If you missed this group, take a trip down to the Living Theatre in Greenwich Village, where another kind of histrionic experimentation is being attempted with real success—and on a picture-frame stage).

2 The picture-frame stage "confines the theatre as an art . . . to variations on the styles of plays written by Ibsen and Chekhov." Although we would have a healthy theatre indeed if our dramatists wrote as well as Ibsen and Chekhov, wrong again. Over the past eighty years, the proscenium has proved perfectly hospitable to the plays of Strindberg, Wedekind, Brecht, Lorca, Pirandello, Synge, O'Casey, Kaiser, Toller, O'Neill, Camus, Beckett and Ionesco, to name only a handful of the playwrights who composed nonrealistic, and sometimes non-illusionistic, plays for the picture-frame stage without any loss of imaginative power. If Broadway has seldom seen their plays, I would suggest the reason has less to do with the poor proscenium than with uncourageous producers and unresponsive audiences. Similarly, though the works of Sophocles and Shakespeare were obviously designed for open stages, they do not suffer as much from proscenium treatment as the critical theorizing would have us believe (remember the Old Vic productions of *Oedipus Rex* and *Henry IV?*), and the plays of Ibsen and Chekov have proved perfectly viable in the round and on the apron. Whenever you feel inclined to blame the proscenium, remember Eric Bentley's valuable rule of thumb: "No play will succeed on an apron stage for which it *was* written unless it has qualities that would make it a success on all types of stage for which it was *not* written." In other words, if the play is sound and the production appropriate, an effective performance could be staged on a leaky raft in the middle of the China Sea.

3 The picture-frame stage, and particularly the box set, leads to "soothing" and "evasive" drama. That charge simply makes no sense to me at all. I do not wish to defend the box-set realism here (it retains a good deal more vitality than its detractors acknowledge), but "soothing" is the last epithet I would apply to it. To be sure, some American plays in the realistic mode—like those of Inge and Chayefsky, for example—are indeed "soothing" and "evasive" because, despite their fidelity to surface authenticity, they are much closer to romance; but the realism of Ibsen, Chekhov, Shaw, and O'Neill is designed to cut below the flattering surface to the harsh and rock-ribbed reality beneath. I suspect, in fact, that one of the reasons Ibsen is never performed on Broadway is that he is never soothing *enough* for the audience, and that the elaborate formal experiments of Wilder and MacLeish have become popular partly because underneath the unconventional surface you often find thick sentiment and easy affirmations. In short, the determination of the dramatist to confront or evade a specific problem is a question of conscience and vision, and has almost nothing to do with the stage for which he writes.

The whole proscenium controversy, then, strikes me as an elaborate evasion of the real problems of our theatre, shifting our attention to purely formal considerations when we should be examining Broadway economics, Broadway timidity, Broadway opportunism, the hit-flop mystique, the general imitation of what is current and fashionable, and the absence of any commitment to anything higher than mere survival and success. Chekhov—who is now almost as maligned by the critics as the theatre he wrote for—probably had the last word to offer the detractors of the proscenium when, sixty-four years ago, he had his Treplev say, "I come more and more to the conviction that it is not a question of new or old forms, but that what matters is that a man should write without thinking about forms at all, write because it springs freely from his soul." It is this urge of the spirit and strength of conviction alone—and not formal experimentation or new theatre buildings—that will turn our theatre at last from a cheap and gaudy side show into a temple of enduring art and truth.

Designing random focus
Hugh Hardy

Hugh Hardy, an architect with Hardy Holzman Pfieffer Associates in New York, has designed several theatres, including those for the Cincinnati Playhouse and the University of Toledo, which he uses here as examples to describe architecture that demands more than single-focus performance.

P eople gather in two different basic ways. Fixed focus. Multiple focus. In the fixed focus relationship the audience and the performers are locked together within a clearly defined limit, like TV in a bar, the math professor at the blackboard, or a cock fight. The event is fixed between limits. The TV camera moves to keep the football "on camera." The professor will not write on the floor. The cocks will not be let out of the pit. The Stratford, Ontario theatre, the San Francisco Opera House, the Washington Arena Stage, and your local Loew's are all fixed focus.

Fixed focus relationships come basically in three shapes: frontal, thrust, arena.

Multiple focus is more diffuse, more ambiguous. In a track meet, the event may be three or more things happening simultaneously. Riding a helicopter down to the top of the Pan Am Building, you see the upright Chrysler Building needle, the burgeoning heliport roof slab, the opening street canyons, and the increasing noise—the event of landing changes its spatial orientation as you undergo it.

The University of Toledo theatre was designed with these ambiguities in mind. The audience is fragmented and each group sees the events differently; the limits of performance are ambiguous. The events may come from anywhere and go to anywhere in the room. Lacking a clearly defined center stage, the space requires more than one action to compose an event. The same is true of the Space Theatre when arranged for simultaneous action. Although fixed in position, the audience is watching different events which, like street life, occur behind and to the sides as well as in front of the spectator.

In both fixed and multiple focus relationships, the audience and the performer are gathered in clearly defined spaces, with the audience firmly in place. Even in so-called "flexible theatres," the purpose of the flexing is to make one clearly defined relationship into another.

Architecture is on firm ground in such contained spaces. It can shape and heighten the experience. True, architects must give up the candy of ornament, learn that there is no shame in an exposed lighting instrument, remember to admit actors generously to the stage (or stages) from many places, find various means of organizing the audience without the hard rules of sightline studies.

But all this is not enough. Our fragmented society requires a theatre and an architecture that can come to terms with ambiguities for which no great play, nor any great architectural space, offers precedent. Take the experience of driving a car. Cars are the most common elements of the contemporary landscape. Americans love cars and we drive them through the damned middle of everything. In doing so, we experience multiple images, some reflected in mirrors, some a judgment between taillights, some the moving graphic jungle of the turnoff we just missed, some the hubbub of a midtown (anytown) traffic jam, some the passing interstate landscape. This polyglot of overlapping motions teaches us to see and understand abstractions which are based on fragments in motion.

Contemporary theatre production explorations come from the violence, jumble, beauty, and brutality of this complicated landscape. We live surrounded by power and energy in motion, not domesticated nature. Perhaps the ambiguities, discontinuities, and absurdities of this landscape cannot be presented adequately in architectural space.

We are not like the Victorians who traveled by train or carriage, sumptuously surrounded by upholstered versions of their drawing rooms, observing the landscape rolling leisurely by their windows. We do, however, still watch performances in Victorian theatres, spaces which are contained and sequential, focused on the performer so expertly that from center stage he can give essentially the same statement to each member of the audience. We also still mount the Victorian play in which performance is controlled by an ordered sequence of events. But these artful conventions of storytelling now seem static, unreal. We are not telling it like it is.

Thus the third basic relationship between audience and performer. Random focus. This may seem to be a contradiction; really, it is very much like driving a car. What you see while driving depends upon what you see through the windshield coming towards and going away from you; what you see in the rear-view mirror going away and coming towards you; whatever fill-ins you get from the side-view mirror; occasional glances at the dashboard; and the sound from the radio.

Architecture should be able to cope with this random focus experience. It should use the rich landscape of industry, the rank invention of roadside America.

But no such luck.

Everyone knows why. Architecture makes beauty, it is expensive and forever. Architecture is serious business.

Let's assume that an architecture of random focus could be made. What would it be like? First, it would require a new idea of architectural space. A performance hall for random focus cannot be shaped like some gigantic pie. Indeed, there's no reason to believe that it should be *a* place; it may be one inside another, or a maze. Certainly it will be ambiguous. Neat distinctions between audience and performer provided by fixed seats are useless and unnecessary. Much as the happening exploits ambiguity between the planned and the unplanned, the performer and the spectator, the architectural space must reinforce the possibility that sometimes there need be no distinction between walls, floors, and ceilings. The space may be needed to reinforce motion, not restrict or define it. Walking inside a cube, the most dynamic events are the corners and they're the same four times over. Walking around inside the Statue of Liberty poses more questions than it answers (until you climb past her armhole). The IND subway station at 34th Street—escalators, galleries, stairs, ramps, and moving people—is a better image for this new architecture than anything since the prison etchings of Piranesi.

The conscious achievement of such spaces will require new images of order. Not static abstractions based on Euclid, but new ideas taken from the clover-leaf and the forms of collision.

The ceiling of the theatre in Cincinnati is an indication of what's required. Here the elements of enclosure and utility are made into contrasting patterns set against one another. But perhaps Euclid is still too much with us. It would be even better to use the random forms of an auto dump. All head-on collisions occurring at the same speed produce roughly the same form. This is just as much an order as piling bricks together in a cube.

Finally, an architecture of random focus could exploit the intricacies and varieties of utility. The jumbled exuberance of highway America seems to shame us, and in some excessive act of atonement architecture has laid on layers of design. We design the outside of buildings, their insides, their equipment, their landscapes—and all with different points of view. Less design would be better. The exposed steel beams do not impede the experience of seeing *Man of La Mancha* at the "temporary" ANTA-Washington Square theatre. I wouldn't cover up the cars on the Golden Gate Bridge, nor the air-conditioning ducts at the Cincinnati theatre.

Thought
Louis H. Sullivan

Louis H. Sullivan, the great American thinker and architect, designed over one hundred buildings from 1880 to 1895, including the Chicago Auditorium. Viewing art as act, his emphasis on visual rather than verbal thought and on reality as the present tense have special relevance for the director as well as for the architect.

"Thought" by Louis Sullivan, from *Kindergarten Chats*. George Wittenborn, Inc., "Documents of Modern Art No. 4," New York, 1947. Reprinted by permission of George Wittenborn, Inc.

I am quite a little impressed by what you say concerning our search for realities rather than mere words. It sounds straightforward and penetrating in one sense and illuminating in another. It seems to direct the faculties straight ahead of one, to focus them on something definite, something that I feel sure must exist and must be true. Still, for all that, we must use words, must we not?

Not necessarily. You need words only when you are to communicate with others by that special method called written or spoken language. Music, painting, sculpture, architecture are manifestly wordless forms of communication; so is gesture, so is facial expression. Words, however, are sometimes useful in explaining these and other things; in fact, explanation is one of the chiefest uses of words, if not the most important. By means of words we try to make clear to others our feelings, thoughts, intentions, recollections, and a great number of other things—in short, our mental or emotional attitude at any time on any subject, and for these purposes words are pretty well adapted, especially where purely human relations are concerned. But there is a vast domain lying just beyond the reach of words; and, to express our impressions of it, our insight into it—our contact with that which lies beyond man—the fine arts enter and carry on a form of language, of expression, of communication, of explanation, that lies beyond words.

But in passing I may say that real thinking is better done without words than with them, and creative thinking *must* be done without words. When the mind is actively and vitally at work, for its own creative uses, it has no time for word-building: words are too clumsy: you have no time to select and group them. Hence you must think in terms of *images*, of pictures, of states of feeling, of rhythm. The well-trained, well-organized, well-disciplined mind works with remarkable rapidity and with luminous intensity; it will body forth combinations, *in mass*, so complex, so far-reaching that you could not write them down in years. Writing is but the slow, snaillike creeping of words, climbing, laboriously, over a little structure that *resembles* the thought: meanwhile the mind has gone on and on, here and yonder and back and out and back again. Thought is the most rapid agency in the universe. It can travel to Sirius and return in an instant. Nothing is too small for it to grasp, nothing too great. It can go in and out of itself—now objective, now subjective. It can fasten itself most tenaciously on a fact, on an idea; or sublimate and attenuate itself with ethereal space. It will flow like water; it may become as stable as stone. You must familiarize yourself, my boy, with some of the possibilities of that extraordinary agent we call thought. Learn its uses and how to use it. Your test will always be—results; for real thinking brings real results. Thinking is an art, a science of magnificent possibilities. It is like an army with banners, where the horses cry ha! ha! at the sound of the trumpets. After a while you will instinctively learn to know whether a given man is thinking or mooning. It's a great art, my lad, remember this, it's an inspiring art. I mean the real, fluent, active thinking, not the dull stammering and mumbling of the mind: I mean the mind awake.

Words, after all, are but a momentary utterance of thought. They may be, in that utterance, as beautiful as the song of a bird we hear, but they are not the bird: for the bird is flown, and sings elsewhere another song in the forest, ere the first has become a memory with us. Of all the songs sung in the forest how many do we hear? And the forest sings its own song: how many of us hear it? And the song is of the forest, it is not the forest. So, let your thoughts be at times like the songs we hear not, the song of the singer in the solitudes. Therefore I would take your mind away from words, and bend it to thinking.

Thinking is a philosophy. Many people believe that when they are reading in a book they are of necessity thinking; that when they listen to someone's discourse they are thinking; but it does not necessarily follow. The best that reading and listening can do is to *stimulate* you to think your own thoughts, but, nine times out of ten, you are thinking the other man's thought, not your own. What occurs is like an echo, a reflection; it is not the real thing. Reading is chiefly useful in that it informs you of what the other man is thinking, it puts you in touch with the currents of thought among your fellows, or among those of the past. But you must carefully and watchfully discriminate between pseudo-thinking and real thinking. Pseudo-thinking is always imitative, real thinking is always creative. It cannot be otherwise. You cannot create unless you think, and you cannot truly think without creating in thought. Judge our present architecture by this standard and you will be amazed at its poverty of thought, its falsity in expression, its absence of manhood. Moreover, real thinking is always in the *present tense*. You cannot think *in* the past, you can only think *of* the past. You cannot think *in* the future, you can think only *of* the future. By great power of imagination you may think of the past and of the future *almost* in terms of the present: the one is the function of the historian, the other that of the prophet. But *reality* is of, in, by, and for the present, and the present only. Bear this strictly in mind, it is highly important, it must lie at the very root of your new education, for it is with the present only that you are in physical, vital contact, and I have told you that real thought, vital thought, is born of the physical senses. It is in the present, only, that you *really live*, therefore it is in the present, only, that you can *really think*. And in this sense you think organically. Pseudo-thinking is inorganic. The one is living, the other dead. The present is the *organic moment*, the *living moment*. The past and future do not exist: the one is dead, the other unborn. The present is that twinkling of an eye that separates death from life, as time moves on: but thought is quicker than the twinkling of an eye.

Excerpts from
An interview with Grotowski
Jerzy Grotowski

From "An Interview with Grotowski," by Richard Schechner. First published in *The Drama Review*, Vol. 13, No. 1 (T41). Copyright © 1968 by *The Drama Review.* Reprinted by permission. All Rights Reserved.

S*chechner* You often talk about the "artistic ethic," what it means to live the artistic life. . . .

Grotowski During the course I did not use the word "ethic," but nevertheless at the heart of what I said there was an ethical attitude. Why didn't I use the word "ethic?" People who talk about ethics usually want to impose a certain kind of hypocrisy on others, a system of gestures and behavior that serves as an ethic. Jesus Christ suggested ethical duties, but despite the fact that he had miracles at his disposal, he did not succeed in improving mankind. Then why renew this effort?

Perhaps we should ask ourselves only: Which actions get in the way of artistic creativity? For example, if during creation we hide the things that function in our personal lives, you may be sure that our creativity will fail. We present an unreal image of ourselves; we do not express ourselves and we begin a kind of intellectual or philosophical flirtation—we use tricks and creativity is impossible.

We cannot hide our personal, essential things—even if they are sins. On the contrary, if these sins are very deeply rooted—perhaps not even sins, but temptations—we must open the door to the cycle of associations. The creative process consists, however, in not only revealing ourselves, but in structuring what is revealed. If we reveal ourselves with all these temptations, we transcend them, we master them through our consciousness. That is really the kernel of the ethical problem: Do not hide that which is basic, it makes no difference whether the material is moral or immoral; our first obligation in art is to express ourselves through our own most personal motives.

Another thing which is part of the creative ethic is taking risks. In order to create one must, each time, take all the risks of failure. That means we cannot repeat an old or familiar route. The first time we take a route there is a penetration into the unknown, a solemn process of searching, studying, and confronting which evokes a special "radiation" resulting from contradiction. This contradiction consists of mastering the unknown—which is nothing other than a lack of self-knowledge—and finding the techniques of forming, structuring, and recognizing it. The process of getting self-knowledge gives strength to one's work.

The second time we come to the same material, if we take the old route we no longer have this unknown within us to refer to; only tricks are left— stereotypes that may be philosophical, moral, or technical. You see, it's not an ethical question. I'm not talking about the "great values." Self-research is simply the right of our profession, our first duty. You may call it ethical, but personally I prefer to treat it as part of the technique because that way there is no sense of its being sweet or hypocritical.

The third thing one could consider "ethical" is the problem of process and result. When I work—either during a course or while directing—what I say is never an objective truth. Whatever I say is a stimulus which gives the actor a chance to be creative. I say, "Fix your attention on this, search for this solemn and recognizable process." You must not think of the result. But, at the same time, finally, you can't ignore the result, because from the objective point of view the deciding factor in art is the result. In that way, art is im- moral. He is right who has the result. That's the way it is.

But in order to get the result—and this is the paradox—you must not look for it. If you look for it you will block the natural creative process. In looking, only the brain works; the mind imposes solutions it already knows and you begin juggling known things. That is why we must look without fixing our attention on the result. What do we look for? What, for example, are my associations, my key memories—recognizing these not in thought but through my body's impulses, becoming conscious of them, mastering and organizing them, and finding out whether they are stronger now than when they were unformed. Do they reveal more to us or less? If less, then we have not structured them well.

One must not think of the result and the result will come; there will be a moment when the fight for the result will be fully conscious and inevitable, engaging our entire mental machinery. The only problem is when.

It is the moment when our living creative material is concretely present. At that point one can use one's mind to structure the associations and to study the relationship with the audience. Things which were prohibited earlier are inevitable here. And, of course, there are individual variations.

There is the possibility that someone will begin with the play of the mind and then later leave it for a time and still later come back to it. If this is your way, still do not think of the result but of the process of recognizing the living material. . . .

Schechner Is there anything you would like to add?

Grotowski I want to underline certain points. What is unity of action in a production? Unity of action is not unity of action of the play. The audience knows that they are not seeing the real Hamlet in Denmark. One must always look for the word-for-word truth. The audience can watch the process of confrontation—the story and its motives meeting the stories and motives in our lives. If there is this contradictory action, this meeting, if the audience sees all these small details which lift the confrontation into flight, if they, as spectators, become part of this confrontation, we have the essential unity of action.

Next, the problem of ethics. There is only one thing that can be considered as ethics, everything else is technique. I do not believe that one can really create if one is not condemned to create. It must be for us the only thing possible in life, the essential task. But one cannot accomplish one's life-task and always be in disaccord with it. If, at certain moments, we do things that are in complete disaccord with our artistic task, something creative in us will be destroyed. Do not take this as a kind of sermon. This question must be treated with a great deal of healthy reasoning and with a sense of humor.

Finally, creativity in theatre does not exist if there is no score, a line of fixed elements. Without these there is only amateurism. One can esteem amateurism as one esteems a lovely rock that one has found at the beach, but it's not a work of art. What is an acting score? That is the essential question. The acting score is the element of contact. To take and to give the reactions and impulses of contact. If you fix these, then you will have fixed all the contexts of your associations. Without a fixed score, a work of mature art cannot exist. That's why a search for discipline and structure is as inevitable as a search for spontaneity. Searching for spontaneity without order always leads to chaos, a lost confession because an inarticulate voice cannot confess.

One cannot achieve spontaneity in art without the structuring of detail. Without this, one searches but never finds because too much freedom is a lack of freedom. If we lack structured detail we are like someone who loves all humanity, and that means he loves no one.

Creativity: a multi-faceted phenomenon
Donald W. MacKinnon

Donald W. MacKinnon has been director of the Institute of Personality Assessment and Research since its founding in 1949 at the University of California, Berkeley. The Institute has focused primarily on the study of creativity. He presented this paper as part of a symposium organized by Gustavus Adolphus College in Minnesota titled, "Creativity: A Discussion at the Nobel Conference."

"Creativity: A Multi-Faceted Phenomenon," by Donald W. MacKinnon, in *Creativity,* ed. by John D. Roslansky © 1970. North-Holland Publishing Company, Amsterdam. Reprinted by permission of the North-Holland Publishing Company and Donald W. MacKinnon.

M any are the meanings of creativity. Perhaps for most it denotes the ability to bring something new into existence, while for others it is not an ability, but the psychological processes by which novel and valuable products are fashioned. For still others, creativity is not the process but the product. Definitions of creativity range all the way from the notion that creativity is simple problem-solving to conceiving it as the full realization and expression of all of an individual's unique potentialities. One would be ill advised to seek to choose from among these several meanings the best single definition of creativity, since creativity properly carries all of these meanings and many more besides. Creativity is, indeed, a multi-faceted phenomenon.

What I am suggesting is that we think of creativity, not as a theoretical construct to be precisely defined, but rather as a rubric or a chapter heading under which a number of related concerns quite naturally fall. Conceived of in this way, there are at least four major aspects of creativity which deserve attention: (1) the creative process, (2) the creative product, (3) the creative person, and (4) the creative situation. Each of these can be formulated as a question to which empirical research, if it has not already done so, can provide some answers: (1) What is the nature of the creative process? What are the qualities and kinds of psychological processes by which creative solutions to problems are achieved? (2) What are creative products? By what qualities can they be identified? (3) What are the distinguishing traits and characteristics of creative persons? (4) What are the specifications of the creative situation, the life circumstance, or the social, cultural, and work milieu which facilitate and encourage the appearance of creative thought and action?

THE CREATIVE PROCESS

Those who have been fortunate enough to experience moments of high creativeness, as well as psychologists who have sought to understand the process whereby creative solutions to complex problems are achieved, are in remarkable agreement as to how the creative process is to be described. Both have noted certain distinguishable phases or stages in the process. Those that I would emphasize are the following: (1) a period of preparation during which one acquires the elements of experience and the cognitive skills and techniques which make it possible for one to pose a problem to himself, (2) a period of concentrated effort to solve the problem which may quickly be solved without much delay or difficulty, but which perhaps more often involves so much frustration and tension and discomfort that, out of sheer self-protection, one is led to (3) a period of withdrawal from the problem, a psychological going-out-of-the-field, a period of renunciation of the problem or recession from it, a time away from the problem that is often referred to as a period of incubation, which is followed by (4) a moment of insight that is accompanied by the exhilaration, glow, and elation of the restructuring "a-ha" experience, and (5) a period of verification, evaluation, elaboration, and application of the insight that one has experienced.

The creative process starts always with the seeing or sensing of a problem. The roots of creativeness lie in one's becoming aware that something is wrong, or lacking, or mysterious. One of the salient traits of a truly creative person is that he sees problems where others don't, and it is this that so often makes him unpopular. He insists on pointing out problems where others wish to deny their existence. A constantly questioning attitude is not an easy one to live with, yet in its absence many problems will not be sensed and consequently creative solutions of them will not be achieved. It has been said of Einstein that a part of his genius, like that of all great creative thinkers, was his inability to understand the obvious.

Creativity, although presently much emphasized in psychological research and in the thinking of many intelligent persons, as evidenced by the theme of this conference, has been one of the most neglected topics in the history of mankind. For far too long the creative process was thought of as inherently mysterious and unanalyzable, and the creative person as too sensitive and precious to be subjected to study. Today the creative process is recognized as scientifically researchable, and the creative person as capable of being assessed as any other human being.

It is misleading to refer to the creative process as though it were a single, unitary process. The term should be thought of as no more than a convenient summary label for a complex set of cognitive and motivational processes, and emotional processes too, that are involved in perceiving, remembering, imagining, appreciating, thinking, planning, deciding, and the like. Such processes are found in all persons, not merely in a chosen few, though obviously there are wide differences in the quality of these processes as well as in the degree to which persons are creative.

There are several factors that serve to block or inhibit a person's creativeness, first among them being the failure to see a problem where one exists. He who is overly satisfied with himself or with the situation in which he finds himself will be blind to shortcomings in himself or in his surroundings. Some measure of dissatisfaction with the present state of affairs—because it isn't clear or is incomplete or is in some sense disturbing—is a prerequisite for any attempt at transformation and improvement. There is the necessity in the creative person for what the poets have called "divine discontent" and what Voltaire chose to call "constructive discontent."

But becoming aware of a problem either by sensing it oneself or by having it pointed out by another will not insure that the problem will be solved creatively or even that it will be solved at all. There is the necessity that the problem be properly perceived and correctly defined. When it is, the very statement of the problem carries within it hints or suggestions as to how it may be solved. Improperly formulated, the problem may appear to be insolvable and, indeed, because of that very fact alone, it may be so. The first task, then, for one who is going to solve a problem creatively is to make a sufficient analysis of the complex situation, narrowing-down and simplifying it, until the crucial difficulty in the task is isolated.

Since most problems are neither clearly perceived nor correctly defined, the first task of a creative person, after becoming aware of a problem, is to see it in a light different from that in which it is originally presented. He must, in other words, be cognitively flexible, capable of reorganizing and restructuring the problem so that possibilities of the solution are carried within the new reformulation of it, if he is ever to solve it creatively.

Another important factor that may hamper attempts to solve problems creatively is the amount and availability of information or knowledge pertinent to the solution. Obviously, too little information or unavailable information will impede or even make impossible the solution of a problem; one must have the relevant and necessary information if the problem is to be solved. It is equally true, however, that too much information can interfere with the attainment of a creative solution. An excessive input of information can produce a state of what has been called "mental dazzle" which makes the problem look more complex than in actuality it is.

In many fields of endeavor the day has long since passed when the "primitive" is likely to be highly creative. In our scientifically and technologically advanced society the well-trained and highly educated professional must possess a large body of expertise. But, as just noted, too much knowledge can be a dangerous thing for creativity. It is not by chance that most of the major inventions have been made by persons who have not been experts in the field of their inventions. The expert, all too often, "knows" both on theoretical grounds and on the basis of empirical findings that certain things are not so or just cannot be done. The naive novice ventures what the expert would never attempt, and often enough succeeds. Some of the most creative scientific achievements have been accomplished by men who, trained in one field, enter upon another, there to formulate new problems and execute novel experiments with the expertise gained from earlier training and experience but at the same time with the naive perception of a stranger in a foreign land. The creative person is one who in his intellectual endeavors reconciles the opposites of expert knowledge and the childlike wonder of naive and fresh perception.

As a result of our training as well as of our experience most of us are disposed to approach any problem with as analytical an attitude as we can muster. We would be ill advised to do anything else, yet paradoxically, efficient, economical, and analytical perception is sometimes the enemy of creative insight. Analysis disassembles a whole into its parts, separating out from one another the elements of a problem. At a certain stage this is necessary, if progress is to be made; but in the course of analyzing a problem certain attributes which pertain to the phenomenon as a whole may be destroyed with the danger that eventually one "cannot see the woods for the trees." What is then needed, if there is to be a creative reorganization, is a compensating, free, spontaneous look at the whole situation, a naive and childlike apprehension of what is there. Such an attitude encourages the use of imagination in the form of analogies, and similes, and metaphors which are so crucial in the insightful reorganization of any problem.

There is much more to say about the creative process; other aspects of it will come to view as we turn our attention to the other facets of creativity.

THE CREATIVE PRODUCT

Anything that is experienced or made by man—an idea, a work of art, a scientific theory, the design of a building—may be a creative product; but if they are to qualify as true creations they must first meet certain criteria.

The first requirement of a creative product is novelty; it must be original. But novelty and originality need further specification, for one must at once ask, within what frame of reference or range of experiences is the product original—that of an individual, or of a group, or of mankind. Much that a young child experiences and many of his ideas will be new to him and in that sense creative for him, but if these experiences and ideas are had by practically all children they are not creative products for the society in which the child lives. Similarly, a man may think a thought new to him, yet it may be one of the most common thoughts in the whole world. Thus the creativeness of a product when judged in terms of novelty, originality, or statistical infrequence is always relative to a given population of products. Those that are most creative are the ones that are novel or original in the experience of an entire civilization or of all mankind.

Mere novelty of a product does not, however, justify its being called creative. There is a second requirement, namely, that the product be adaptive to reality. In other words, it must serve to solve a problem, fit the needs of a given situation, accomplish some recognizable goal. And this is as true for the expressive arts as for scientific and technological enterprises; in painting, the artist's problem is to find a more appropriate expression of his own experience; in dancing, to convey more adequately a particular mood or theme, etc.

A third requirement that a fully creative product must meet is that the insightful reorganization which underlies it be sustained, evaluated, elaborated, developed, and communicated to others—in other words, the creative product must be produced.

These, as I see it, are the three absolute criteria of a creative product. There are additional and, if you will, optional criteria. The more of them that are met, the more creative the product, for, though there may be many correct solutions to a problem, not all solutions are equally good. Some are more elegant than others. Thus there is a fourth criterion, met by a truly creative product, which demands that the answer which the product yields be an aesthetically pleasing one. The solution must be both true and beautiful.

The fifth and highest criterion for a creative product is seldom met since it requires that the product create new conditions of human existence, transcending and transforming the generally accepted experience of man by introducing new principles that defy tradition and change radically man's view of the world. Products of this level of creativeness would include the heliocentric theory of Copernicus, Darwin's theory of evolution, and Freud's psychoanalysis.

A distinction is frequently made between two kinds of creativity and creative products—artistic and scientific. Artistic creativity, it is said, results in products that are clearly expressions of the creator's inner states, his needs, perceptions, emotions, motivations, and the like. In creating them he has a deeply moving emotional experience or encounter. In scientific creativity, it is argued, the product is unrelated to the creator as a person, who in his creative work acts mainly as a mediator between externally defined needs and goals, operating on some aspect of his environment so as to produce a novel and appropriate product, but he adds little of himself or of his style as a person to the result. Such a description of scientific creativity is, however, more appropriate to technological and inventive activity in which the affective life of the worker plays relatively little role. In the highest reaches of science as well as of art it seems clear that there is a connection, albeit a mysterious one, between affectivity and the creative process. In the arts, the great productions appear to be exquisite attempts to resolve an internal turbulence. In the sciences, the important theoretical efforts seem to be personal cosmologies as much as anything else (witness Einstein, the prime example; Sherrington, Cannon, Born, Schrödinger, and others). The validity of the creative product thus is almost (but not quite) incidental to the forces driving its expression. And the forces are largely affective.

There is another sense in which the distinction between artistic and scientific and technological is often obliterated, for surely there are domains of creative striving in which the practitioner must be both artist and scientist-technologist; architecture would be a good example. Great architectural designs are surely expressions of the architect and thus very personal products, at the same time that they impersonally meet the demands of external problems. Surely, however, creative products are not limited to the realms of art and science and technological invention, but include such intangibles as those educational, social, business, and political climates which permit and encourage those who are in them to develop, and to express to the full, their creative potentials. In some cases even a person may be thought of as a creative product. These are the persons who have been variously called, by Goldstein and Maslow, the self-actualizing person, by Jung, the individuated person, by Rogers, the fully functioning individual, by Fromm, the productive character, and by Rank, the artist, the man of will and deed who makes a work of art out of his own life.

THE CREATIVE PERSON AND THE CREATIVE SITUATION

The other two facets of creativity, the creative person and the creative situation, I shall discuss together rather than separately, for it is to the answering of these two related questions that the researchers in the Institute of Personality Assessment and Research have contributed most directly and importantly. Our present concern with creativity is the most recent expression of the continuing research objectives of the Institute, namely, the delineation of the characteristics of individuals, who, in their personal lives and professional careers, function with high effectiveness, and the discovery in the life history, in the present life circumstance, and in the structure personality, of those factors which contribute to and make possible personal and professional effectiveness.

Although our researchers have revealed differences among creative workers in the several fields we have studied, our most impressive finding is the large number of attributes which they share in common. I shall therefore, and especially in view of the constraints of time, limit my remarks to a presentation of a few of the more salient characteristics of all the creative groups we have studied, emphasizing what is most generally true of creative persons.

Few would doubt that it is the events of the early years of life, and the social and intellectual climate in which a child grows up, that are most crucial for the nurturing of creative potential. However, again due to the constraints of time, in discussing the creative situation, I shall restrict myself to suggesting, mindful of the traits of creative persons, ways in which colleges might structure the curriculum and provide intellectual climates most likely to foster the creative potential of their students.

Creative persons are, in general, intelligent, whether their intelligence is estimated from the quality of their accomplishments of measure by standardized tests. Yet we have found essentially zero correlation between the measured intelligence of our creative subjects and the judged creativeness of their work; and, similarly, little relationship between their academic performance both in high school and in college, and their judged creativeness. One obvious implication of this finding is that a college which desires to nurture creativity should perhaps start by examining its admissions policy. If it wishes to admit mainly those who will do well academically it should, as most colleges in the past have done, give preference to those whose grades in high school are good and whose scores on tests of scholastic aptitude are high, since it has been repeatedly shown that these are the best predictors of academic achievement in college. If, however, a college seeks students with creative potential, it will inquire about the creative accomplishments of its applicants during the high school years or even earlier, for these are the best predictors of creative achievement in college and thereafter.

A certain level of intelligence is required for satisfactory academic achievement in college, and we should not delude ourselves into thinking that we can lower drastically the level of intelligence required for admission and still have students capable of meeting the standards of higher education as we have known them in the past. Traditionally there has been an overemphasis on intellect and aptitude in college admissions. The need to right that imbalance by giving more weight to factors of interest and motivation is clear; it is important, however, not to move so far as to substitute a new imbalance for the old. Non-intellective factors are no more the sole determinants of creative performance than intellective factors were in an earlier day thought to be, but they obviously need to be taken into account in selecting students.

Creative persons are independent in thought and action, and it is this independence of spirit that may well account for the lack of correlation between their high school and college grade-point averages and their subsequently demonstrated creativeness. Typically, they earn high grades in courses which interest and challenge them and poor grades in those that do not. Thus I would suggest that in selecting students at both the graduate and undergraduate levels more attention be paid to the pattern of grades earned rather than to mere grade-point average or rank in class.

Since it is a fundamental characteristic of those with creative potential that they are strongly motivated to achieve in situations in which independence of thought and action are called for and have much less interest or drive to achieve in situations which demand conforming behavior, as much opportunity as possible should be provided for independent study and research. All too often, however, in most colleges independent study is restricted to honor students, and while they too can profit from such a program, there would seem to be little justification for excluding from such opportunities the very students likely to profit most from them.

Creative persons are open to experience both of the inner self and the outer world. As between perceiving (becoming aware of something) and judging (coming to a conclusion about something) creative persons are on the side of perception, receptive, and seeking to know as much about life as possible. Their perceptive attitude expresses itself in curiosity; it is the hallmark of their inquiring mind. Moreover, creative persons are discerning, observant in a differentiated fashion; they are alert, capable of concentrating attention and shifting it appropriately; they are fluent in scanning thoughts and producing those that serve to solve the problems they undertake; and, characteristically, they have a wide range of information at their command. From an associationistic viewpoint, creativity is putting the elements of one's experience into new combinations, and the more bits of information one has and the more combinations that are formed, the more likely it is on purely statistical grounds that some of them will be creative.

Colleges can nurture and reward the perceptiveness and curiosity of their students by providing a wide variety of courses of study. All too often, though, they curb the far-ranging interests of their students by demanding that an excessive number of units of study be taken in the major subject. In all education, and especially in professional education, an openness of mind, and thus the creative potential of students, can be fostered by a broadening of their experience in fields of study beyond their specialty. Such wanderings should be encouraged, for they provide the student with that range of information and knowledge without which the highest levels of creative achievement are unlikely to be reached.

The creative person's perceptive openness to his inner life, to his feelings and emotions, to his imagery and symbolic processes, and to much that in others remains unconscious, provides not only multiplicity and richness of experience but also the experience of conflicting opposites and at times even of chaos. But without such psychic turbulence combined with an independence of spirit, one is not likely to grow creatively. We who are teachers need constantly to remind ourselves that students who combine these traits will often enough act in ways that are disturbing to us. What we need at such times is some of the tolerance that they show, if we are genuinely to support and encourage them in their creative striving.

Creative persons are intuitive both in their perceptions and in their thinking. Keenly perceptive as they are, they do not remain unimaginatively focused upon what is given by the senses. Rather, they immediately grasp the deeper meanings, the implications, and the possibilities for use or action of that which they experience.

Traditional emphases in education—rote learning, learning of facts for their own sake and unrelated to other facts, repeated drill of material, precise memorization—are often enough valuable and required, but they contribute little to the nurturance of the processes of intuition and, indeed, seem almost designed to inhibit them. If intuitive powers are to be strengthened, quite different exercises are required, for example, transferring of training from one subject to another; searching for common principles in terms of which facts from quite different spheres of knowledge can be related; developing a feeling for analogies, similes, and metaphors; seeking the symbolic equivalents of experience in the widest number of sensory and imaginal modalities; engaging in imaginative play; training in retreating from the facts in order to see them in larger perspective and in relation to more aspects of the larger context thus achieved.

Creative persons prize most highly the theoretical and the aesthetic. Their valuing of the theoretical is congruent with their intuitiveness, for both orient them to seek a deeper and more meaningful reality beneath or beyond that which is present to their senses.

The theoretical value is the highest value in scientific and scholarly research. One of the best ways for a professor to nurture the theoretical interests of his students is to engage them in his own researches, and not merely as laboratory assistants or technicians, but as full-fledged collaborators in all phases of the research and most importantly in its conceptualization and planning. An even better way of fostering the development of students' theoretical interests is, of course, to encourage them to formulate their own problems and to design and execute their own researches.

The truly creative person is not satisfied with the solutions to his problems unless they are also aesthetically pleasing—unless, to use the mathematician's term, they are elegant. The aesthetic viewpoint permeates all of the work of the creative person, and it should find expression in the teaching of all skills, and disciplines, and professions if creativity is to be nurtured.

The Swiss psychologist Carl Jung described human nature as ruled by a law of complementariness: the tendency for every trait of man's conscious and manifest personality to be matched or complemented by its opposite in his unconscious and undeveloped self. Those aspects of self and experience which are unconscious and unexpressed in man partake of these character- istics for one of three reasons: either they have been neglected because con- scious attention was never paid to them, or they have been repressed or suppressed because to experience them would be too painful, or they have remained undeveloped and unexpressed because the conscious ego, the per- son, is not yet mature enough to experience them. To experience what is unconscious and to give expression to it in a fully conscious manner is not easy and often enough painful and frightening. Consequently, most persons live a sort of half-life, giving expression to only a very limited part of them- selves, and realizing only a few of their potentialities. In contrast, the creative person has the courage to experience the opposites of his nature and to attempt some reconciliation of them in an individuated expression of himself.

The most salient mark of a creative person, the central trait at the core of his being is, as I see it, just this sort of courage. It is not physical courage of the type that might be rewarded by the Carnegie Medal or the Congressional Medal of Honor, although a creative person may have courage of this kind, too. Rather, it is personal courage, courage of the mind and spirit, psycho- logical or spiritual courage that is the radix of a creative person: the courage to question what is generally accepted; the courage to be destructive in order that something better can be constructed; the courage to think thoughts unlike anyone else's; the courage to be open to experience both from within and from without; the courage to follow one's intuition rather than logic; the courage to imagine the impossible and try to achieve it; the courage to stand aside from the collectivity and in conflict with it if necessary; the courage to become and to be oneself.

If my assessment of the creative person is correct, our task as educators, whether we be parents or professors, is not so much to teach creativity as it is to encourage our charges by ourselves being those creative persons in whom the opposites of our nature have been reconciled, creative persons with whom they can identify. Thus we each would become an educator in the original meaning of the word—one who brings forth or educes from another that which exists as a potentiality within him through being an example of that which is desired.

Foreword to
They became what they beheld
Edmund Carpenter
and
Ken Heyman

Edmund Carpenter is an anthropologist and the author, with Ken Heyman, of *They Became What They Beheld,* a book heavily influenced by Marshall McLuhan, that explores changing modes of perception in contemporary society. The book includes fascinating photographs by Ken Heyman.

recently came across the following rules of communication, posted in a school of journalism:

1 Know your audience and address yourself directly to it.
2 Know what you want to say and say it clearly and fully.
3 Reach the maximum audience by utilizing existing channels.

Whatever sense this may have made in a world of print, it makes no sense today. In fact, the reverse of each rule applies.

If you address yourself to an audience, you accept at the outset the basic premises that unite the audience. You put on the audience, repeating clichés familiar to it. But artists don't address themselves to audiences; they create audiences. The artist talks to himself out loud. If what he has to say is significant, others hear and are affected.

The trouble with knowing what to say and saying it clearly and fully, is that clear speaking is generally obsolete thinking. Clear statement is like an art object: it is the afterlife of the process which called it into being. The process itself is the significant step and, especially at the beginning, is often incomplete and uncertain. Columbus's maps were vague and sketchy, but showed the right continent.

The problem with full statement is that it doesn't involve: it leaves no room for participation; it's addressed to consumer, not co-producer. Allan Kaprow posted a few small posters about Berkeley: "*Suppose* you were interested in designing a primer, in mixed media, etc. . . . Allan Kaprow will be in Berkeley in July and August." No phone, address, dates, terms. He found, however, that those who wanted to work with him, and those he wanted to work with, located him without difficulty.

Reaching the maximum audience may be the last thing one wants to achieve. George Segal says, "I don't give myself to everybody, I give myself very intensely to my work, my wife, my kids, my few friends. I can't begin to give myself indiscriminately to all. It's the only thing that makes me pause about, say, Ginsberg's preachings of universal love or even California ideas about Esalen and touching."

Utilizing existing channels can wipe out a statement. There is a widely accepted misconception that media merely serve as neutral packages for the dissemination of raw facts. Photographers once thought that by getting their photographs published in *Life*, they would thereby reach large audiences. Gradually they discovered that the only message that came through was *Life* magazine itself, and that their pictures had become but bits and pieces of that message. Unwittingly they contributed to a message far removed from the one they intended.

The same thing occurs on TV guest shows. Guests accept invitations to appear on programs in the hopes their messages will reach new and wider audiences, but even when they are treated in a friendly manner, they generally come away with a sense of failure. Somehow the message transmitted is far removed from the message intended. The original message has been declassified by an alien medium. "Oh, what a blow that phantom gave me!" cries Don Quixote.

The young today shun the hardware of the past. Marx thought the big question was: Who owns the presses? Software makes hardware obsolete, an encumbrance, creating a false sense of power and security. The young package their messages in media that fit their messages, that is, they create new media to fit their messages. In so doing, they create their own audiences. Some of these audiences may be very small at the beginning. In Houston I met film makers producing films for audiences of no more than six. The point was that they would reach the right people in the right way with the right message.

It is one of the curiosities of a new medium, a new format, that at the moment it first appears, it's never valued, but it is believed. What it offers, I believe, is a sudden insight, an unexpected glimpse into a reality that, at most, was merely suspected but never before seen with such clarity.

Like guerrillas, the young are in a favored position; they don't need or want the hardware and audiences of yesterday.

Funerals, celebrations and novelty
Jean-Claude van Itallie

Jean-Claude van Itallie is best known as a playwright whose work with the Open Theatre led to such plays as *American Hurrah* and *The Serpent*. Many of his plays are short, a dramatic form rediscovered in the 1960's, and all are tied directly to our modern age, the problems of which he discusses here.

A couple of months ago I was invited to Brown University where they were having a smorgasbord of playwrights: in a large room in separated arm-chairs, our names crayonned and pinned to the nearest wall, were Michael Smith, Rochelle Owens, Israel Horovitz, Arthur Sainer, Meg Terry, Richard Schechner, Susan Yankowitz, and me. The students wandered freely from group to group, to partake of us so to speak. Not much happened. The only black student snapped his fingers in justifiable disgust and left. I followed him and asked why he had come in the first place to such a meeting. "The ball is with you white boys," he said. "I want to find out some things I can use."

I told him he was mistaken. There is no more ball here. We're pretending to throw it around. About five years ago, or seven, the vital energies of a lot of young people did go into theatre, a new kind of theatre, and we were happy about it. Off-off-Broadway blossomed spontaneously, untended by grants or other institutional encouragements. But even by the time the media discovered us, the vital stomping ground had moved elsewhere, to rock, then into life-styles (the hippies), until that too was invaded and tamed and the form became direct political action: the Yippies, the Weathermen. Now that's fading. Political groups are transforming into consciousness-raising groups, a creative separatism has set in (the Blacks, the women, the gays, the Jews) and many who are twenty-five or so are running out to the country communes to breathe a little clean air.

Developments in the theatre parallel the Movement, and the Movement is responding, of course, to the changing desperations of the country. To me there seems at the moment to be a pall over the theatre as there is a pall over the country. We are in mourning for ourselves, our past, our future, and most particularly our present. We have the president we deserve, the president we have conjured out of our worst mechanistic nightmares, and that president casts his dark shadow over the land and the world. There is nothing forthcoming from the great living playwrights (Beckett, Genet), or the good ones even (Pinter). What we hear from Williams and Albee is no longer in joint with the times.

In the Old Days, six or seven years ago, it seemed important to use theatre to point up where things were at, to shock ourselves out of a lethargic insouciance to our own self-created environment, and to put our hacked-up selves into focus. But it no longer seems to the point to provide shocks. Shocks are everywhere. Violence is less and less hidden, and our duplicity with it more and more in the open. The Washington Mayday police maulings—which, although not more violent than many other events, are still more shocking than anything which can be put on the stage—were publicly acknowledged by Nixon as his own. In a play I started to write a couple of years ago a character tells of how he saw a giant centipede fixed in the sky over Cambridge, Massachusetts, and of how, when he over-casually mentioned the fact in a bar, nobody would hear him. Today, however, everyone sees the centipede blacking out the skies over the cities. There is no need anymore to put it all on a stage. *MacBird, Viet Rock,* and *America Hurrah* are past forms. There is a need to take action, but that is different from writing plays. What I do as a citizen—demonstrate, march, talk, publicly declare my sexual preferences—is beside the point of what it is timely to do in the theatre. It's fruitless to try to shock an American audience in 1971.

It's not insignificant that students at Brown and elsewhere want to learn from playwrights and actors rather than from plays, that what they want in fact to know is how to make their own plays. Both the theatre and the Movement are going toward what I would venture to call a greater and greater authenticity of experience, an expression of that experience. There is a kind of truth abroad, often called "testimony," and often confused with art. Plays which have stirred the most interest in universities in the past couple of years are so-called group plays in which the commitment of the actor is to his material rather than to his character, and is political rather than pseudo-psychological. The actors of troupes like the Open Theatre, the Performance Group and the Polish Lab often appear indistinguishable from the material they perform. The players, at best, appear to be the play, and the playwright non-existent. What is in fact happening is that both players and playwright are in a more revolutionary attitude toward material they are handling, toward questions they are asking themselves. Of course the moment a single word or gesture is repeated even once it becomes art rather than life, and it must be planned for. The actors in pieces like *The Serpent* and *Terminal* must give up some of their ego in favor of the ensemble acting, and the playwright must give up some of his in favor of a collective exploration of the material, but both are still, at least to date, performing their traditional functions, in that it is the actors who confront the audience, the playwright providing words and structure to the material. Much as the original hippies took the Movement one step away from the establishment by choosing to embody art rather than to create it, some of the theatre groups are trying to demonstrate by their very existence that there is an alternative way of living that is possible, a different form from the old family ones which is viable. Living Theatre has gone even a step further, paralleling the Movement into direct political action: the art of the Living Theatre now *serves* their politics. In a sense Bob Wilson has succeeded in staging "himself" very authentically in *The Life and Times of Sigmund Freud.*

Marcuse said in a lecture that the function of art in revolutionary or disorderly times (and I am only paraphrasing) is to demonstrate order. The creative question is *which* order to demonstrate, and how. As a single individual, a playwright cannot do much in his own being, except perhaps in teaching situations in which, if he is lucky and has the power, he may manage to turn himself "on" for students, and consequently turn them on (this is what Allen Ginsberg does, sometimes best in absolute silence). But I have been conditioned to "produce" something other than creative silence, and I can't shake that. Also words and the structure of events fascinate me. I like to write plays rather than only try to be one.

In terms of the form of plays there is a certain "demonstration of order" I would like to try. I'd like a theatre of transportation, not an escapist theatre but one which would transport people from the death-dealing rhythms of their lives into another state of being. I would like, as an example, to present a play which would start in different rooms for different people (why should everyone always arrive at the same time?), which would include breathing, touching, a change of clothes perhaps, possibly water-drinking or immersion as in many temple rituals, and words, words economically chosen for their poetry and directness (and not invented on the spur of the moment by the actors). The audience might unite at last in some large room for some planned celebration of awareness.

Another way to transport an audience, traditionally, is through words. But we would have to use words differently than we use them now. We have to rediscover them. There is an understandable but frightening mistrust of words everywhere, because they are used as lying tools of the power forces. And yet, in the longer view, they are the only tools we have yet devised, we humans, to communicate precisely to one another. It seems to me it is not now a question of casting out words but of renewing language to serve our best selves.

The theatre may indeed have just begun to stir in these directions: the Bread and Puppet Theater serves bread at its communions; the Company Theatre of Los Angeles had a wonderful evening, or the first half of a wonderful evening called, aptly enough, the *James Joyce Memorial Liquid Theatre*. No one has yet liberated the theatre as James Joyce did the novel, but people are thinking about it. Peter Handke, the strongest new voice I hear on any continent, seems obsessed with the necessary reinvention of language.

Another kind of theatre, however, will demand another kind of participator, a different social context. The most action a bourgeois, city audience-member performs today is paying money and sitting down. And a "new" piece of theatre happening today, in the smogged and habit-bound confines of New York City, say, is likely to be greeted, at very best, as yet another gimmick, a novelty.

Theatre is truly linked to its times. The times are dark; their most expressive form: a funeral. If we're to change the theatre then we must simultaneously change everything: our social context and ourselves. Personally, at thirty-five I have the feeling of being in a cocoon. I have no idea how I'm going to come out, but I sense the first stirrings in the dark.

Just at this moment Alice felt a very curious sensation, which puzzled her a good deal until she made out what it was: she was beginning to grow larger again, and she thought at first she would get up and leave the court; but on second thought she decided to remain where she was as long as there was room for her.

APPENDIX I
PLAYS FOR PLAYING

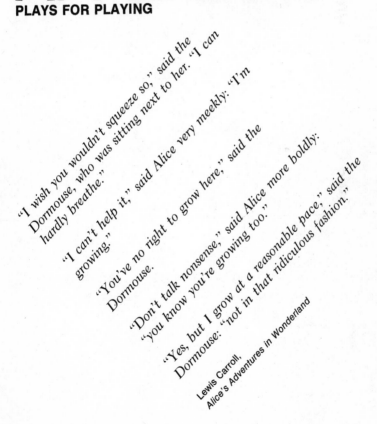

"I wish you wouldn't squeeze so," said the Dormouse, who was sitting next to her. "I can hardly breathe."

"I can't help it," said Alice very meekly: "I'm growing."

"You've no right to grow here," said the Dormouse.

"Don't talk nonsense," said Alice more boldly: "you know you're growing too."

"Yes, but I grow at a reasonable pace," said the Dormouse: "not in that ridiculous fashion."

Lewis Carroll,
Alice's Adventures in Wonderland

Rehearsal
Benjamin Bradford

Character

CLIFTON MATTINGLY

The play takes place in Clifton Mattingly's apartment, an unfurnished converted flat in the far reaches of the East Village. Only the living room, if one could call it that, can be seen or suggested. There is no furniture at all. After a moment Clifton enters. He is twenty-two, painfully shy. He walks about anxiously for a moment, then girding his shoulders, makes a ringing noise and mimes opening the door.

CLIFTON

(*Enthusiastically*) Hello. How are you? Have any trouble finding the place? (*A beat*) It's easy when you follow instructions. Not the best part of town, I guess, but it's good enough for me. Here, let me have your coat. (*Mimes taking a coat from his imaginary visitor*) Very nice coat. I like the color. (*A beat*) Is it blue? (*Again a slight pause*) Looks blue under the light. Actually, I don't have very good color sense. Can't tell blue from green, and sometimes red. I guess I don't pay enough attention. (*Slight laugh*) When I was in kindergarten, I'd as well draw an elephant yellow as gray or whatever. (*Faltering*) You know. (*Mimes hanging up the coat*) Do you mind if I hang it here? (*Small laugh*) It's perfectly safe . . . I'd do the sky red and the grass orange. I failed kindergarten art, and that's really failing. Did you have a good day? (*A moment*) Oh, the usual things. You know how it is in a hardware store . . . busy sometimes, not so busy at others. I guess you're not too interested in that. (*Gently*) Did you have a nice day? Oh, I asked you that. You did, you said you did. It's very nice of you to come all the way down here . . . in the rain. I wouldn't have asked you if I'd known it was going to rain. If I didn't want you to come, I wouldn't have asked . . . You know. (*Suddenly*) I guess you want to sit down. (*Crossing left*) I'll get you a chair. (*He exits left but continues to speak*) I keep the chairs in the kitchen. Don't keep much out there. Well, the truth is, I don't have much. You know. (*He returns carrying a folded metal chair*) It's a folding chair . . . (*Quickly*) But it's perfectly safe . . . and comfortable. I think it's guaranteed to support three hundred pounds. (*Embarrassed laugh*) Of course, I don't think you weigh three hundred pounds . . . or anywhere near it. I mean . . . if I did, I wouldn't have asked you at all. I keep trim by climbing all those stairs. Very good exercise, you know. I go up and down them all the time. When I moved in here two and a half months ago, I could barely get up the first three flights without stopping for breath, but . . . now, I don't have any trouble at all . . . just breeze up and down like I was on the street floor. (*A beat*) You're out of breath, I should have noticed. (*Opening the chair*) Here, I'll fix the chair for you. You just sit down and be comfortable. Well, it's not as comfortable as some, but it's more comfortable than the floor. (*A laugh*) It's not as far down as the floor. You know what I mean. Your color's getting better all the time. (*Quickly*) You want a drink, don't you? I asked you for a drink and you want it. You see, I'm not really used to having company. I hardly know anyone, and when you don't know anyone, you don't have much company. I hope you like vodka. (*A pause*) It's all I have. Wait a minute, I have a small bottle of red wine . . . it's sort of sour. (*A smile*) You like red wine? But you'd rather have vodka? Wonderful. I got some quinine water. I hope you like quinine water. Do you think it's too cold? Well, I mean, it's a drink for summer, and now it's winter, and well, I'm not used to company. (*A brief pause*) Especially when they are so pretty. (*Quickly*) I'm not making fun. I think you are pretty. I like a girl that's filled out. (*A small leer*) Especially in the right places. I'm going to get some furniture up here as soon as I can or I'll find another place. I'd rather live uptown, you know, by the museum, but I just took the first place I looked at. I guess it's not too bad. (*A beat*) It's not too good either. When I have time to look around, I'll find another place. And I'll want you to come there too. I have another chair. It's in the kitchen too. You just sit there and be comfortable and I'll be right back. (*He exits left and continues to speak*) Can you hear me out there? Sound carries nicely in here . . . these thin walls. I bet you were busy today, being Friday. I didn't come in for lunch because I took a pimiento cheese sandwich . . . and an apple. The pimiento cheese was getting old and if I didn't eat it today, I'd just have to throw it out. And I knew I'd see you tonight anyway. I plan to be in Monday . . . same table. (*He enters with one vodka and tonic*) I forgot. Monday's your day off. I'll see you Tuesday then. Here's a nice, cool drink. I'm going to have one too. (*He slowly drinks the vodka*) I had the ice and everything ready to go. I was really prepared for . . . you know. Say, you've got nice legs. I never noticed in the restaurant. You've got on a shorter skirt. Knees are nice too. You still have your baby dimples. (*A beat*) I'm twenty-two. That's not so young. I've lived a long time. Twenty-two years is a long time any way you look at it. (*A slight laugh*) You don't look as if you could possibly be that old. You're not much over thirty, are you? Why should I care? (*He finishes the drink*) Well, age is relative, very relative. I meant to bring my own chair in here. I'll be right back. (*He finishes the drink*) You lean back and wait a minute, please. (*He exits and quickly returns with another chair and another drink*) See, I have two just alike. They're a matched set. (*A beat*) I went to college because I didn't have anything better to do for four years. I didn't learn a thing I didn't know already. (*A slight pause*) You drink very fast. (*He is drinking the second vodka*) I could have taught school. I have a teacher's certificate. But if you want to know the truth, I think I'd be scared of children. (*A laugh*) And I wanted a little excitement in the big city first. You know. Do you think the big city is exciting? (*A beat*) I guess it wouldn't be to you. You have nice knees, do you mind if I . . . ? (*Quickly*) I guess you want to finish your drink. Do you always drink so fast? Of course, you're thirsty after all those stairs. Now, here you are, and here I am. Do you like it here? Are you comfortable? I don't mind if you take off your shoes. Wow, I believe in being comfortable. I'll loosen my tie. (*He does*) Wow, that's better, isn't it? I bet you never thought you'd be up here in my apartment, drinking vodka, with your shoes off. I bet you didn't think that a week ago, when I walked in your place and ordered a bowl of vegetable soup. That was doggone good soup. You know I'm terribly attracted to your knees. (*A beat*) You're welcome. (*Pulling the chairs very close together*) You feel warm. (*A pause*) Are you warm? Must be the drink. I'm a little warm too, even with my collar unbuttoned. (*He unbuttons all the shirt buttons*) There, I'm not hirsute. (*A laugh*) That means hairy. I'm not very hairy. Of course I have hair some places . . . but not on my chest. One or two maybe. You want another drink? Wow, you drink faster than any girl I ever saw. (*He rises*) Oh sure. I've known lots of girls. Not at college, it was a boy's school. But I went out on weekends . . . when I wasn't studying. (*Pause*) Yeah, it was pretty sexy being in college. I'll get you another drink. (*He finishes the drink and chokes on it*) Excuse me. You know, when you said you'd like to know me better, I was really amazed. Not a lot of people want to know me better. I'm really very shy. I don't seem to be, I know, but I am . . . and quiet, very quiet. (*Boyishly*) Your hair looks clean. You must have washed it. Feels good, too. You don't mind, do you? The way the light shines on it, I could tell it was clean. (*Suddenly*) You want another drink . . . already? Sure, if you want one. (*He exits and returns with another drink*) I bet you're feeling very warm now . . . all over. I know I am. My lower lip feels numb when I drink too much. (*He drinks*) Say, I just bought a pint of vodka. I could go out and get some more. (*A pause*) Those stairs . . . I'm feeling pretty good. (*A pause*) I thought you were. I could tell. Wow, why don't we just let our hair down? You know what I mean. (*He mimes handing her the drink and drinks it himself*) God no. I'm not trying to get you drunk. (*A beat*) Or me either. I guess I could do most anything I want with you. (*Quickly*) That's not what I meant. No I meant . . . Wow, I didn't mean that at all. I just meant, I'd like doing things to you. (*Suddenly*) No, that's not what I meant. I mean, I'm glad you're here. (*He is getting a little high*) Yeah, they called me the quiet one. Can you believe that? I've been talking like a breeze to you. I guess you have to meet the right person to talk to. Yeah, I knew I'd come here and meet someone . . . that liked me. Yeah, I guess my leg is hot too. (*Quickly*) I'll get a better job when I have time to look for one. I'm just getting my bearings now. (*A moment*) I could always go back home, I suppose. I don't much want to. Talking to my mother is like talking to nobody. It's more listening than talking anyway. (*A pause*) It's next door . . . really part of the kitchen. That's why the kitchen is so small. They put the bathroom in half of it. (*Rising*) Just pull the chain when you're through. Don't worry about the noise, I'll hum or something. And don't worry about the door either, I won't come in there. I'm not that kind. I guess they just didn't think a door was necessary. (*Singing*) "Roses are blooming in Picardy La de da, la de da, la de da, Roses are blooming in Picardy." (*He completes the verse whistling*)

There you are. Didn't take long at all. Yeah, it does sound like a waterfall. Say, you know what it really sounds like? We had a cyclone in Georgia when I was growing up. That's exactly the way it sounded. Boy, I won't forget that noise. Didn't touch our house at all, but blew two houses across the street completely away. (*He sits*) I don't know where they went. Somewhere, I guess. First thing you know, more houses were put up, and before I could remember how it looked before . . . I'd forgotten. (*Seriously*) The bedroom is through the kitchen. Nicest room I've got. I brought the chest all the way up here by myself. I'm going to paint it when I find the time. (*A pause*) Probably blue. Well, I don't really have a bed yet. I don't even know how I'll get it up the stairs. You saw how narrow the turns are. The army cot folds up. I can take it when I leave. (*Very close to her*) It's narrow and it's hard, but you get used to it. Why, I've been sleeping on it over two months, since I moved out of the YMCA. (*A pause*) Wow, I sure didn't think I looked that young. I guess I ought to grow a beard or something. (*Laughs*) As slow as it grows it'd take five or six years then I wouldn't need to look older. (*Earnestly*) I shave at least twice a week. If you're all that hot, you could take off your dress. I sit around here with nothing on most of the time. Sure, it'd be fine with me. (*A beat*) If I'd known you like to drink that much, I'd have bought a bigger bottle. Say, how'd you like the red wine? What's it matter, alcohol is alcohol. (*He exits and continues to speak*) Wait a minute. Just hang your dress on that nail by your coat. I usually put my jacket there when I come in. (*Offstage*) If you want to take something else off, feel free. I just want you to be comfortable, really comfortable. (*He returns with a glass of wine*) I thought we could share this . . . make it a loving cup. You know, you take a drink and I'll take a drink. (*He drinks*) You've got the biggest breasts I've ever seen . . . or imagined. No honest, I think they're horribly attractive. Fascinating really. (*Sitting*) Do you mind? (*Drinking*) I hope . . . well, I hope you won't think I'm too skinny. Never have been able to gain weight. Well, if you are too fat, I'm too thin. Doesn't make any difference when two people are . . . You know. (*Taking off his shirt*) I could put a towel on the chair if you're really cold. I mean, I don't want you to be cold. Here, just put my shirt on the seat. (*He puts his shirt on the other chair*) Better? (*A beat*) Too much light out here. I'll take off my pants in the bedroom. (*Laughing*) Wow. No, I mean . . . if you don't think you'd fit on a cot, I could bring a blanket in here. Yeah, the floor is full of splinters. I learned that the first week I was here. Boy, I wouldn't walk on that floor

without shoes for anything. (*Earnestly*) When I get up and go to the bathroom, I always put on my shoes. I have a thick blanket. A birthday present
from my mother. She was scared I'd freeze up here. (*A beat*) I guess I'm
not warm all the time, but I haven't frozen. (*Laughing*) Well, you can see
that. (*Seriously*) Why don't you look at the cot . . . ? You can make up
your mind then. (*Rising*) Now? (*A beat*) Yeah, I'm ready if you are. Wow.
I'd be happy to kiss you. (*A long pause*) I've never been kissed like that. I
didn't know people did. Aren't you afraid of germs and colds and things?
(*A beat*) No, I'm not afraid of anything. (*Crossing left*) Sure I'm certain.
(*Softly*) Say, wait a second . . . Afterward . . . (*A beat*) I mean . . . well,
you know . . . (*A wistful, boyish smile*) You know . . . after . . . I hope
you still like me. (*He exits quickly*)

Curtain

The tiger, the man, and the mouse

adapted by **Richard Aumiller** *from an East Indian folk tale,*
The Tiger, the Brahman, and the Jackal

The stage is bare except for a large wooden cage hanging from the ceiling. The raising and lowering of the cage is controlled from offstage. In general, each character speaks the narration that pertains to himself and acts out the story as he tells it by doing what he says.

Tiger (*enters, prowling*). Once upon a time, there was a ferocious tiger (*growl*) who was very hungry. One evening, he decided to prowl around the jungle and see if he couldn't find someone to eat. He listened very carefully, but he couldn't hear anything. Then he sniffed the air, but he couldn't smell anything. Finally, he looked one way . . . and then, he looked the other way; but he didn't see anything. He was just getting ready to give up and try another part of the jungle, when . . . (*the cage falls over the tiger, who has been backing into position during all of this*) . . . he found himself caught in a trap. He tried to get out *through* the bars, he tried to ram *into* the bars, he even tried to *chew* the bars! But he just couldn't get out.

Man (*enters*). Just then, who should come walking through the jungle but a man, on his way home from working in the fields.

Tiger When the tiger saw the man, he cried out to him, "Help! I'm trapped in this cage; I can't get out. Please help me. Let me out and I will become your servant. I'll do anything you say; only set me free."

Man "Oh no, no! I know what you'd do if I set you free—you'd eat me for supper, that's what you'd do. I'm not going to let you out."

Tiger (*sobbing and crying*) Oh, I could never do *that*! Let me out and I'll prove it; I'll be your friend forever. (*the man does not respond; the tiger tries a different angle*) Oh, what am I going to do? Don't leave me trapped in this cage. They'll come and take me far away. They'll put me in a circus or a zoo. I'll never see my family again.

Man   Now the man had begun to cry, too. Men cannot stand to see tigers cry. (*the tiger hands the man a handkerchief through the bars; the man blows his nose very loudly and hands it back*) "All right, all right! Since you put it that way, I'll let you out." (*the man starts to lift the cage*)

Tiger   But the man had no sooner lifted the cage, then the tiger leaped out with a mighty roar and landed on top of the poor man. "You fool! Now what is to prevent me from eating you? After being trapped in that cage, I'm hungrier than before. I'm so hungry I could eat you in one bite." (*the tiger grabs the man's hand and prepares to take a big bite; but he is halted by the entrance of the mouse*)

Mouse   (*entering in a hurry-scurry fashion*) But just as the tiger was about to begin his supper, a little mouse came scurrying through the jungle. When he saw what was about to happen (*the mouse stops dead and stares at the tiger and the man*), he shouted out in his loudest squeek: "Wait!"

Tiger   "What?"

Mouse   "Wait!"

Tiger   "Why?"

Mouse   "Why?"

Tiger   "Why!"

Mouse   (*thinking fast*) "Uh . . . I'm confused. I don't understand what's happening here."

Man   "The tiger here was trapped in the cage there; I set him free and now the ungrateful beast is going to eat me for dinner. It is really quite simple."

Mouse   (*acting very flustered*) "Not so simple, not so simple at all! Oh, my poor brain, my poor brain. Now, let me see, let me see; how did it all begin? You (*indicating the man*) were in the cage, and the tiger came walking by. . . ."

Tiger   "Phooey. What a fool you are, mouse. *I* was in the cage!"

Mouse   "Oh, yes, of course, how stupid of me. (*the mouse pretends to tremble in fear*) Yes, I was in the cage—no, I wasn't. Dear, dear! Where are my wits? Let me see, the tiger was in the man, and the cage came walking by—no, no; that's not it either. I'm afraid you'd better go ahead and finish your dinner. I'm never going to understand."

Tiger   (*in a rage over the mouse's stupidity*) "I'll make you understand. Look here, I'm the tiger. . . ."

Mouse   "Yes, I understand that."

Tiger   "And this is the man. . . ."

Mouse   "Yes, I understand that."

Tiger   "And that is the cage. . . ."

Mouse   "Yes, I understand that."

Tiger   (*triumphantly*) "And I was in the cage. Do you understand?"

Mouse   (*makes a gesture as though he is going to say "yes" again, but at the last moment reconsiders*) "No! Please sir?"

Tiger   (*impatiently*) "Well?"

Mouse   "Please sir; how did you get in the cage?"

Tiger   "How? Why in the usual way!"

Mouse   "Oh, dear me; my head is beginning to spin again. Please don't be angry, but what is the usual way?"

Tiger   (*jumping into the cage*) "This way, you fool. Now do you understand?"

Mouse   "Perfectly!" (*he closes the cage over the tiger*) "I understand that you are back in the cage where you belong; and I understand that that is where you will stay *this* time."

Mouse and Man   And with that, the Mouse and the Man shook hands and continued on their separate ways.

Blackout

Master of all masters

adapted by **J. Robert Wills**
from an English folk tale as told by Joseph Jacobs

GIRL A girl once went to the fair to hire herself for a servant.

MAN At last a funny looking old gentleman hired her, and took her home to his house.

GIRL When she got there, he told her that he had something to teach her, for in his house, he had his own name for things. He said to her:

MAN What will you call me?

GIRL Master or mister, or whatever you please, sir.

MAN You must call me "master of all masters." And what would you call this, he said, pointing to the bed.

GIRL Bed or couch, or whatever you please, sir.

MAN No, that's my barnacle. And what do you call these?

GIRL Breeches or trousers or pantaloons, or whatever you please, sir.

MAN You must call them squibs and crackers. And what would you call her?

GIRL Cat or kitten or whatever you please, sir.

MAN You must call her white-faced simminy. And now, what would you call this?

GIRL Fire or flame, or whatever you please, sir.

MAN You must call it hot cockalorum. And what this?

GIRL Water or wet, or whatever you please, sir.

MAN No, pandalorum is its name. And what do you call this?

GIRL House or cottage, or whatever you please, sir.

MAN You must call it high topper mountain.

GIRL And with that, he sent her away and went to bed.

MAN Later that night the servant woke her master up in a fright.

GIRL Master of all masters, get out of your barnacle and put on your squibs and crackers. For whitefaced simminy has got a spark of hot cockalorum on its tail and unless you get some pandalorum, high topper mountain will be all hot cockalorum.

Mathematics
Hrant Alianak

This play is about one day
(any day)
in the life
of a normal
fairly well-to-do
married
childless
couple
(any couple).

"Mathematics" is divided into six scenes.

There is a ten second pause between each scene, before the first scene, and after the last scene.

There are five objects in every scene.

There is a five second pause between every object in every scene.

The defined objects are to be thrown onstage but the throwers themselves should not be visible.

The stage should be divided into six areas.

Each scene should have a clearly defined and separate stage area.

Every object should be clearly visible, after being thrown onstage.

The entire length of the play should have a musical accompaniment.

The musical accompaniment should have a constant and methodical beat.

The exact duration of this play is 190 seconds, or, three minutes and ten seconds.

Scene one

A duster . . . a dust pan . . . a pail . . . a bottle of detergent . . . a bottle of coffee

Scene two

A brief case . . . an umbrella . . . a raincoat . . . a hat . . . a bunch of flowers

Scene three

A glass . . . a plate . . . a spoon . . . a bag of spaghetti . . . a roll of toilet paper

Scene four

A newspaper . . . a shoe . . . a *TV Guide* . . . a beer can . . . a bag of potato chips

Scene five

A dress . . . a pair of trousers . . . a sock . . . a brassiere . . . a toothbrush

Scene six

A pillow . . . a copy of Playboy magazine . . . a pair of pyjama bottoms . . . a pack of cigarettes . . . an alarm clock

Good question
Allen J. Koppenhaver

Lights come up on an empty stage. After a 10-second pause, the first character comes down center aisle to stage. When he is on stage, staring into the audience, second actor comes down right aisle. Same procedure—third actor comes down left aisle, fourth down middle. When all are on stage, they stand for another 10-20 seconds staring into audience until they sense uneasy tension on the part of the audience. Gradually they begin to look around and at each other.

First actor comes down into audience strolling, looking around. All four will come down at 5-second intervals, and at different places in the theatre they try out new sounds, difficult at first, but gradually with ease. One finds a sound he likes, repeats it. Another hears this and repeats same sound. They begin to converse by repeating the sound with developing enthusiasm. The other pair in counterpoint also hits upon a shared sound. The two pairs come down to stage in a dance of joy over these sounds, but it doesn't take them very long to begin to make dissonant sounds which in turn leads to anger and eventually a physical fight.

When they pull out of this fight, they draw back to their first positions on stage and in pantomime, slam the doors of their imaginary boxes, stand perfectly still and stare. Once inside, they have second thoughts, open their doors slowly, look out, see the others, and slam the doors. They turn, reach up and unlock their windows, raise the windows, look out, see each other again and quickly slam and lock the windows, and stand. Eventually boredom sets in. Then accidentally one knocks the side of his box, likes the sound, knocks a pattern (♩ ♩ ♫ ♩) repeats (♩ ♩ ♫ ♩). Another picks it up and replies. In short order the four are rapping, making a joyful mixture of sounds with knuckles, knees, elbows, etc. in a dance of joy. In the midst of all this, two of them open their windows, look out to see each other to find out what each of them was saying. They close their windows and come out, slowly approach each other and then rush into an embrace and go out once more into the aisles trying sounds. Just as they start out, the other two also emerge, grasp hands and proceed down center aisle.

We are now back to the beginning design in which they both try out sounds, find those they like, exhange sounds and proceed to front in dance of joy, which once more leads to dissonance and fight.

Only this time one of them very quickly recognizes that "she's been there before" and withdraws, slamming her door (underscored by big musical climax). Then only do the others realize that she is missing. They "see" the door closed on the box, come up, rap on it, very quickly in anger, they shout, pound on the house, shake it, rattle the doorknob. Nothing. Their anger subsides and soon they all stand dejected around the house.

One of the outsiders gets the idea of knocking and does so (no sound here until insider knocks.) Tries again. The insider looks up, stands, raises hand and knocks (♪♩), hesitates (♪♩). The outsider quickly answers. In short order the others are knocking and the dance is on as before.

Finally the insider turns to the window, slowly unlocks and raises it and looks out. One of the outsiders motions to her to come out and join them. Now, the only line in the play:

Insider: (slowly, pleading and questioning) Let me be me.

The others don't know what to make of this and turn away, and gradually one by one drift away down the center aisle. The insider slowly closes her window and locks it, sits down. When all are down the aisle, one of them returns, slowly, tries the doorknob. The insider sees, opens door. They look at each other. Insider finally smiles, comes out and rushes down aisle, ecstatic, to join the others. The one who opened the door, looks around in surprise and joy and follows after.

9 parts in 7 circumstances with conclusion and epilogue
J. Robert Wills

No. 1:

Man, dressed in white choir robe, white beret, with white boxes on his feet, stands before white painted lectern, with cross, and reads—King James Version of Bible—beginning with the Gospel of John, 1-1, and continuing throughout entire performance.

His voice should be exceedingly even, his hands should remain at all times over his ears, and his sunglasses should be white.

Midway through the performance his voice goes dumb but his lips continue to move.

Woman, dressed in white leotards stands waiting. Man, also dressed in white leotards, wraps her entirely with white wrapping paper.

She sobs while he mixes paint in large white paint bucket.

Sobbing ceases when he begins to paint wide white stripes on the wrapping paper.

When completed, he carries her off. He sobs.

White telephone begins to ring and continues throughout performances.

No. 2:

Woman, dressed in white tights, white mini-skirt, long-sleeved white blouse and white scarf, her face painted white, begins, when the Man reaches Chapter 2, Verse 1, to hang white toilet paper streamers from ceiling to floor, side by side, over entire width of performing area. She moves the ladder for every streamer.

No. 1 continues through this.

No. 3:

Begins two minutes after No. 2

Woman, in white uniform, white leotards, white high heels with large white bows on her ankles and hair and white lines painted on her face and arms, enters to answer telephone. She hesitates, and takes two minutes and thirty seconds deciding not to answer it. During this period of decision she sits cross-legged on the floor. After, she sleeps.

Man, in white long underwear, with all visible skin painted in white squares, enters with fifty-foot length of white clothesline. He measures carefully and cuts this into one-foot lengths, making a pile before him. He then ties the pieces together, end to end, and uses resulting length of rope to hang himself while sitting on a stool.

No. 4:

Begins one minute, thirty seconds after No. 3.

Three men, three women—a team. Dressed in white tights, white raincoats, with white ribbons on their heads cascading over their shoulders and reaching the floor.

Team takes white cloth, full width and depth of performing place in size, holds it over audience for one minute, then flaps it to floor, then rolls on it. Team then wads cloth into ball, places it on white stretcher, and carries it off.

During this the team hums a single note in unison.

9 parts in 7 circumstances with   287
conclusion and epilogue
J. Robert Wills

No. 5:

Begins when team (No. 4) has rolled on white cloth for one minute.

Man, dressed in white tennis shoes, white socks, white shorts, white T-shirt and white gloves, enters with small horn. Conducts himself 4/4 time, blowing the horn on the first beat of every measure. The tempo gradually increases.

Couple, encased in white sheet—with only two heads and three feet showing—hop in and commence to throw (wildly) white confetti in all directions. They hop out.

No. 6:

Begins when confetti is exhausted.

Woman, dressed in white negligee and carrying white umbrella open, enters. She does the following: cuts rope of hanging man; wakes sleeping woman; takes horn from musician; lifts telephone from receiver; tears down white toilet paper streamers; closes Bible. (Performers freeze in turn.) After closing Bible, woman stands with back to audience, arms stretched high.

No. 7:

Smoke envelops the entire performing place.

Love lace
Robert Patrick

(The setting is a bare stage. A man and woman in modern dress enter.)

HE   This place. This place is a dead-end street.

SHE   This place is an emergency ward where we bring people who throw fits in public places.

HE   This place is your Mafia hangout where you've brought me to rub me out because you're not supposed to fall in love with outsiders.

SHE   This place is a psychiatrist's office where I have to listen to your ravings.

HE   This place is a museum where I stand around as exhibit A, the first in your line-up of past works.

SHE   This place is a ladies' room in a swank night-club where you, a weeping drunk blonde, have been brought by your girl-friend after an attack of the Martini maudlins.

HE   This place is the underground laboratory of a militant dyke organization where you've brought me to castrate me.

SHE   This place is a street-corner where you stand around in a beanie yelling insults at every girl that passes.

HE   This place is a family therapy office where we get it all out throwing accusations at each other.

SHE   This place is a stalled elevator on the way to a divorce court where you make one last desperate try to win me back.

HE   This place is a party in a penthouse where you throw dry epithets at a cast-off gigolo.

SHE   This place is the waiting room at an expensive insane asylum where I wait helplessly for them to come and get you.

HE   This place is the waiting room at an expensive insane asylum where I have brought you and where you think you have brought me, causing me the pain that only a devout and puzzled lover can know as the only woman for him disintegrates before his eyes.

SHE   This place is a campus soda shop where the wittiest boy in Lit 101 wears himself out being clever to a new girl.

HE   This place is a torture-chamber in the basement of a slick-magazine skyscraper where you are trying to extract the secrets of my genius.

SHE   This place is a littered attic where a madman has brought a trusting fan whom he suddenly alcoholically menaces and murders.

HE   This place is a black bar where a jaded white lady goes for a few thrills with a vital stud from a member of a subjugated race.

SHE   This place is a World War I hospital where a gas-crazed lieutenant castigates and derides the nurse who has never heard such language before.

HE   This place is a dude ranch where a lady waiting for a divorce flirts with a wrangler while always clutching her plaited quirt.

SHE   This place is an expensive hotel suite where a girl trying to humor a passing lover finds herself requested to do sick, sado-masochistic games.

HE   This place is a gutter slum where a backstairs maid tries to wheedle her passionate, devoted admirer into flattering her fantasies of grandeur.

SHE   This place is a twenties Ziegfeld Follies revue where a baggy-pants comedian laces into a showgirl and honks his nose.

HE   This place is a mid-western motel where Humbert Humbert labors on the edge of neuralgia trying to amuse his pathetic, petty, uncomprehending Lolita.

SHE   This place is a Los Angeles bungalow where Joan Crawford slowly realizes that the helpless young man she has taken under her wing is in reality a deteriorating psychotic.

HE   This place is an English heath where Joan Fontaine is wracked with crippling suspicion about the marvelous man she will marry.

SHE   This place is a bad play about a brave woman realizing she has grown beyond a man whom she was cruel to let love her in the first place.

HE   This place is a gorgeous cliff beside a Big Sur sunset where Kim Kovak fights her sincere passion for a man she was only out to trick and toy with.

SHE   This place is a Noel Coward drawing-room where two decent people, refined through suffering, meet for one last time and part wistfully like mature adults.

HE   This place is a Bernard Shaw parlor where a lovely and gracious matron seeks the kindest way to tell a young poet that she cannot accept his passion.

SHE   This place is a metropolitan cubbyhole where a working girl and an ambitious boy have tried very hard to be happy, but could find no suitable roles in which to comfort one another.

HE   This place is a famous landmark in the twenty-first century, with a plaque that says: "Here He and She, despite the beleaguering collapse of a corrupt culture, came to a new and fruitful understanding beyond all roles and all differences; here the battle of man and woman died in an historic compromise, and a new millennium was founded from a love that inspired the whole wailing world. Gloria in Excelsis Amo Perpetuum."

SHE   This place is a theatre where we fell in love with one another as lead actors in a romantic play.

HE   This place is the dressing-room after that play where we found it was one another after all.

SHE   This place is a freeway motel where we went after the last performance and found that it was only the roles that we loved.

HE   This place is the chapel where we married one another in the strange cold kaleidoscopic light of a full moon through a florious rose window.

SHE   This place is a theatre we have rented to act out the play again, only to find that our belief is gone.

HE   This place is a secret temple of Venus, where gossamer paisley hangings wave in the faint wind from strumming lutes, and a delicate perfumed fountain splashes and giggles like the multicolored houris who shuffle whispering about, serving our love, gossiping about our love.

SHE   This place is a whorehouse where Svengali hypnotizes Trilby, bringing her again and again to the verge of belief.

HE   This place is a primordial retreat, an immemorial cavern where a wounded wanderer stumbles to fall on his knees before the image of woman triumphant, gorgeous, muliebrious eternal, chthonic, conquering, bold.

SHE   This place is a quiet, small, safe nest away from a garbaged, gutted city, where a woman rests for a moment more, perhaps for the moments that make a few hours, with a tender man in whom there is no harm, to leave his life on the morning no matter what happens.

HE   This place is a quiet time machine, designed to bear one man and woman through the night until dawn, to leave them back where they started, forever reconciling frivolous differences in the quest of an untroubled unity, forever young, forevermore in love.

SHE   This place is a great repository of wisdom, where an opportunistic librarian seduces a poetry-struck youngster.

HE   This place is an interlaced forest glen, where a princess caresses a beggar, and finds she has disenchanted herself from cynicism, and he was her prince all along.

SHE   This place is a place of religious punishment, where a girl too proud and too callow is proved to herself to be human and needful and warm.

HE   This place is a place of psychedelic revelation, where great world-weaving patterns try themselves out like magical tapestries, and are tested by entangled lovers, and frayed and discarded until they find at last the proper patterning to cover and coddle and control them.

SHE   This place is a mess.

HE   This place is the modular, mystic beginning of order.

SHE   This place is a dell where lovers kneel.

HE   This place is a monument.

SHE   This place is a maze spun by a magician.

HE   This place is a nest built by a suitor.

SHE   This place is yours.

HE   This place is yours.

SHE   This place is ours.

HE   This place is cool.

SHE   This place is warm.

HE   This place is anyplace we truly want to be.

SHE   This place is where I want to be.

Curtain

Self-accusation
Peter Handke

This piece is a Sprechstuck for one male and one female speaker. It has no roles. Female and male speaker, whose voices are attuned to each other, alternate or speak together, quiet and loud, with abrupt transitions, thus producing an acoustic order. The stage is empty. The two speakers use microphones and loudspeakers. The auditorium and the stage are lighted throughout. The curtain is not used at any time, not even at the end of the piece.

I came into the world.

I became. I was begotten. I originated. I grew. I was born. I was entered in the birth register. I grew older.

I moved. I moved parts of my body. I moved my body. I moved on one and the same spot. I moved from the spot. I moved from one spot to another. I had to move. I was able to move.

I moved my mouth. I came to my senses. I made myself noticeable. I screamed. I spoke. I heard noises. I distinguished between noises. I produced noises. I produced sounds. I produced tones. I was able to produce tones, noises, and sounds. I was able to speak. I was able to scream. I was able to remain silent.

I saw. I saw what I had seen before. I became conscious. I recognized what I had seen before. I recognized what I had recognized before. I perceived. I perceived what I had perceived before. I became conscious. I recognized what I had perceived before.

I looked. I saw objects. I looked at indicated objects. I indicated indicated objects. I learned the designation of indicated objects. I designated indicated objects. I learned the designation of objects that cannot be indicated. I learned. I remembered. I remembered the signs I learned. I saw designated forms. I designated similar forms with the same name. I designated differences between dissimilar forms. I designated absent forms. I learned to fear absent forms. I learned to wish for the presence of absent forms. I learned the words "to wish" and "to fear."

I learned. I learned the words. I learned the verbs. I learned the difference between being and having been. I learned the nouns. I learned the difference between singular and plural. I learned the adverbs. I learned the difference between here and there. I learned the demonstrative pronouns. I learned the difference between this and that. I learned the adjectives. I learned the difference between good and evil. I learned the possessives. I learned the difference between mine and yours. I acquired a vocabulary.

I became the object of sentences. I became the supplement of sentences. I became the object and the supplement of principal and subordinate clauses. I became the movement of a mouth. I became a sequence of letters of the alphabet.

I said my name. I said I. I crawled on all fours. I ran. I ran toward something. I ran away from something. I stood up. I stepped out of the passsive form. I became active. I walked at approximately a right angle to the earth. I leapt. I defied the force of gravity. I learned to relieve myself outside my clothes. I learned to bring my body under my control. I learned to control myself.

I learned to be able. I was able. I was able to want. I was able to walk on two legs. I was able to walk on my hands. I was able to remain. I was able to remain upright. I was able to remain prone. I was able to crawl on my stomach. I was able to play dead. I was able to hold my breath. I was able to kill myself. I was able to spit. I was able to nod. I was able to say no. I was able to perform gestures. I was able to question. I was able to answer questions. I was able to imitate. I was able to follow an example. I was able to play. I was able to do something. I was able to fail to do something. I was able to destroy objects. I was able to picture objects to myself. I was able to value objects. I was able to speak to objects. I was able to speak about objects. I was able to remember objects.

I lived in time. I thought of beginning and end. I thought of myself. I thought of others. I stepped out of nature. I became. I became unnatural. I came to my history. I recognized that I am not you. I was able to tell my history. I was able to conceal my history.

I was able to want something. I was able not to want something.

I made myself. I made myself what I am. I changed myself. I became someone else. I became responsible for my history. I became co-responsible for the histories of the others. I became one history among others. I made the world into my own. I became sensible.

I no longer had to obey only nature. I was supposed to comply with rules. I was supposed to. I was supposed to comply with mankind's historic rules. I was supposed to act. I was supposed to fail to act. I was supposed to let happen. I learned rules. I learned as a metaphor for rules "the snares of rules." I learned rules for behavior and for thoughts. I learned rules for inside and outside. I learned rules for things and people. I learned general and specific rules. I learned rules for this world and the afterworld. I learned rules for air, water, fire, and earth. I learned the rules and the exceptions to the rules. I learned the basic rules and the derivative rules. I learned to pretend. I became fit for society.

I became: I was supposed to. I became capable of eating with my hands: I was supposed to avoid soiling myself. I became capable of adopting other people's practices: I was supposed to avoid my own malpractices. I became capable of distinguishing between hot and cold: I was supposed to avoid playing with fire. I became capable of separating good and evil: I was supposed to eschew evil. I became capable of playing according to the rules: I was supposed to avoid an infraction of the rules of the game. I became capable of realizing the unlawfulness of my actions and of acting in accordance with this realization: I was supposed to eschew criminal acts. I became capable of using my sexual powers: I was supposed to avoid misusing my sexual powers.

I was included in all the rules. With my personal data I became part of the record. With my soul I became tainted by original sin. With my lottery number I was inscribed in the lottery lists. With my illnesses I was filed in the hospital ledger. With my firm I was entered in the commercial register. With my distinguishing marks I was retained in the personnel records.

I came of age. I became fit to act. I became fit to sign a contract. I became fit to have a last will.

As of a moment in time I could commit sins. As of another moment I became liable to prosecution. As of another moment I could lose my honor. As of another moment I could oblige myself contractually to do or to abstain from doing something.

I became duty-bound to confess. I became duty-bound to have an address. I became duty-bound to make restitution. I became duty-bound to pay taxes. I became duty-bound to do military service. I became duty-bound to do my duty. I became duty-bound to go to school. I became duty-bound to be vaccinated. I became duty-bound to care. I became duty-bound to pay my bills. I became duty-bound to be investigated. I became duty-bound to be educated. I became duty-bound to give proof. I became duty-bound to be insured. I became duty-bound to have an identity. I became duty-bound to be registered. I became duty-bound to pay support. I became duty-bound to execute. I became duty-bound to testify.

I became. I became responsible. I became guilty. I became pardonable. I had to atone for my history. I had to atone for my past. I had to atone for the past. I had to atone for my time. I came into the world only with time.

Which demands of time did I violate? Which demands of practical reason did I violate? Which secret paragraphs did I violate? Which programs did I violate? Which eternal laws of the universe did I violate? Which laws of the underworld did I violate? Which of the most primitive rules of common decency did I violate? Which and whose party lines did I violate? Which laws of the theater did I violate? Which vital interests did I violate? Which unspoken law did I violate? Which unwritten law did I violate? Which command of the hour did I violate? Which rules of life did I violate? Which common-sense rules did I violate? Which rules of love did I violate? Which rules of the game did I violate? Which rules of cosmetics did I violate?

Which laws of aesthetics did I violate? Which laws of the stronger did I violate? Which commands of piety did I violate? Which law of the outlaws did I violate? Which desire for change did I violate? Which law of the world and the afterworld did I violate? Which rule of orthography did I violate? Which right of the past did I violate? Which law of free fall did I violate? Did I violate the rules, plans, ideas, postulates, basic principles, etiquettes, general propositions, opinions, and formulas of the whole world?

I did. I failed to do. I let do. I expressed myself. I expressed myself through ideas. I expressed myself through expressions. I expressed myself before myself. I expressed myself before myself and others. I expressed myself before the impersonal power of the law and of good conduct. I expressed myself before the personal power of God.

I expressed myself in movements. I expressed myself in actions. I expressed myself in motionlessness. I expressed myself in inaction.

I signified. I signified with each of my expressions. With each of my expressions I signified the fulfillment or disregard of rules.

I expressed myself by spitting. I expressed myself by showing disapproval. I expressed myself by showing approval. I expressed myself by relieving nature. I expressed myself by discarding useless and used objects. I expressed myself by killing live beings. I expressed myself by destroying objects. I expressed myself by breathing. I expressed myself by sweating. I expressed myself by secreting snot and tears.

I spat. I spat out. I spat with an aim. I spat at. I spat on the floor in places where it was improper to spit on the floor. I spat on the floor in places where spitting was a violation of health regulations. I spat in the face of people whom it was a personal insult of God to spit at. I spat on objects which it was a personal insult of human beings to spit upon. I did not spit in front of people when spitting out before them allegedly brought good luck. I did not spit in front of cripples. I did not spit at actors before their performance. I did not use the spittoon. I expectorated in waiting rooms. I spat against the wind.

I expressed approval in places where the expression of approval was prohibited. I expressed disapproval at times when the expression of disapproval was not desired. I expressed disapproval and approval in places and at times when the expression of disapproval and the expression of approval were intolerable. I failed to express approval at times when the expression of approval was called for. I expressed approval during a difficult trapeze act in the circus. I expressed approval inopportunely.

I discarded used and useless objects in places where discarding objects was prohibited. I deposited objects in places where depositing objects was punishable. I stored objects in places where storing objects was reprehensible. I failed to deliver objects I was legally obligated to deliver. I threw objects out the window of a moving train. I failed to throw litter into litter baskets. I left litter lying in the woods. I threw burning cigarettes into hay. I failed to hand over pamphlets dropped by enemy planes.

I expressed myself by speaking. I expressed myself by appropriating objects. I expressed myself by reproducing live beings. I expressed myself by producing objects. I expressed myself by looking. I expressed myself by playing. I expressed myself by walking.

I walked. I walked purposelessly. I walked purposefully. I walked on paths. I walked on paths on which it was prohibited to walk. I failed to walk on paths when it was imperative to do so. I walked on paths on which it was sinful to walk purposelessly. I walked purposefully when it was imperative to walk purposelessly. I walked on paths on which it was prohibited to walk with an objective. I walked. I walked even when walking was prohibited and against custom. I walked through passages through which it was an act of conformity to pass. I stepped on property on which it was a disgrace to step. I stepped onto property without my identity papers when it was prohibited to step on it without identity papers. I left buildings which it was a lack of solidarity to leave. I entered buildings which it was unseemly to enter without a covered head. I stepped on territory which it was prohibited to step upon. I visited the territory of a state which it was prohibited to visit. I left the territory of a state which it was a hostile act to leave. I drove into streets in a direction it was undisciplined to enter. I walked in directions it was illegal to walk in. I went so far that it was inadvisable to go farther. I stopped when it was impolite to stop. I walked on the right of persons when it was thoughtless to walk on their right. I sat down on seats that were reserved for others to sit on. I failed to walk on when ordered to walk on. I walked slowly when it was imperative to walk quickly. I failed to get on my feet when it was imperative to get on my feet. I lay down in places where it was forbidden to lie down. I stopped at demonstrations. I walked on by when it was imperative to offer help. I entered no-man's land. I lay down on the floor with R during her period. I delayed people's flight by walking slowly in narrow hallways. I jumped off moving streetcars. I opened the train door before the train had come to a complete stop.

I spoke. I spoke out. I spoke out what others thought. I only thought what others spoke out. I gave expression to public opinion. I falsified public opinion. I spoke at places where it was impious to speak. I spoke loudly at places where it was inconsiderate to speak loudly. I whispered when it was required to speak up. I remained silent at times when silence was a disgrace. I spoke as a public speaker when it was imperative to speak as a private person. I spoke with persons with whom it was dishonorable to speak. I greeted people whom it was a betrayal of principle to greet. I spoke in a language which it was a hostile act to use. I spoke about objects of which it was tactless to speak. I suppressed my knowledge of a crime. I failed to speak well of the dead. I spoke ill of absent persons. I spoke without being asked to. I spoke to soldiers on duty. I spoke to the driver during the trip.

I failed to observe the rules of the language. I committed linguistic blunders. I used words thoughtlessly. I blindly attributed qualities to the objects in the world. I blindly attributed to the words for the objects words for the qualities of the objects. I called objects dead. I called complexity lively. I called melancholy black. I called madness bright. I called passion hot. I called anger red. I called the ultimate questions unanswerable. I called the milieu genuine. I called nature free. I called horror frightful. I called laughter liberating. I called freedom inalienable. I called loyalty proverbial. I called fog milky. I called the surface smooth. I called severity Old Testament-like. I called the sinner poor. I called dignity inborn. I called the bomb menacing. I called the doctrine salutary. I called darkness impenetrable. I called morality hypocritical. I called lines of demarcation vague. I called the raised fore-finger moralistic. I called mistrust creative. I called trust blind. I called the atmosphere sober. I called conflict productive. I called conclusions futuristic. I called integrity intellectual. I called capitalism corrupt. I called emotions murky. I called the picture of the world distorted. I called the view of the world fuzzy. I called criticism constructive. I called science unbiased. I called precision scientific. I called eyes crystal-clear. I called results easily obtain-able. I called the dialogue useful. I called dogma rigid. I called the discussion necessary. I called opinion subjective. I called pathos hollow. I called mysti-cism obscure. I called thoughts unripe. I called horseplay foolish. I called monotony oppressive. I called solutions obvious. I called being true. I called truth profound. I called lies insipid. I called life rich. I called money of no account. I called reality vulgar. I called the moment delicious. I called war just. I called peace lazy. I called weight dead. I called conflicts irreconcilable. I called the fronts fixed. I called the universe curved. I called snow white. I called ice cold. I called spheres round. I called a something certain. I called the measure full.

I appropriated objects. I acquired objects as property and possessions. I ap-propriated objects at places where the appropriation of objects was pro-hibited on principle. I appropriated objects which it was an act hostile to society to appropriate. I claimed objects as private property when it was inopportune to claim I owned them. I declared objects to be public property when it was unethical to remove them from private hands. I treated objects without care when it was prescribed to treat them with care. I touched ob-jects which it was unaesthetic and sinful to touch. I separated objects from objects which it was inadvisable to separate. I failed to keep the required distance from objects from which it was imperative to keep the required distance. I treated persons like objects. I treated animals like persons. I took up contact with living beings with whom it was immoral to take up contact. I touched objects with objects which it was useless to bring into touch with each other. I traded with living beings and objects with which it was in-human to trade. I treated fragile goods without care. I connected the positive pole to the positive pole. I used externally applicable medicines internally. I touched exhibited objects. I tore scabs off half-healed wounds. I touched electric wires. I failed to register letters that had to be sent registered. I failed to affix a stamp to applications that required a stamp. I failed to wear mourning clothes upon a death in the family. I failed to use skin cream to protect my skin from the sun. I dealt in slaves. I dealt in uninspected meat. I climbed mountains with shoes unfit for mountain climbing. I failed to wash fresh fruit. I failed to disinfect the clothes of plague victims. I failed to shake the hair lotion before use.

I looked and listened. I looked at. I looked at objects which it was shameless to look at. I failed to look at objects which it was a dereliction of duty to fail to look at. I failed to watch events which it was philistine to fail to watch. I failed to watch events in the position prescribed to watch them. I failed to avert my eyes during events it was treasonable to watch. I looked back when looking back was proof of a bad upbringing. I looked away when it was cowardly to look away. I listened to persons whom it was unprincipaled to listen to. I inspected forbidden areas. I inspected buildings in danger of collapse. I failed to look at persons who were speaking to me. I failed to look at persons with whom I was speaking. I watched unadvisable and objectionable movies. I heard information in the mass media that was hostile to the state. I watched games without a ticket. I stared at strangers. I looked without dark glasses into the sun. I kept my eyes open during sexual intercourse.

I ate. I ate more than I could stomach. I drank more than my bladder could hold. I consumed food and drink. I ingested the four elements. I inhaled and exhaled the four elements. I ate at moments when it was undisciplined to eat. I failed to breathe in the prescribed manner. I breathed air which it was below my station to breathe. I inhaled when it was harmful to inhale. I ate meat during fast days. I breathed without a gas mask. I ate on the street. I inhaled exhaust gases. I ate without knife and fork. I failed to leave myself time to breathe. I ate the Host with my teeth. I failed to breathe through my nose.

I played. I misplayed. I played according to rules which, according to existing rules, were against convention. I played at times and places where it was asocial and ingenuous to play. I played with persons with whom it was dishonorable to play. I played with objects with which it was unceremonious to play. I failed to play at times and places where it was unsociable to fail to play. I played according to the rules when it was individualistic not to play according to the rules. I played with myself when it would have been humane to play with others. I played with powers with whom it was presumptuous to play. I failed to play seriously. I played too seriously. I played with fire. I played with lighters. I played with marked cards. I played with human lives. I played with spray cans. I played with life. I played with feelings. I played myself. I played without chips. I failed to play during playtime. I played with the inclination to evil. I played with my thoughts. I played with the thought of suicide. I played on a thin sheet of ice. I played and trespassed at one and the same time. I played despair. I played with my despair. I played with my sex organ. I played with words. I played with my fingers.

I came into the world afflicted with original sin. My very nature inclined toward evil. My innate viciousness expressed itself at once in envy of my fellow suckling. One day in the world, I was no longer free of sin. Bawling, I craved my mother's breasts. All I knew was to suck. All I knew was to gratify my desires. With my reason I refused to recognize the laws that were placed in the universe and in myself. I was conceived in malice. I was begotten in malice. I expressed my malice by destroying things. I expressed my malice by trampling live beings to death. I was disobedient out of love of play. What I loved in playing was the sense of winning. I loved in fantastic stories the itch in my ear. I idolized people. I took greater delight in the trivia of poets than in useful knowledge. I feared a solecism more than the eternal laws. I let myself be governed solely by my palate. I only trusted my senses. I failed to prove that I had a sense of reality. I not only loved crimes, I loved committing crimes. I preferred to do evil in company. I loved accomplices. I loved complicity. I loved sin for its danger. I did not search for truth. The pleasure I took in art was in my pain and my compassion. I pandered to the desires of my eyes. I failed to recognize the purpose of history. I was godforsaken. I was forsaken by the world. I did not designate the world as *this* world. I also included the heavenly bodies in the world. I was sufficient for myself. I cared only for worldly things. I took no cold bath against melancholy. I took no hot bath against passion. I used my body for wrong ends. I failed to take notice of the facts. I failed to subordinate my physical nature. I denied my nature. I ran up against the nature of things. I indiscriminately sought power. I indiscriminately sought money. I failed to teach myself to regard money as a means. I lived in excess of my means. I failed to have the means to put up with the state of affairs. I myself determined how I would fashion my life. I did not overcome myself. I did not toe the line. I disturbed the eternal order. I failed to recognize that eveil is only the absence of good. I failed to recognize that evil is only an abuse. I gave birth to death in my sins. I made myself, with my sins, one with the cattle that is to be slaughtered in the slaughter-house but snuffles at the very iron designed to slaughter it. I failed to resist the beginnings. I failed to find the moment to stop. I made myself an image of the highest being. I sought not to make myself an image of the highest being. I refused to divulge the name of the highest being. I only believed in the three persons of grammar. I told myself that there is no higher being so as not to have to fear it. I looked for the opportunity. I did not use the chance. I did not submit to necessity. I did not count on the possibility. I did not learn from bad examples. I did not learn from the past. I abandoned myself to the free play of forces. I mistook freedom for license. I mistook honesty for self-exposure. I mistook obscenity for originality. I mistook the dream for reality. I mistook life for the cliché. I mistook coercion for neces-sary guidance. I mistook love for instinct. I mistook the cause for the effect. I failed to observe the unity of thought and action. I failed to see things as they really are. I succumbed to the magic of the moment. I failed to regard existence as a provisional gift. I broke my word. I did not have command of the language. I did not reject the world. I did not affirm authority. I was a naive believer in authority. I did not husband my sexual powers. I sought lust as an end in itself. I was not sure of myself. I became a puzzle to myself. I wasted my time. I overslept my time. I wanted to stop time. I wanted to speed up time. I was in conflict with time. I did not want to grow older. I did not want to die. I did not let things come toward me. I could not limit my-self. I was impatient. I could not wait for it. I did not think of the future. I did not think of *my* future. I lived from one moment to the next. I was domineering. I behaved as though I was alone in the world. I proved illbred. I was self-willed. I lacked a will of my own. I did not work on myself. I failed to make work the basis of my existence. I failed to see God in every beggar. I did not eradicate evil at its roots. I irresponsibly thrust children into the world. I failed to adapt my pleasures to my social circumstances. I sought for bad company. I always wanted to be at the center. I was too much alone. I was not enough alone. I led my own life too much. I failed to grasp the mean-ing of the word "too." I failed to regard the happiness of all mankind as my ultimate aim. I did not place the common interest before the individual interest. I did not face the music. I disregarded orders. I failed to disobey unjustifiable orders. I did not know my limits. I failed to see things in their relationship with one another. I made no virtue of necessity. I switched convictions. I was incorrigible. I failed to put myself at the service of the cause. I was satisfied with the status quo. I saw no one by myself. I yielded to insinuations. I decided neither for one nor the other. I took no stand. I disturbed the balance of power. I violated generally acknowledged principles. I did not fulfill the quota. I fell behind the goal that had been set. I was one and everything to myself. I did not take enough fresh air. I woke up too late. I did not clean the sidewalk. I left doors unlocked. I stepped too near the cage. I failed to keep entrances free. I failed to keep exits free. I pulled the safety brake without good reason. I leaned bicycles against forbidden walls. I solicited and peddled. I did not keep the streets clean. I did not take off my shoes. I leaned out the window of a moving train. I handled open fires in rooms that were firetraps. I paid unannounced visits. I did not get up for invalids. I lay down in a hotel bed with a lighted cigarette. I failed to turn off faucets. I spent nights on park benches. I failed to lead dogs on a leash. I failed to muzzle dogs that bit. I failed to leave umbrellas and coats in the cloakroom. I touched goods before I bought them. I failed to close containers immediately after use. I tossed pressurized containers into the fire. I crossed on the red. I walked on superhighways. I walked along the railroad bed. I failed to walk on the sidewalk. I failed to move to the rear in streetcars. I did not hold onto the straps. I used the toilet while the train was stopped in the station. I did not follow personnel instructions. I started motor vehicles where it was prohibited to do so. I failed to push buttons. I crossed the rails in railroad stations. I failed to step back when trains were coming in. I exceeded the load limit in elevators. I disturbed the quiet of the night. I affixed posters to forbidden walls. I tried to open doors by pushing when they could only be pulled open. I tried to open doors by pulling when they could only be pushed open. I roamed the streets after dark. I lit lights during blackouts. I did not remain calm in accidents. I left the house during curfew. I did not stay in my place during catastrophes. I thought of myself first. I indiscriminately rushed out of rooms. I activated alarm signals without authorization. I destroyed alarm signals without authorization. I failed to use emergency exits. I pushed. I trampled. I failed to break the window with the hammer. I blocked the way. I put up unauthorized resistance. I did not stop when challenged. I did not raise my hands above my head. I did not aim at the legs. I played with the trigger of a cocked gun. I failed to save women and children first. I approached the drowning from behind. I kept my hands in my pockets. I took no evasive action. I did not let myself be blindfolded. I did not look for cover. I offered an easy target. I was too slow. I was too fast. I moved.

I did not regard the movement of my shadow as proof of the movement of the earth. I did not regard my fear of the dark as proof of my existence. I did not regard the demands of reason for immortality as proof of life after death. I did not regard my nausea at the thought of the future as proof of my nonexistence after death. I did not regard subsiding pain as proof of the passage of time. I did not regard my lust for life as proof that time stands still.

I am not what I was. I was not what I should have been. I did not become what I should have become. I did not keep what I should have kept.

I went to the theatre. I heard this piece. I spoke this piece. I wrote this piece.

Eight poem-plays
Ruth Krauss

RE-EXAMINATION OF FREEDOM

ONE
If I were FREEDOM
I'd be an apple

TWO
If I were FREEDOM
I'd be hurricanes
of sugarcanes

THREE
If I were FREEDOM
I'd navigate all the drunken rivers
and if I drown I go down
in a carnival of sky
and if I ride
the World rides with me
over the sunken drunken sun and whee-ee-ee-ee-eeeeeeee-

FOUR
If I were FREEDOM
I'd never be Aunt May
who thinks she is the U.S.A.
and her left leg is Florida

May: or is it my right
        no my left
        I'll have a Civil War
        I'll sell Louisiana to Napoleon

Louisiana flies away

Left Leg: Napoleon Napoleon
            la la la la la—

FIVE
If I were FREEDOM
I'd be that mud puddle
where Walter Raleigh laid his cloak
no I mean I'd be that cloak
laid by Sir Walter in the puddle of Queen Elizabeth I mean
the puddle for Queen Elizabeth I mean
once there was a puddle and there was a queen and
along came Sir Walter Somethingorother and laid
down his cloak for her
if I were FREEDOM
I'd be that cloak
and the World my Queen
I mean

SIX
If I were FREEDOM
I'd be a small tree
at the edge of night
in the wild skyscrapers
then a lonely sea
and the blue waters rushing
would do your heart good
I'd be

SONG
If I were FREEDOM
I'd love you
in the demented batteries

I'd love you
on the sidewalk
I'd love you
and glasses are empty but
I'd love you I'd love you

abandoned thus to the fury of symbols
If I were FREEDOM
and suddenly there is the wilderness
I'd love you
yes all hands are lost when the ship goes down but
I'd love you
the shadows crowd on the shore
I love you
tell me before the ferryman's return
I love you I love you
and everything is full of the sea

If I were FREEDOM
I'd love you
dirty calabash
I'd love you
my lion
I'd love you I'd love you
if I were FREEDOM
on feathers in my head if there were snow
on cards on the tables on the chairs
the waves distill you
and the night

salt white stuff on stones
I love you
so that one discovers strawberries at the rim of fire everyday
I love you I love you
which is a condition that becomes a festival

QUESTIONS OR MAYBE ANSWERS

in a cottage kitchen

CHILD: Mother, was a skyscraper
once a little cottage
like ours?

MOTHER: No, dear. Of course not.

(the COTTAGE begins to grow . . .

PRACTICAL MOTHER'S GUIDE

BELL: begins ringing

CHILD: Mama Mama,
is that the bell for springtime?

MOTHER: No, silly, that's the door bell.
Would you answer it please.

DIRECTIONS: CHILD runs to the door

CHILD: Mama Mama, it's a man with the sun.

MOTHER: Well, dear, tell him to leave it.

CHILD: He says it's C.O.D.
And Mama, it's all tied up in ribbons and moths.

MOTHER: Ask him to bring it back tomorrow please.
We have no money in the house.

CHILD: Mama, he should leave it anyway.
It *was* the bell for springtime
and if we don't take it in but
send it away—
Mother Mother, the sun—
what will happen to it?

MOTHER: Well, I don't know.
Shells are full of the sea
the sea is full of waterbabies
and if you look in the eyes of the waterbabies . . .
. . . .
Tell the man to take away the sun
and bring you a waterbaby.

CHILD: Sir, we have no money for the C.O.D.
Could you please leave the sun
and it shine anyway?

MAN: Why not.
Here.

DIRECTIONS: CHILD takes the sun
and does a sun dance

A BEAUTIFUL DAY

GIRL: What a beautiful day!

THE SUN falls down onto the stage

end

PLAY 1

NARRATOR: in a poem you make your point with pineapples

PINEAPPLES fly onto the stage from all directions

SPY: and it would be nice to have a spy going in and out

PLAY 2

NARRATOR: in a poem you make your point with lemons-on-fire

LEMONS-ON-FIRE fly out overhead across the
horizons over into onto the stage from all
directions the people run out and bow lie down
and roll in the grass on the rooftops in the sand

ICEBERG: and it would be nice to have an iceberg going
in and out

PLAY 3

NARRATOR: in a poem
you make your point with—

NIGHT flies onto the stage
from all directions however
it is summer
and full of tree-toads
car-brakes
Mack-the-Knife
and dog howl

THIS BREAST

This breast Mexican poetry
This breast Chinese history
This breast Odyssey

This breast Eugenie Grandet at the age of seven
This breast a resort in the Black Forest
This breast was acquainted with the King of Monataccata
This breast given special permission to settle in Geneva
This breast Dostoevskian Masterpiece

This breast Hegelian
This breast little acorn does to mighty oak tree grow

This breast as the Irish Statesman so shrewdly remarked
                most unabashed explorer of the crypts of the soul
This breast —but we have nothing but the word of Mr. Snooks
This breast a dove
This breast the flower of Gum Swamp
This breast a little confused by this possibility
This breast suggesting by turns the mother the mistress
            the father the Church Ireland India Greenland
            Tierra Del Fuego Africa and the boot of Italy
This breast apostrophe to the cathedral of night

This breast Olé

This breast Shakespeare
This breast Picasso
This breast Einstein
This breast I seen it in the papers

This breast in Egypt the Pharoah
This breast we must emphasize the fact that a man should bid
                farewell before going to his death
This breast with the historic city near the entrance to
            the Hellespont

This breast composed entirely of scraps of historic fact
This breast giant devil troll sorcerer cannibal
This breast earliest form of the ballad in France
This breast the field and wood blossom thereat

This breast would you like to know how it started
This breast then we shall have to take an exciting trip
This breast boom-boom yippee slurp strawberries cabanas
This breast as we go whizzing along
This breast thousands of years go by
This breast we have a fine view of everything that happens
This breast like the time the star
This breast there has also been some attempt to correlate
              its activity with changes in the time of the
              migration of swallows with wheat yields and
              even with social revolutions
This breast suddenly
              waves quiverings storms lightnings shining
              music apple-blossoms green grass blue days
              like forget-me-nots

This breast surveyors at first considered flatlands
This breast the train service was never there
This breast following the dedication service there will be
              a reception for old-timers
This breast serve as a reminder of the famous Railroad
              That Went Totemic
This breast celebration parades fiesta a circus
              state-of-the-state message one touchdown favorite
              walloped the Philadelphia Eagles U.S. representatives
              on the scene should have ah-ha! Doe not mock me
              in thy bed while these cold nights freeze me dead
              in the supernatural dark of Main Street West
              under the trestle with dreams broke down
              tobacco haze

This breast volta! he is suddenly galvanized by the announcement
This breast to go to a special performance
This breast of predilection the legendary radiance the wanton
This breast between the final stations of revolutionary orbit
            no day no night summer or winter thermal radiation
            transmissions megacycles and as to the Eastern
            flank the encroachment of the North American
            continent complicates matters
This breast needs timetable
This breast early one morning Gothic, Gothic on a vernal sea

The big welling
Paul Reps

"Hello. Will you give me some information?"

"Will try."

"In, out of mind, we experience this and that.
Tell me, could there be a big welling
including ordinary experience—
as if unexpected, effortless,
as if seeing many things at once invisibly,
as if watching a play unmoved in moving?"

"Could be."

"An immense refreshing? How does even a little
freshening come?"

"Before • moving •
    let
     •

any   stir
    •

start   through."

"O thank you
                and might it
        in dark
                or
                    turning?"

"Might."
                "In fragrancing,
                rain
                spat

                    snow
                    fall
        bird   cry
                    or
            placing   branch
                with
                        others

pouring
cup   in
                        glance,

> with
> step
>   through
>   feet
>   head
>   hand,
>   welling
>   includingly—
>   in it
>   the
>   galaxy
>   the
>   dust
>   feet
>
>   touch—"

"Much."

Great waves, small waves
Paul Reps

Woman walking on her hands
While giving birth to a child.

CHILD   Where am I?
WOMAN   Dear child, you are being born here.
CHILD   Let me out.
WOMAN   Let yourself out.

Help
a stereophonic narrative for authorial voice
John Barth

"Help," by John Barth, from *Esquire Magazine*, September, 1969. Reprinted by permission of Esquire Magazine, © 1969 by Esquire, Inc.

R = Right channel of disc or tape recording, separately recorded.
C = Central voice, either recorded equidistant between stereo microphones, in synchrony with and superimposed on *R* and *L*, or live interlocutory between *R* and *L*.
L = Left channel, separately recorded in synchrony with *R*.

R: Help! help! HELP! **HELP!**

C: Help! *help* HELP **HELP!** Help *help!* HELP! ... Hel (et cetera at random pitches, volumes, frequencies, timbres, and inflections for 30 sec.) LP!

L: HELP! **HELP!** Help! Help! Help *help* HELP!

R: 11-second pause | **HELP!** (exclamatorily) | 8-second pause | (unison shouts) HIP-hip **HELP!** **HELP!** 2-second pause **HELP!** 2-second pause **HELP!** 3-second pause LP!

C: 14-second pause | **HELP.** (declaratively) | 5-second pause | **HELP!** HIP-hip **HELP!** 1-second pause **HELP!** 2-second pause **HELP!** 3-second pause

L: 7-second pause | **HELP?** (interrogatively) | 12-second pause | **HELP!** HIP-hip **HELP!** 1-second pause **HELP!** 2-second pause HIP-hip **HELP!** 1-second pause **HELP!** 3-second pause

R | Help.....help....help...help..help..helphelphelphelp!
(peremptorily: gradual accelerando from very slow to very fast, 15 seconds)
3-second pause | (read as if from list, about one per second) | Assistance Aidance Boot Providence Ministration Favor Shot in the arm Mercy Encouragement

C | Help? Help help? HELP? Helphelphelp?..Assistance?
(interrogatively: random intervals, 15 seconds) *(last time)*
3-second pause | Fosterage Charity Guidance Sustenance Nourishment Manna Provision Alleviation Easement

L | Help help help help help help ....HELP!
(crescendo from whisper to shout, about twice/second, 15 seconds)
3-second pause | Redress Reinforcement Pardon Shrift Abettance Succor Cast Subvention Ministry Boost

---

R | Good turn Clemency Therapy Protection Auspice Benevolence Championship Sustenation Nutrition Subsidy Relief Comfort Deliverance Indemnification Stay | **5-second pause** | **Unnnh!** *(groan)* | **3-second pause**

C | Befriendment Amnesty Obligement Aid Lift Accommodation Supportance Furtherance Hand Beneficence Rescue Care Sanctuary Goodwill Countenance | **5-second pause** | **Oy veh.** *(wearily)* | **3-second pause**

L | Maintenance Eutropy Bounty Migration Ease Remedy Deus ex machina Indulgence Absolution Boisterance Help | **5-second pause** | **Whew!** *(sigh)* | **3-second pause**

R | Aiudo Aiudo, aiudo, per piacere, aiudo! AU SECOURS? **AU SECOURS** ... *(evenly)* | **AU SECOURS AU SECOURS** ... | **AU SECOURS** ...

C | mayday mayday mayday mayday mayday mayday *(tersely)* | mayday mayday mayday mayday mayday mayday | mayday mayday mayday mayday

L | ¡Socorro!¡Socorro! ¡Socorro, por Dios! **¡BAH!** *(flatly)* | **HELP HELP HELP** | **HELP HELP HELP**

Zu Hilfe, bitte. Zu Hilfe?

repeat 3 more times

repeat 1 more time

repeat 2 more times

tsk t-t-tsk   tsk t-t-tsk   tsk t-t-tsk   tsk t-t-tsk   tsk t-t-tsk ∶

unh - - - -   unh - - - -   unh - - - -   unh- - - -   unh - - - -

(conversationally)
Help help help help   help help help help   help help help

help

help-help   help

Help   help   help

bones ad lib

R Tsk-tsk-tsk-tsk-tsk-tsk-tsk-tsk- · · · · · · -tsk
(rapidly, 15 seconds)

no pause
(♩ = 116)   ¾

C My, my, my, my, my, my . . . . . . my.   *5-second pause*
(concernedly, 10 seconds)

snap fingers
starting at R's
5th bar   ¾

L Unh.   Unh.   Unh unh unh . . . . . unh.   *5-second pause*
(desperately, 10 seconds)

grunt rhythmically
starting at R's
3rd bar   (♩ = 116)   ¾

brightly, to rhythm
of Waiting on
the Levee

Help-help
tamb. ad lib.

R no pause   (♩ = 116)   4/4
tambourine   4/4

HELP!

C (♩ = 116)   4/4
snap
fingers   4/4

HELP!

L (♩ = 116)   4/4
bones   4/4

HELP!

brightly, to rhythm of Johann Fischer Augsburgiensis, Tafelmusik, Ouverture: 2nd & 3rd movements. Vivace (♩ = 192)

Help! **H-E-L-P**   **H-E-L-P-H-E-** elp!   Help! **H-E-L-P**

help help help help,diddly   helphelp,diddly   Help! **H-E-L-P**

(resignedly)   **E-L-P** help! *Helphelp!*   **H-E-L-P-H-E-** elp!

3/4 Dear God   (resignedly)   (sigh)   Help! **H-E-L-P** help help help helphelpDiddly -elp!
(groan)

3/4

3-second pause
end tamb.

Et cetera!
end finger snap

3-second pause
end bones

R Help-help help help-help
(etc. ad lib.)

C (booming Interlocutory voice)

Help   Help
(etc. ad lib.)

L Help   Help
(etc. ad lib.)

Grave ($\quad = 102$)

help! *Helphelp!* Help.

help! Help help!

H-E-L-P!

help help help help!

help! *helphelp*, help

H-E-L-P!

Help, **H-E** -L-P help help help!

Help-E-elp help help!

help! *Helphelp* Help

help! E-L-P help! Help

Help help! Help

H-E-L-P!

help! Help

H-E-L-P

(sustained crash-
ing sounds,
5 seconds)

(add sirens &
penetrators,
5 seconds)

(thuds, grunts, ouches, oofs, other
urgent noises, 10 seconds)

(sustained
splashing &
gurgling,
5 seconds)

(add alarm bells
& buzzers,
5 seconds)

help! E-L-P-H-E-L-P

H-E-L-P

Help!

(1 small crash
& tinkle)

5-second pause

(1 short & 1
long blast of
police whistle)

10-second pause

10-second pause

help! **H** - **E-L-P**

help! Help help!

H-E-L-P-H-E-L-P

(1 small splash
& gurgle)

5-second pause

10-second pause

10-second pause

HELP.

(matter-of-factly)

10-second pause

6-second pause

He-e-e-elp!

(croak, 3 seconds) *3-second pause*

6-second pause

(...faintly, sound of horses &
bugles, growing louder as if
approaching from R, building to a
tremendous crescendo as it reaches
C, sustained for several seconds at
C, then moving toward L and growing
ever fainter and fainter until it recedes
entirely into silence at L....)

10-second pause

10-second pause

10-second pause

1-second pause

1-second pause

R

C

L

R

C

L

R

C

L

Graphic Design by Rudolph De Harak

Bo
Michael Smith

Scene: A fig grove just outside Nazarene, Calif. BO TREE stands alone centerstage.

Enter JESUS E. LEE DON JUAN CROCKETT DE LA MANCHA.
Young, generously encrusted with sunburn and grit, he walks with the unmistakable Death-Valley-Days prospectors's clatter of shovels, picks, handsaws, gongs, slide rule, frying pan, surfboard and railroad tie. A large offstage kazoo-and-castanet band announces his entrance with an excruciating first few bars from an appropriate anthem, such as "O Bury Me Not on the Lone Prairie" or "Malaguena." The music stops abruptly when JESUS discards his equipment to duck under the shade of BO TREE.

BO   Drachma for your thoughts.
JESUS *(leaping back)*   Hah! FoooWAP! *(circles BO TREE, making threatening noises and attacking with castanets).*
BO   Not bad for a biped. Try concentrating.
JESUS   Con-cen-tricating. *(Pause)* This tree is telling me—
BO   Thoughts. Drachma for your thoughts.
JESUS *(pressing thumbs to eyes, squinting in thought)*   Stars.
BO   What's that?
JESUS   Stars. Just inside the eyelids. *(Wanders in small circle, thumbs still jammed into his eyes. Bumps into BO TREE, blinks)* Every night they're different. A whole skyful of blueprints.
BO   You are referring, I take it, to these? *(Stage grows dark).*
JESUS *(looks up, presses thumbs to eyes, opens again, looks up):*   These, yeah. See? Instruction kits, clear across the galaxy. Look at all of 'em! Tipis. Geodomes. Chicken coops.
BO   Chicken coops?

JESUS   Sure. Just connect the dots, star-to-star. Like a giant erector set. Houseboats. Grain elevators.

BO   Build things, do you?

JESUS   No getting around it. Whole correspondence course beaming down at you like that every night. Rain barrel. Printing-press. All it takes is raw materials. Rocking chair. Electron microscope. Kazoo—look at the size of that kazoo! (*Points to one corner of the sky*). Handcarved: beautiful. Music of the spheres. (*Kazoo band is heard very faintly in background.*) I'll do it! (*Begins crawling about.*) Wood . . . wood . . . my kingdom for a tree! (*Comes up against BO TREE, stares, grins, fetches handsaw from his bag, begins sawing.*)

BO   Wrong, wrong, wrong. (*A flash of light, handsaw has turned into a fiddlestick.*) You can't cut me down, cretin—I'm the Flowering BO TREE. And where's my drachma?

JESUS   Jesus here (*shakes hands with fiddlestick*). Now, what's this about "your drachma?" It was my thought. My saw, too.

BO   Your thought, my time. I offered, you accepted, I listened. Fee one drachma. Next consultation tomorrow.

JESUS   Usurer. Here (*He takes an impossibly rusted pocketwatch from his jacket, opens it: dozens of springs, bedspring-size leap out. JESUS catches one, offers it to BO TREE.*)

BO   That's no drachma.

JESUS   Spirals! Shape of the lunar orbit. Source of all form and substance. It's an archetype.

BO   It's a scrap of spun rust. Worthless.

JESUS   Priceless. Galaxies patterned after it—earring of the universe. (*Tries on one or two springs*).

BO   Extended session—revised fee, two drachmas. Please pay now.

JESUS   (*slipping a misshapend hacksaw from his bag*) Sorry, no coins. Don't believe in 'em.

BO   You don't believe in coins?

JESUS   Nope. Too flat. (*Thrusts hacksaw at BO TREE.*)

BO   In that case it's my turn—role reversal. Stop sawing and listen.

JESUS (*listening*)   Coyotes. Diesel truck, steep incline. Figs ripening. More coyotes. (*Frantically begins sawing again.*) (*BO TREE crashing to the ground.*)

BO   Not to them—to me. To my thought. It's the least you can do.

JESUS   I've done less. Let's hear it.

BO   Sit down.

JESUS   That's your thought?

BO   I think (*clears its equivalent of throat*): I think you should sit down (*JESUS finds himself abruptly down*)—and drink Bodhi tequila. (*Hacksaw becomes a wineskin. JESUS aims, squirts.*) Then I think you should go out and enlighten the world.

JESUS (*gurgling*)   Hra?

BO   Just for a while. Role reversal. I need a rest.

JESUS (*sloshing his words*)   I don't want to enlighten the world. I want to carve that honcho kazoo.

JESUS points to kazoo constellation, drinks Bodhi tequila while watching the sky. Faint kazoo music.

A red radish sprouts up from his hair.

Two radishes.

Three.

A rush of radishes spill out from his head and begin spinning around BO TREE above him.

White radishes launch out. Green paisley radishes. Old junior-high school madras radishes. Radishes of every color and creed appear and orbit BO TREE.

A fig leaf flies out.

More radishes.

More fig leaves.

Hummingbirds.

Woodapples.

Harpsichord jacks.

Gyroscopes.

Fanfares of cherry bombs whirl from his head and surround the tree/ the BO leaves explode into tiny galloping fire stallions.

A thousand wildfinch shadows fly out in finch-flock calligraphies.

Fleets of rainbow trout flash upstream into the sun, describing fish-tetrahedrons above the tree.

A billion black tulips appear.

Water clocks.

Lions' manes leaping through burning hoops and disappearing.

Internal combustion engines square-dancing with the President of
    the United States.
Astrolabes.
The Great Wall of China.
All the children in the world riding dolphins and pewter bicycles
    and brass giraffes through a rain forest at sunset appear.
A brushfire handsprings out disguised as the child Krishna.
The Rocky Mountains snakedance from his head, playing bagpipes
    and spoons and chanting and stomping and hornpiping themselves
    into boulders into pebbles into dust.
The Seven Oceans transmogrify into strawberries and surf across
    themselves into the tree.
One hundred forty-four thousand saloongirls burst out from double
    doors inside the tree with strawberries between their teeth.
The Entire Universe leaps from his head, claps its hand, spins
    about the BO TREE at the speed of light in watchspring spirals.
The BO TREE becomes a kazoo, joins the Universe, dancing/shouting
    around itself above his head.
JESUS E. LEE DON JUAN CROCKETT DE LA MANCHA sits in the
    center of the Universe above himself, laughs 186,000 times
    per second/holds his Breath for a thousand geologic eras.

JESUS (*exhaling*)   oxowowmomoxoHA!

EPILOGUE: *The Ascension*

JESUS E.L.D.J.C. de la M. parachutes down toward the stage from impos-
    sible heights. He removes a French horn from his head, blows on it: bil-
    lions of exotic vegetables rush out into the audience from the bell of the
    horn in breathless vegetable polyphonies. Kazoo-and-castanet band ac-
    companies with four-part angel choir rendition of the Hallelujah Chorus,
    or perhaps "California Here I Come." JESUS continues to drift down.
JESUS   Truly I say to you, hoosha—
PARACHUTE   Whosoever.
JESUS   —whosoever does not receive the Kingdom of God like a child shall
    not enter it. Luke eighteen seventeen.

PARACHUTE (*barely audible above kazoos*)   The scene you are witnessing is an illusion: I am suspended motionless several light years above the stage/ the entire theatre is rising to meet us. I, of course, am the BO TREE; the body dangling pitifully beneath me is that of Jesus E. Lee Don Juan Crockett de la Mancha.

JESUS (*as his feet disappear through the stage floor*)   Ridiculous. I am the Bo Tree, the Parachute is Jesus E. Lee Don Juan Crockett de la—

PARACHUTE   Truly I say to you—

JESUS (*as he, French Horn, and finally PARACHUTE sink slowly into the stage*):   Truly *I* say—

PARACHUTE   —*I* say to you—

JESUS   —*I*—

Both disappear from sight. Only a single red radish remains on the stage.

SINGLE RED RADISH   Curtain!

CURTAIN   Single Red Radish!

A STAGEHAND enters, salts the CURTAIN, eats it/he then draws the RADISH shut, disappears behind it.

", or REQ
Ronn Smith

", or REQ by Ronn Smith. Originally presented by Center Theatre Group of Los Angeles as part of the Laboratory Program of the Mark Taper Forum. July, 1973. Reprinted by permission of Ronn Smith, to whom inquiries about rights should be addressed care of Box 8073, Columbus, Ohio, 43201.

(this play should not be performed on a flat or systematically steeped surface, although such a space might not prove to be a hindrance to a competent cast if, for instance, oranges are served to the audience, cast size and running time is left to the discretion of the director. perform without intermission.)

(may the production of this play be dedicated to a.a.)

: : : : : : : : : : : :

!

- - - - - - - - - -

;!!   (blackout)

(req
uest)   (illuminate slowly)

&   //
&   //
&   //
///.
/&
/
/
/
&

(should a large wire basket, holding
crumbled newspaper, fall over. the
paper blows away)

!

(req
quired)   (blackout)

%   (highlight)   %   %
 % $$$$
$ ¢
¢
¢
(spotlight)   : : : : : : : : : : :
!
; ! !

.

.

.

.

. :
&   (blackout)

(should a radio be heard)
(fade radio)
(such a variety of color and
light above the audience)
(and from the dark space)   !
(blackout)

(gentle lighting up)

/ /
# # # #
# # #
*
/ /,
*
/ /

(gentle lighting down and out)

- - -
#
- -
# #
-
# # #
- -
# #
- - -
#

(floodlight)
     ′ ′ ′ ′
&   &
   / / /

(req
uisition)

: : : ;*   (blackout)

(illuminate slowly as)

```
!
&
&/
. ///
//          &,
//          &,
//          &
! ! ;
- - - - - - - - - -
!
: : : : : : : : : : :
"
: : : : : : : : : : :
!      (!)
```

APPENDIX II
Evaluating process and product

Evaluating a director's effectiveness can serve at least two purposes: exploration of current competence and analysis for potential future growth. Yet evaluation is difficult, not only because the director's best work is often his least visible, but also because judgments about directing usually rely more on subjective than an objective criteria. Written critical reviews, analysis of audience response, formal sessions of oral criticism, informal comments, the observed artistic growth of actors, the welcome and unwelcome observations of colleagues—all can lead to a highly subjective, often romanticized, concept of artistic effectiveness. Furthermore, the overall sense of a performance often outweighs its individual elements, which may be desirable for an audience, but blurs areas of concern for the director, making it difficult to identify strengths and weaknesses.

To improve their effectiveness, directors, while very much concerned with overall results, need to concentrate on specific problems in both the process and the product of their work. The following forms, when used by actors for their director or when used by a director for self-evaluation, can help to pinpoint expertise (or lack of it) by focusing attention on the craft elements of directing and by isolating individual areas of competence. Such an evaluation naturally cannot provide a truly objective measure of effectiveness, nor can it measure the degree of excellence achieved in performance, but it can reveal a perceived overall shape of how well the director has performed. It can also stimulate the pursuit of excellence by providing a springboard for further written evaluation or focused critical discussion. The forms themselves should be treated with a good deal of flexibility, and adapted to suit different kinds of directing experiences. Not every item will apply to every production.

Directing evaluation
Form A

Indicate your response to each item by *circling* the number which most clearly expresses your considered opinion.

5 = Outstanding
4 = Above average
3 = Average
2 = Below average
1 = Poor

Title of play _____

Name of Director _____

I. ABOUT THE DIRECTOR

1.	Knowledge of directing	1	2	3	4	5
2.	Skill in directing	3	2	1	4	5
3.	Preparation for production	5	2	1	3	4
4.	Communication with actors	2	3	4	5	1
5.	Concern for the audience	2	5	3	1	4
6.	Interest in the production	5	4	3	2	1
7.	Level of creativity	3	4	2	1	5
8.	Organization	2	5	4	1	3
9.	Ability to stimulate actors	4	1	5	3	2
10.	Openness to disagreement	1	2	5	3	4
11.	Attitude toward actors	5	4	1	2	3
12.	Sense of humor	1	5	4	3	2
13.	Working relationships with co-artists other than actors	2	4	5	3	1
14.	Efficiency	3	5	4	1	2
15.	Level of expectation	5	4	3	1	2
16.	Punctuality	2	1	4	3	5

17.	Helpfulness to you as an actor	3	2	5	1	4
18.	Patience	2	4	1	3	5
19.	Concern for the total production	5	2	3	1	4
20.	Overall effectiveness	4	3	1	2	5
21.	Understanding of the script	5	4	3	1	2
22.	Understanding of actors	3	1	2	4	5
23.	Understanding of the technical aspects of production	5	4	1	2	3
24.	Encouragement of production growth	2	5	3	4	1
25.	Handling of human problems	4	1	3	5	2
26.	Try-out procedures	1	5	2	4	3
27.	The level of creativity he expected of you	4	3	1	5	2

II. ABOUT YOU

1.	Your enthusiasm for rehearsal	1	2	3	4	5
2.	Your enthusiasm for performance	5	4	1	3	2
3.	Your concentration in rehearsal	2	1	5	4	3
4.	Your preparation for rehearsal	3	5	4	2	1
5.	Your punctuality	4	2	3	1	5
6.	Your artistic growth through rehearsal and performance	5	1	3	2	4
7.	Your growth in the crafts or skills of acting	3	2	4	5	1
8.	Your growth in knowledge of and appreciation for theatre	1	5	4	3	2
9.	Your overall effort	2	3	5	1	4
10.	Your overall results	3	5	4	2	1

III. ABOUT REHEARSAL

1.	The atmosphere of rehearsals	1	3	2	5	4
2.	The efficiency of rehearsal periods	2	1	5	3	4
3.	The scheduling of rehearsals	4	5	1	2	3
4.	Working relationship between actor and director during rehearsals	3	4	5	1	2

IV. ABOUT THE PERFORMANCE

1.	Quality of the performance score	5	4	2	3	1
2.	Quality of the finished production	1	4	2	3	5
3.	Quality of directing	2	5	4	3	1
4.	Sense of ensemble	3	4	2	1	5
5.	Quality of acting	4	1	3	2	5
6.	Sense of theatrical unity	2	1	5	4	3
7.	Audience appreciation of and involvement with performance	4	2	1	5	3
8.	Your *awareness* of audience response	3	5	2	1	4
9.	Your *concern* for audience response	3	2	1	5	4

V. GENERAL

Compared to all theatre experiences you have had, how would you rate this experience? 2 1 5 4 3

Compared to all directors you have known, how would you rate this director? 5 4 2 3 1

Other Comments:

Directing evaluation
Form B

Please circle the appropriate response, leaving blank any items not applicable:

5 = Outstanding   2 = Below average
4 = Above average   1 = Poor
3 = Average

Casting	1	2	3	4	5
Acting	1	2	3	4	5
Movement	1	2	3	4	5
Picturization	1	2	3	4	5
Use of stage areas	1	2	3	4	5
Use of body position	1	2	3	4	5
Use of level	1	2	3	4	5
Use of plane	1	2	3	4	5
Emphasis	1	2	3	4	5
Focus	1	2	3	4	5
Business	1	2	3	4	5
Rhythm1	1	2	3	4	5
Tempo	1	2	3	4	5
Ground plan	1	2	3	4	5
Mood	1	2	3	4	5
Aural effectiveness	1	2	3	4	5
Kinetic effectiveness	1	2	3	4	5
Clarity	1	2	3	4	5
Variety	1	2	3	4	5
Sense of unity	1	2	3	4	5
Overall effectiveness	1	2	3	4	5

Comment:

SUGGESTED READING

The reading suggested here can provide both a further beginning point and expanded exploration for the contemporary director. Most truly current information, of course, will be found primarily in periodicals, so while only a few specific journal articles are noted, a list of useful periodicals has been included.

Albright, Hardie. *Stage Direction in Transition.* 1972.

Appia, Adolph. *The Work of Living Art.* 1960.

Artaud, Antonin. *The Theatre and Its Double.* 1958.

Bakshy, Alexander. *The Theatre Unbound.* 1923.

Barrault, Jean Louis. *The Theatre of Jean Louis Barrault.* 1962.

Beck, Julian. *Paradise Now,* "A Collective Creation of The Living Theatre Written Down by Judith Malina and Julian Beck." 1971.

Beck, Julian. *The Life of the Theatre.* 1972.

Benedikt, Michael. *Theatre Experiment: An Anthology of American Plays.* 1967.

Benedetti, Robert. "The Director As Gardener," *Southern Theatre,* Fall 1973.

Berne, Eric. *Games People Play.* 1964.

Berne, Eric. *Transactional Analysis in Psychotherapy.* 1961.

Biner, Pierre, *The Living Theatre.* 1972.

Blau, Herbert. *The Impossible Theatre.* 1964.

Braden, William. *The Age of Aquarius.* 1970.

Brecht, Bertolt. *Brecht on Theatre.* Tr. and ed. by John Willet. 1964.

Brook, Peter, *The Empty Space.* 1969.

Brustein, Robert. *Revolution as Theatre.* 1971.

Brustein, Robert. *Seasons of Discontent.* 1967.

Burke, Kenneth. *A Grammar of Motives.* 1945.

Burnham, Jack. *The Structure of Art.* 1971.

Cage, John. *Silence.* 1966.

Carpenter, Edmund, and Ken Heyman. *They Became What They Beheld.* 1970.

Chaikin, Joseph. *The Presence of the Actor.* 1972.

Clark, Brian, *Group Theatre.* 1972.

Clay, James, and Daniel Krempel. *The Theatrical Image.* 1967.

Clurman, Harold. "The New Theatre, Now," *Harpers Magazine,* February 1971.

Cole, Toby, and Helen Krich Chinoy, eds. *Directors on Directing.* 1963.

Corrigan, Robert W. *New American Plays.* Vol. 1, 1965.

Corrigan, Robert W. *The Theatre in Search of a Fix.* 1973.

Corrigan, Robert W. *Theatre in the Twentieth Century.* 1963.

Craig, Edward Gordon. *On The Art of The Theatre.* 1911.

Croyden, Margaret. *Lunatics, Lovers and Poets.* 1974.

Dietz, Norman D. *Fables, Vaudevilles and Plays.* 1968.

"Directing Issue," *The Drama Review* (T54), June 1962.

Dukore, Bernard, Jr., and Daniel C. Gerould. *Avant Garde Drama.* 1969.

"Environmental Theatre," *Theatre Crafts,* September 1971.

Esslin, Martin. *Brecht: The Man and His Works.* 1960.

Esslin, Martin. *Reflections.* 1971.

Fabun, Don. *The Dynamics of Change.* 1967.

Fergusson, Francis. *The Idea of a Theatre.* 1949.

Ghiselin, Brewster. *The Creative Process.* 1952.

Gilman, Richard. "The True and Only Crisis of the Theatre," *New American Review #4,* 1968.

Gottfried, Martin. *A Theatre Divided.* 1967.

Greene, Naomi. *Antonin Artaud: Poet Without Words.* 1970.

Gropius, Walter, ed. *The Theatre of the Bauhaus.* 1961.

Grotowski, Jerzy. *Towards A Poor Theatre.* 1968.

Guthrie, Tyrone. *A Life In the Theatre.* 1959.

Hansen, Al. *A Primer of Happenings and Time/Space Art.* 1966.

Hirschman, Jack, ed. *Antonin Artaud Anthology.* 1965.

Hodgson, John, and Ernest Richards. *Improvisation: Discovery and Creativity in Drama.* 1966.

Hoffman, William M., ed. *New American Plays.* Vols. 2 and 3, 1968 and 1970.

Huizinga, Johan. *Homo Ludens.* 1955.

Ionesco, Eugene. *Notes and Counter Notes.* 1964.

Isaac, Dan. "The Death of the Proscenium Stage," *Antioch Review.* Vol. 31, No. 2. 1971.

Ives, Charles. *Essays Before a Sonata.* 1920.

Jellicoe, Ann. *Some Unconscious Influences in the Theatre.* 1967.

Jones, Robert Edmund. *The Dramatic Imagination.* 1941.

Kaprow, Allan. *Assemblages, Environments and Happenings.* 1966.

Kerr, Walter. "How Playwrights Lose," *Harper's Magazine,* September 1966.

Kirby, E. T., ed. *Total Theatre: A Critical Anthology.* 1969.

Kirby, Michael. *Happenings.* 1965.

Kirby, Michael. *The Art of Time.* 1969.

Kirby, Michael. "The New Theatre," *The Drama Review* (T30), Winter 1965.

Kloman, William. "And the Damned Spaceship Just Sat There, Like a McCarthy Button, Asking to be Dug," *Motive,* January 1969.

Knapp, Bettina L. *Antonin Artaud: Man of Vision.* 1969.

Koestler, Arthur. *The Act of Creation.* 1964.

Kostelanetz, Richard. *The Theatre of Mixed Means.* 1968.

Krauss, Ruth. *The Cantilever Rainbow.* 1965.

Krauss, Ruth. *There's a Little Ambiguity Over There Among the Bluebells.* 1968.

Krauss, Ruth. *This Breast Gothic.* 1973.

Kubler, George. *The Shape of Time.* 1962.

Lahr, John. *Astonish Me: Adventures in the Contemporary Theatre.* 1973.

Lahr, John. *Up Against the Fourth Wall.* 1970.

Lahr, John, and Jonathan Price. *Life-Show.* 1973.

Lahr, John, and Jonathan Price. *The Great American Life Show.* 1974.

Laing, R. D. *The Divided Self.* 1960.

Laing, R. D. *The Politics of Experience.* 1967.

Leonard, George B. "Language and Reality," *Harper's,* November 1974.

Lesnick, Henry. *Guerilla Street Theatre.* 1973.

Ley, Maria Piscator. *The Piscator Experiment.* 1967.

Macgowan, Kenneth. *The Theatre of Tomorrow.* 1921.

McLuhan, Marshall. *Counter-Blast.* 1969.

McLuhan, Marshall. *The Medium is the Massage.* 1967.

McLuhan, Marshall. *Understanding Media.* 1965.

Marowitz, Charles, and Simon Trussler. *Theatre At Work.* 1967.

Meyerhold, Vsevelod. *Meyerhold on Theatre.* Tr. and ed. by Edward Braun. 1969.

Mitchell, Roy. *Creative Theatre.* 1929.

Munk, Erika, ed. *Brecht*. 1972.

Neff, Renfreu. *The Living Theatre USA*. 1970.

Nelson, Stanley. *The Scene*. Two books: 1972, 1974.

Oldenburg, Claes. *Store Days*. 1967.

Ono, Yoko. *Grapefruit*. 1971.

Orzel, Nick, and Michael Smith. *Eight Plays from Off-Off Broadway*. 1966.

Papanek, Victor. *Design for the Real World*. 1967.

Parone, Edward. *Collision Course*. 1968.

Parone, Edward. *New Theatre for Now*. 1971.

Parone, Edward. *New Theatre in America*. 1965.

Pasolli, Robert. *A Book on the Open Theatre*. 1970.

Plays for a New Theatre. New Directions Books, 1962.

Pound, Ezra. *Guide to Kulchur*. 1938.

Prince, George M. *The Practice of Creativity*. 1969.

Read, Herbert. *The Forms of Things Unknown*. 1960.

Reich, Charles A. *The Greening of America*. 1970.

Reps, Paul. *Unwrinkling Plays*. 1965.

Reynerston, A. J. *The Work of the Film Director*. 1970.

Ridley, Clifford A., ed. *The Arts Explosion*. 1972.

Roose-Evans, James. *Experimental Theatre*. 1970.

Rosenthal, Raymond, ed. *McLuhan: Pro and Con*. 1968.

Roslansky, John D., ed. *Creativity: A Discussion at the Nobel Conference*. 1970.

Rostagno, Aldo, with Julian Beck and Judith Malina. *We, The Living Theatre*. 1970.

Roszak, Theodore, *Pontifex*. 1974.

Roszak, Theodore. *The Making of a Counterculture*. 1969.

San Francisco Mime Troupe. *Radical Theatre Festival*. 1969.

Sarris, Andrew. *Interview with Film Directors*. 1967.

Schechner, Richard, ed. *Dionysus in 69*. 1970.

Schechner, Richard. *Environmental Theatre*. 1973.

Schechner, Richard, ed. *Makbeth and Commune*. 1970.

Schechner, Richard. "Post Proscenium," *American Theatre 3*, 1971.

Schechner, Richard, Jerry N. Rojo, and Brooks McNamara. *Environmental Theatre Design*. 1973.

Schevill, James. *Break Out: In Search of New Theatrical Environments*. 1973.

Schotter, Richard. *The American Place Theatre: Plays*. 1973.

Schroeder, Robert J., ed. *The New Underground Theatre*. 1968.

Seltzer, Daniel, ed. *The Modern Theatre*. 1967.

Smith, Michael. *The Best of Off-Off Broadway*. 1969.

Spolin, Viola. *Improvisation for the Theatre: A Handbook of Teaching and Directing Techniques.* 1963.

Stein, Gertrude. *Geography and Plays.* 1922.

Steward, Dwight. *Stage-Left.* 1970.

Sullivan, Dan. "The Open Theatre Is Dead—Long May It Live," *Los Angeles Times,* December 9, 1973.

Sullivan, Louis H. *Kindergarten Chats.* 1947.

Swenson, May. "To Make A Play," *Theatre: The Annual of the Repertory Company of Lincoln Center,* 1965.

Tairov, Alexander. *Notes of a Director.* 1969.

Temkine, Raymonde. *Grotowski.* Tr. by Alex Szogyi. 1972.

"The Future of the Arts," *Saturday Review/World,* September 1974.

"The Theatre: Does It Exist?" *Arts in Society,* Fall-Winter 1971.

Toffler, Alvin. *Future Shock.* 1971.

Toffler, Alvin, *The Culture Consumers.* 1964.

"Total Theatre," *World Theatre,* Vol. 14, No. 6. (1965) and Vol. 15, No. 1 (1966).

Vilar, Jean. "The Director and the Play," *Yale French Studies,* III, No. 1 (1949).

Weisman, John. *Guerilla Theatre.* 1973.

"What's Next In Theatre?" *The Drama Review* (T20), Summer 1963.

Youngblood, Gene. *Expanded Cinema.* 1970

Periodicals
Arts in Society
Black Theatre
Canadian Theatre Review
Cue of Theta Alpha Phi
Dramatics
Educational Theatre Journal
Empirical Research in Theatre
Mime Journal
New Theatre Magazine
Performance
Players: The Magazine of American Theatre
Plays and Players
Scripts
Theatre Crafts
Theatre Design and Technology
Theatre Quarterly
The Drama Review
Village Voice
World Theatre
YalesTheatre

INDEX

This index is designed to supplement the Table of Contents, and it does not duplicate the descriptive information to be found in the titles of individual articles. Nor does it list individual contributors' names.